Industrial Politics

Industrial Politics

ROBERT
CURRIE

CLARENDON PRESS · OXFORD
1979

Oxford University Press, Walton Street, Oxford OX2 6DP

OXFORD LONDON GLASGOW
NEW YORK TORONTO MELBOURNE WELLINGTON
IBADAN NAIROBI DAR ES SALAAM CAPE TOWN
KUALA LUMPUR SINGAPORE JAKARTA HONG KONG TOKYO
DELHI BOMBAY CALCUTTA MADRAS KARACHI

*Published in the United States by
Oxford University Press, New York*

British Library Cataloguing in Publication Data

Currie, Robert
  Industrial politics.
    1. Industrial relations — Great Britain — History
  — 19th century 2. Industrial relations — Great
  Britain — History — 20th century
  I. Title
  331′.0941   HD8391   78–40480

  ISBN 0–19–827419–X

*Printed and bound in Great Britain by
Morrison & Gibb Ltd., London and Edinburgh*

social institutions are the visible expression of the scale of moral values which rules the minds of individuals, and it is impossible to alter institutions without altering that valuation.

R. H. TAWNEY, *The Acquisitive Society*

In general, we may say that in capitalist democracies a greater part of the workers' struggle takes place in the realm of ideas.

JOHN STRACHEY, *What Are We to Do?*

our working class . . . is naturally the very centre and stronghold of our national idea, that it is man's ideal right and felicity to do as he likes.

MATTHEW ARNOLD, *Culture and Anarchy*

Preface

IN THIS book I have tried to show how utilitarian liberal-democratic individualism has shaped both trade unions and the Labour Party, and, to that degree, the whole character of society in industrial Britain. The first chapter illustrates the significance of cultural factors in the study of social organizations, including labour organizations; and attempts to demonstrate how these factors have operated in Britain, both by a brief comparison with German and Japanese thought and culture, and by examination of the individualist *laissez-faire* ideology. The next four chapters study the history of individualism; the corporatist compromise, and its vicissitudes in the first half of the twentieth century; the movement for workers' control, and its failure to overcome the persistent *laissez-faire* orthodoxies of trade unionism; and the labour sectionalism of the last thirty years. A concluding chapter summarizes the argument; considers the problematical nature of current proposals for industrial democracy; and looks at some present-day problems for British society and for the political aspirations of the British people.

The book breaks new ground in one or two places. I am a trade unionist; have quite often voted Labour; and think that the labour movement, in the broadest sense, has done much good to the economic, social and political life of the best of all countries. But in some respects I feel a greater scepticism about the apparently eternal verities of the labour credo in particular, and the British liberal-democratic tradition in general, than I detect in certain books about labour history, left-wing politics, and industrial relations: and this scepticism may from time to time be perceptible to the reader.

To that extent the tone of the book may be unfamiliar. I believe, however, that greater difficulties will arise from the methodological innovation of concentrating more or less on the implications of labour history and industrial relations for *political theory*. In attempting to show the *theoretical* significance, not merely of labour doctrines, but of the *minutiae* of trade union and party affairs, I have used the concepts of 'collectivism', 'individualism', and 'corporatism', both 'unitary' and 'bipartite'. None of these is very easy to define. I have outlined my notion of 'collectivism' on pp. 18–19 and 47; and have discussed 'individualism' at some length on pp. 19–25, 26–31, and 240–1. 'Corporatism' in general is considered on pp. 48–50; 'unitary' and 'bipartite' corporatism on pp. 52–6.

As this may seem a somewhat individualistic book, it is perhaps not a very good place to note any similarity there may be between my approach and that of other scholars; but I am glad of the opportunity to record my debt to the great mainstream works in British labour history and industrial relations, and, above all, to the writings of Allan Flanders, Hugh Clegg, Alan Fox, and A. F. Thompson. In writing this book I have benefited in particular from the advice of George Bain, Ian Brownlie, and Michael Surrey. I would be very surprised to find that their views coincide with mine; and still more surprised to find that I had equalled either their exactitude or their learning.

Contents

I

Individualism and the Industrial Revolution

They might take society from two points of view; from that in which they started from the individual who had rights; the other when they started from the citizen who had duties. The first was a conception of society . . . in which they had isolated units each fighting for the ground on which he stood. The second was what had been called the biological view of society, where they regarded it not as a mass of isolated atoms but as an organic whole, a growth with a common life running through it. In the first they had a society which was composed of isolated people, each claiming his own rights, in which each man demanded 'How much can I get?' In the second conception they had organic growth and a common life, in which each man demanded 'What is my duty to that self which is greater than my own personality?' This second was the Socialist conception of human society. The first was the Individualist conception.

ANNIE BESANT, 25 October 1890

LABOUR AND THE THEORETICIANS

Most people would agree that a social organization is not exhaustively described by mere recital of its formal procedures and public goals. A trade union, for example, might define its objectives as protection and furtherance of the interests of its members as workers and employees. Yet its life might be so directed, by those that had power within it, that its practical policy was calculated first and foremost to fill the pockets of its elected leaders, or, to overthrow existing social and political order. Moreover, even if a trade union could be shown to adhere as closely as possible to such objectives as protection and furtherance of its members' interests, we would perhaps be less instructed by that proof than by an analysis of the way in which the organization perceived and interpreted such interests.

Various devices can be employed to give the bare bones of organizational conventions, constitutions and methods at least a scholarly versimilitude of life. An organization may, for instance, be located within a historical process deemed to inform the organization's purpose and tendency. The current renewal of interest in German idealism suggests that Hegel's scheme of history presents a concept of historical process highly pertinent to modern historiography; and, though Hegel's enthusiasm for great men allowed social organizations little place in his system (other than as passive instruments of great men), his writings on history can be generalized into historical schemas in which social organizations have a major role. Thus Hegel can be said to see history as the development of *laws*, that proceed by phases and counter-phases: each phase forming its own historically distinctive organizations, which, as the phase comes into being, assume a progressive aspect that is lost when, the phase being taken up in the counter-phase, new organizations are formed in opposition to those already existing, which perforce must now be seen as reactionary institutions.

Wherever ideas of 'progress' and 'reaction' are acceptable, some such historical model is very likely to be found. Thus, for instance, the Webbs' *History of Trade Unionism* assumes the existence of easily differentiable periods characterized, in one case, by the 'New Model' trade societies, and, in another, by 'New Unionism'. The Webbs interpreted the New Model as the product of a constrained working-class culture during an era of restricted political franchise and rapid expansion of the factory system. The New Model trade unions, developing after 1840, were characterized by a self-help system of social security, and by intense practicality of approach. Internally they provided, in the Webbs' eyes, an admirable self-education in democracy; externally, they achieved, if only within certain narrow limits, a significant measure of control over the trades in which they operated.

But by about 1890, the factory system relied much more on workers less skilled than the members of New Model unions.

Meanwhile, the rapid growth of productivity had assisted the emergence of enormous urban areas, marked by severe differentials of income and wealth; and, at the same time, working men had grown more conscious of themselves and the world, and had, indeed, in many cases received the vote. In these changed circumstances the New Model unions adopted, according to the Webbs, an 'exclusive and apathetic policy', and sank into an 'almost cynical fatalism'. Historiographically, they were demoted to the status of 'Old Unionism'; and the Webbs showed how a 'New Unionism' sprang up, to organize the poorer and less skilled workers, and to preach, as a 'gospel of deliverance', the implementation of 'Collectivist ideals and Collectivist principles' through the exploitation of the political opportunities newly opened to the working classes.[1]

Much of what the Webbs said about the New Model, and about New Unionism, was derived from empirical observation. The historical method, by means of which they ordered and explained their empirical material, enables us the better to understand organizations such as, say, the Amalgamated Society of Engineers, and the Gasworkers' and General Labourers' Union. But this understanding arises from a historical method that receives whatever validity it possesses, not from the data employed, but from certain theoretical assumptions. The method is, in any event, unlikely to be the only useful technique for dealing with empirical historical data, partly because of the difficulty of subsuming all available evidence under any one argument, however instructive, but partly also because of deficiencies in the theory that prompts the argument. The problems of applying such a method to the historical study of organizations have aroused, in those that have used it, a desire to establish which factors do change organizations; and much of post-Hegelian historiography has been concerned with precisely this issue.

Marx's attempt to show that 'the productive organs of men' are 'the material basis of all social organization' is justly the most famous of these efforts. 'Revolutionizing the instruments of production' meant, Marx claimed, revolutionizing 'thereby the relations of production, and with them the whole relations

---

[1] S. and B. Webb, *The History of Trade Unionism*, London, 1920, pp. 387, 388, 413, 414.

of society'. So, said Marx, in a well-known epigram, 'the hand-mill gives you society with the feudal lord; the steam-mill, society with the industrial capitalist'. But Marx concerned himself not so much with technology as with the system of property within which any particular technology evolved and was put to commercial use. For he held that the world was increasingly dominated by the power of the owners of capital to make those without capital their servants or even their slaves. So long as the relation of wage labour to capital existed, he wrote, 'there will always be a class which will exploit and a class which will be exploited'; and out of that system would develop an inevitable 'antagonism between industrial capitalists and wage workers'. In this way, the 'wage workers', the proletarians of Marx's theory, gained class consciousness and a class purpose which came to shape the growth of labour organization.[1]

This argument has greatly influenced the writing of labour history. One example of the use of the Marxist argument to elucidate the structure and policy of trade unions is J. B. Jefferys' *The Story of the Engineers*. Jefferys did not doubt that productive technique had had a considerable effect on the formation and development of engineers' unions, since he was sure that changes in that technique had inexorably changed the union. Thus, he concluded his analysis of technological change in engineering in the first half of the nineteenth century with the statement that 'the engineering industry was emerging from the chrysalis stage and with it the organization of the engineers'; and he completed his survey of the 'revolution in the means, methods, organization and products' of the engineering industry after 1890, by declaring that, 'it was necessary for the engineers to re-mould their traditional views on organization, policy and skill'.[2]

Jefferys believed that these changes in productive technique should be seen in the context of a system of property ownership which produced antagonism between 'capitalists' or 'employers' on one hand, and the 'working class' or the 'workers' on the

[1] Karl Marx, *Capital*, vol. 1, Moscow, 1961, Chapter 15, Section 1, p. 372; K. Marx and F. Engels, *Manifesto of the Communist Party*, London, 1938, Chapter 1, p. 12; K. Marx, *The Poverty of Philosophy*, Moscow, n.d., Chapter 2, Section 1, p. 109; Appendix, 'On the Question of Free Trade', p. 221.

[2] James B. Jefferys, *The Story of the Engineers, 1800–1945*, London, n.d., pp. 15, 126.

other. He emphasized that the profit motive corrupted both employers and employees. The capitalists became 'grasping and obstinate' and were indifferent to 'the misery' that they caused 'thousands of working class families'. Meanwhile the worker sank into a state of slavery, on whatever conditions the capitalist dictated, because 'the consequence of not coming to terms with the employer was the "freedom and right" of the worker to starve'.[1]

The workers' degradation necessarily issued in 'conservatism', failure of 'vision', and immersion in 'sordid' disputes among themselves. But Jefferys was certain that, through organization, the workers would slowly come to know their position as a class over against the capitalist class; and he wished to demonstrate that the history of labour revealed a struggle to overthrow the capitalists. Thus he wrote of the Engineers and other unions after the First World War that 'from 1923 until 1926 workers' organizations were still on the defensive, but searching for ways and means to resist further attacks from the employing classes and build their organizations to the pitch where they could challenge the capitalist system with a socialist alternative'.[2]

Marx's emphasis on technical factors (and especially on change therein), his overriding concern with the distribution of property in the industrial process, his identification of conflict as the chief characteristic of industrial life, have profoundly influenced the study of labour organization, especially in Britain, the country whose conditions he knew best. Yet the apparent failure of some of his prognostications, together with a certain abstract quality in his notions of 'class', 'class consciousness' and 'class struggle', have aroused various criticisms of a strictly 'Marxist' approach to labour history.

The most notable attempt to devise an analysis of labour organization which goes beyond Marx, so to speak, and indeed, does without parts of Marx's argument, is Selig Perlman's *Theory of the Labor Movement*, published in 1928. Perlman devoted much attention to labour *psychology*; and tended to discount the concept of what Marxists would see as labour's objective class responses to the capitalist system of production. Perlman claimed that trade unionism 'is essentially pragmatic',

[1] Ibid., pp. 82, 226, 95.
[2] Ibid., pp. 156, 107, 158, 217.

but is dominated by 'economic pessimism'. 'Manual groups . . .'
he wrote,

> have had their economic attitudes basically determined by a
> consciousness of scarcity of opportunity. . . . Starting with this
> consciousness of scarcity, the 'manualist' groups have been led to
> practising solidarity, to an insistence upon an 'ownership' by the
> group as a totality of the economic opportunity extant, to a
> 'rationing' by the group of such opportunity among the indi-
> viduals constituting it, to a control by the group over its members
> in relation to the conditions upon which they as individuals are
> permitted to occupy a portion of that opportunity.

Perlman therefore saw labour organization as a series of 'trade
unions enforcing "job control" through union "working rules" '.
Whatever aspect of the job could be regulated, that a trade
union would regulate, according to Perlman, by exerting
pressure both on employers and on workmen.[1]

Perlman based his argument chiefly on the British case; and
his theory has been adopted by many British scholars, particularly under the influence of Allan Flanders, who interpreted
labour organization as a bid for 'job regulation'. Of course,
rules and regulations were not unknown to the Webbs, as the
pages of their *History of Trade Unionism* and *Industrial Democracy*
attest; but in recent years a Perlmanian approach has become
more and more evident in Britain, where the study of labour
history has become, in effect, the analysis of the different
systems of industrial relations arising from different types of
trade-union rules and regulations.

Clegg, Fox, and Thompson's *A History of British Trade Unions
since 1889* exemplifies this trend. The first volume of their work,
which covers the period 1889–1910, begins with the struggle of
craft unions to turn custom 'into a universal and uniform rule
so as to exert a firm control over the size of the labour force';
and traces thereafter the vicissitudes of labour's attempt to
control 'working conditions' through the many different stages
of 'collective bargaining'. Indeed the authors conclude that 'the
development of collective bargaining was the outstanding
feature of this period'; and their narrative describes in great
detail the problems created for labour leaders seeking to parcel

---

[1] Selig Perlman, *A Theory of the Labor Movement*, New York, 1928, pp. 5–7, 241.

out scarce work opportunities, by changes in 'the laying of floors and the fixing of tiles', by the replacement of 'hand-sewing of soles and uppers with machinery', by disputes over the 'trade in untinned sheets', by disagreements over 'the output of linotype machines', and all the rest.[1]

The great virtue of this approach is that it establishes the concrete form and life of labour organization. It allows that historial epochs do bring their own forces to bear on organized labour; that those forces manifest themselves through alterations in productive technique; and that labour tends to view each such alteration as yet a new battle in the great campaign against 'capital'. But it also emphasizes the precise mode of labour's perception of such matters, the real content of labour's policies, and the order of labour's priorities. What is seen in this light is indeed a good deal less grandiose than what is to be seen by the illumination of classical Marxism; yet it may be that labour is a good deal more humdrum than Marx would have us believe.

The weakness of the Perlmanian approach is this. Just as Hegel conceived of a universal historical process, and Marx envisaged a universal proletariat, Perlman saw regulative labour organization as a universal norm, the exceptions to which were mere trifling variants explicable by reference to the characteristics of local labour markets. Perlman's knowledge of labour organization was almost completely confined to the trade unions of the Anglo-American world: and even he was forced to concede that his theory did not apply in its entirety to the case of the United States. Half a century after Perlman, it would be a rash man who would assume the existence of an Anglo-American (let alone an English) norm of universal validity in labour organization—or anything else. The notion that there is a 'normal' state of affairs, and certain 'peculiar' survivals outside it, has diminished intellectual currency; and this is all to the good, both because such social uniformitarianism blinds us to the existence of ways of life quite other than, and independent of, our own; and, still more, because it conceals from us the true particularity of our own way of life, assumed to be universal and unexceptionable, but in fact highly specific and characteristic.

[1] H. A. Clegg, A. Fox, and A. F. Thompson, *A History of British Trade Unions Since 1889*, vol. 1, London, 1964, pp. 5, 6, 133, 199, 209, 439, 471.

APPROACHES TO INDUSTRIALIZATION

During the last ten years or so, different scholars have attempted to extend the study of society, and of social organizations, by examining the *cultural* factors operative in human affairs. Such scholars have not been content with an abstract doctrine of historical change (or progress) in labour organization and industrial relations, a general theory of technical change and property ownership, or indeed a notion of universal labour psychology *à la* Perlman, but have investigated the attitudes and norms which, arising from concrete historical situations, have long continued to shape men's attitudes and responses toward the changing events that confront them. In other words, such scholars grant considerable conceptual significance to the pressure exerted on individuals by diurnal externality, but also try to allow for individuals' ability to resist, or reduce, that pressure by reinterpreting and re-ordering data presented by the external stimuli to which they are subject.

It might seem unnecessary to assert that different men differently perceive, and differently respond to, a workshop, a lathe, a wages agreement or a refrigerator; or to insist that different perceptions and responses can often be aggregated as aspects of given cultural (or indeed national) entities. But such claims are by no means everywhere accepted. Sometimes they are rejected in favour of what Lucien Goldmann calls the '*capital* importance' of 'economic activity' in shaping men's 'way of thinking and feeling'. In many cases they are only admitted as preliminaries to some argument about the universal 'convergence' of local variations upon some supposed, and usually Anglo-American, norm. Meanwhile, grave unease about 'national character' is evinced by writers who, content to despatch such matters to some misty, quasi-genetic realm into which, with great show of intellectual respectability, *they* will not venture, sturdily refuse to reckon how far these variations are attributable to eminently empirical (if complex) factors in the cultural and philosophical life of peoples.[1]

One great exception to all the many examples so readily dismissed by authors of this type is Japan. Most students of Japanese affairs agree without quibble that Japan is 'the out-

[1] Lucien Goldmann, *The Human Sciences and Philosophy*, London, 1969, p. 88.

standing case of non-Western industrialization', a categorization which, though it rests on a schematic bisection of the entire world into 'west' and 'non-west', does at least allow that the world is not culturally one, and therefore not economically one either. In dealing with Japan at least, scholars do allow the relevance—to greater or lesser degree—of 'history', 'cultural tradition', and 'ideological convictions'.[1]

Similarities do of course occur between Japanese and 'western' industrial society. 'Factories look very much alike anywhere', both inside and out; and the unions that operate in these factories, whether in Britain or Japan do have many points in common. Both groups bargain over wages and working conditions; both seek to further the interests of their members. In Britain, most unions are affiliated to the Trades Union Congress, which has strong links with the Labour Party; in Japan, many unions are affiliated to the General Council of Trade Unions, which has links with the Socialist Party.[2]

But such similarities recede beside the differences that at once obtrude themselves. While British trade unionists think themselves situated in a market for labour, a market in which they are free to seek optimum conditions and maximum wages, Japanese trade unionists associate themselves with a company, with which, in many cases, they have a life-long contract, incurring permanent rights and duties. Thus surveys show that most Japanese workers 'identify closely with the company' and 'subordinate individual to group goals'. These workers, many observers report, 'do not conceive of the workshop situation as a straightforward "us" and "them" situation in which the foreman is usually seen as one of "them" '. While 'British workers are more individual workers: Japanese workers are more of a team'. And since these workers largely regard themselves as bound to the company by a life-time commitment, they are much less able than British workers to envisage pressing demands whose satisfaction may harm the company as a whole.[3]

---

[1] A. M. Whitehill and Shin-Ichi Takezawa, *Cultural Values in Management-Worker Relations, Japan*; *Gimu in Transition*, Chapel Hill, North Carolina, 1961, p. 104; Ronald Dore, *British Factory Japanese Factory, The Origins of National Diversity in Industrial Relations*, London, 1973, p. 419.

[2] Ibid., pp. 193, 200; W. W. Lockwood (ed.), *The State and Economic Enterprise in Japan*, Princeton, New Jersey, 1965, pp. 704–7.

[3] Dore, pp. 74, 163, 170, 261; Whitehill and Takezawa, p. 107.

Unions organizing in such a milieu must differ from British unions. True, there are national affiliations of unions in Japan, but these have the allegiance of part only of the 20,000–30,000 Japanese unions, almost all of which recruit, bargain, and maintain themselves in one single enterprise. Whatever the requirements, and grievances, of union members, these enterprise-wide unions must recognize the power of concepts of 'harmony' and 'duty' in factory life; they must reckon with what the British would regard as a highly submissive work force; they must acknowledge, even today, a certain company interest in the personal affairs of its workers; and they must accept powerful restraints upon their bargaining strength.[1]

A 'Marxist' theory of labour might be used to explain the specific features of Japanese trade unions by reference to 'universally' operative economic forces—productive technique and organization, supply of the factors of production, character of the markets for labour and for commodities, and so forth. Writing in 1920, Yosoburo Takekoshi argued that 'man is above all an economic animal'; that 'the strata of human history', and especially economic history, 'are nearly common throughout many countries'; and that Japanese economic history 'is nothing but a part of . . . world history'. Fifty years later, Koji Taira rejected arguments from Japanese cultural peculiarities, and attributed the crucial institution of the life-long labour contract to employers' rational responses to 'acute labour shortage and high labour turnover' during Japanese industrialization. Yet the 'strata' of economic (and other) history do differ from country to country in character, order, and chronological depth. There is, for example, no Japanese parallel to the 400-year period in which the British created a world empire; there is no British parallel to the five-year period in which Japan was conquered, occupied and in certain ways reshaped by the United States. Moreover, men's 'responses' vary even when they do appear to inhabit rather similar historical 'strata'. During industrialization, labour shortage, especially at certain periods and in certain skills, was acute not only in Japan but in England, and even more in New England. But 'employer paternalism', as Taira termed Japanese employers' recruitment

---

[1] Ibid., *passim*; R. J. Ballon (ed.), *The Japanese Employee*, Tokyo, 1969, pp. 25, 201, 203, 228; Dore, pp. 163, 171, 220, 262, 297; Lockwood, p. 660.

policies, was attempted in both Britain and America only half-heartedly—and with no lasting success.[1]

If 'employer paternalism' was a response to labour shortage in industrializing Japan, any assessment of the effectiveness of that response should take account of specifically Japanese circumstances. These would include the preservation in Japan of regulative, paternalistic trade guilds that collapsed in Britain well before 1780, and never established themselves in America; and the survival throughout Japan, right up to industrialization, of a system of feudal obligations entirely destroyed in England in the period of the civil war, and never exported to America. Moreover, Japanese industrialization, quite unlike English or American industrialization, was preceded by a revival of monarchy, as the executive centre of government as well as the object of a religious veneration that gave divine sanction to state authority and to paternalist principles. Finally, as R. J. Ballon argues, 'western industrialization' was by and large 'started and developed by some especially clever individuals . . . who, in order to satisfy their own personal ambitions, created . . . enterprises.' In Japan, on the contrary, the European and American challenge, from 1853 onwards, convinced government and public opinion that industrialization was 'a *sine qua non* of national policy' if the country 'wanted to survive'. For this reason if for no other, Japan was industrialized under government supervision, direct and indirect, and with considerable government assistance.[2]

All these factors are sociological, political or historical in content. They are interconnected with a set of ideas that have continued to exert their influence, not least over Keynes's 'practical business men', into eras in which these factors have quite largely ceased to operate. These ideas were expressed, for example, by Yukichi Fukuzawa, the alleged exponent of 'western' notions in early industrial Japan, who declared, 'in everything I have done my great wish has always been to lead the whole country into the ways of civilization, to make Japan a great nation, strong in military might, prosperous in trade'.

[1] Yosoburo Takekoshi, *The Economic Aspects of the History of the Civilization of Japan*, London, 1930, pp. x–xi; Koji Taira, *Economic Development and the Labour Market in Japan*, New York, 1970, p. 126.

[2] Johannes Hirschmeier, *The Origins of Entrepreneurship in Meiji Japan*, Cambridge, Massachusetts, 1964, pp. 8–9; Lockwood, p. 638; Ballon, pp. 4, 7.

And they were also expressed by Bunji Suzuki, a labour organizer contemporary with Fukuzawa, who remarked that 'in the West everything is individualism, but in Japan we have familism', so that 'the factory becomes exactly like a family'.[1]

The most influential theorist and practitioner of industrialization in Japan was very probably Eiichi Shibusawa, who could scarcely stand much further then he does from, say, Adam Smith. 'I believe', stated Shibusawa, 'that in order to get along together in society and serve the State, we must by all means abandon this idea of independence and self-reliance and reject egoism completely.' Shibusawa favoured what he called the 'objective view' of self, which 'regards society first and the self second. The ego is disregarded to the point where, without hesitation, one sacrifices the self for the sake of society.' Shibusawa insisted that 'the guidance' of the economy 'should be entrusted to the government', and in his own enterprises he was happy to suffer losses 'for the good of the country'.[2]

Shibusawa, and those who supported him, may have been products of their environment: though that environment cannot be defined in exclusively economic terms. But however such theorists are themselves produced, their theories can survive the circumstances in which they were devised, and can, of course, shape even the activities of those who seek more or less consciously to exploit such theories for their own ends. Suppose a more or less Hegelian theory of historical progress be used to analyse labour organization and industrial relations in Japan, such a theory must there display a face it could not wear here. If a Marxist schema of labour, such as has found favour, say, on the Clyde, be introduced into Japan it must undergo major modifications, not merely to find favour, but to fit the facts of a history, and a culture, of industrialization so thoroughly unlike that of the Clyde. And whenever a Perlmanian concept of labour psychology is tested by reference to Japanese data, it must, given the particular character of Japanese assumptions about work, property, industry, and society, find less than total verification. In short, culture does matter, and the significance

---

[1] Carmen Blacker, *The Japanese Enlightenment, A Study of the Writings of Fukuzawa Yukichi*, Cambridge, 1964, p. 121; Byron K. Marshall, *Capitalism and Nationalism in Pre-war Japan, The Ideology of the Business Elite, 1868–1941*, Stanford, California, 1967, p. 79.

[2] Ibid., pp. 26, 34–5; Lockwood, p. 245.

of Japan for the study of 'western' labour, and 'western' industrial relations is the degree to which that country's experience casts doubt upon the theory that there exists in the 'west', as everywhere else of course, one universal, rational, economic norm, if struggling to make itself felt through a morass of inconvenient 'peculiarities' and 'abnormalities'.

The Japanese case has, by its very remoteness and un-familiarity, served to convince some scholars that social structures, labour organizations and industrial relations in-cluded, cannot be adequately explained in terms of a universal norm; but must be related to quite localized specificities, often of cultural origin. There are, however, certain European instances (of which Germany is perhaps the most interesting) that, though still comparatively neglected by the Anglo-American world, can, by their very propinquity, afford us a better understanding of the cultural determinants of social structure than we are likely to derive from the more distant example of Japan.

In Federal Germany, as in postwar Japan, British observers find many well-known features. The Federal Parliament has a Social Democratic plurality (of which trade union deputies form a considerable proportion), and a coalition headed by a Social Democratic chancellor. Industrial relations are conducted by a system of collective bargaining between single employers or groups of employers, on the one hand, and large labour unions of the 'industrial-occupational' type, on the other. These unions are mainly affiliated to the German Confederation of Trade Unions, which expects to find itself in a special relation-ship with Social Democratic ministers.

Yet German unions only organize about 30 per cent of the labour force, while British unions organize about 50 per cent; and during 1968–71, strikes cost British industry 8,000,000 working days a year, but German industry only about 100,000 working days a year. In Germany collective agreements have a statutorily defined legal status and often prohibit industrial action. Moreover, under Acts of 1951, 1952 and 1972, a system of worker-representatives on supervisory boards (first devised, at the prompting of German trade unionists, by British officials for the iron and steel industry in the British occupation zone) has spread to many sectors of manufacturing. As a recent inquiry into European collective bargaining systems noted, German society shares a powerful ideology 'which tries to bind together the interests of all the industrial-relations actors with those of the community at large'; and that ideology's origins can be traced back through the era of Nazism and the German Labour Front, the Weimar Republic's experiments in state arbitration, the authoritarian paternalism of the Wilhelmine Reich, and beyond.[1]

One major influence on the present character of German industry and society is this. As can be seen, in Japanese history, from the continued vigour of Buddhist creeds, of the Shinto religious system, and especially of the imperial cult, a strong religious tradition can have a two-fold significance for industrialization: first, and in general, it may sustain, among the masses of the population, a practical notion of something 'other' and 'higher' than themselves; and secondly, and in particular, it may tend to link that notion with the life of the 'people', the 'society', the 'nation', or the 'state'. Germany, though rather more secularized than Japan at the onset of industrialization, preserved into and beyond that event a strong religious life, in which the approximate equipollence of Catholicism and Protestantism encouraged individuals still further to identify and intensify their own religious loyalties. The idea of the 'other' and the 'higher' was therefore both familiar and forceful to these individuals, who were thus readied to receive, through the medium of German nationalism, the verity of a secular 'other' and 'higher', to which they were inclined to subordinate themselves as they had, all along, been inclined to subordinate themselves to ecclesiastical or theological verities.

Men like Herder and Hegel gave the notions of Pan-Germanism an intellectual cogency rarely granted to the concepts of any nationalist movement. These writers, appealing to the evident facts of a unified German language, German literature, German scholarship, and German arts, over against the fragmented multiplicity of the German states, argued that what was universally 'German' supplied the true worth and significance of individuals, who were nevertheless doomed to

---

[1] Herbert J. Spiro, *The Politics of German Co-determination*, Cambridge, Massachusetts, 1958, *passim*; Institute of Personnel Management, *Collective Bargaining in Western Europe*, London, 1973, p. 50; *The Times*, 27 January 1977.

remain distorted and incomplete men so long as they were divided from each other by citizenship in the separate petty German principalities; and once this analysis gained strength in men's minds, all German states became petty principalities, from Prussia down to Sieghartsweiler. The recurrent French invasions of Germany, culminating in Napoleon's remarkable campaigns, greatly reinforced these nationalist arguments. For, on the one hand, the German states proved utterly incapable of resisting invasions from France; while, on the other hand, Napoleon's France provided—for a few crucial years—an almost overwhelming symbol of the modern, rational, united, popular and powerful state, a state in which, at last, men could be men. It was in this context that Hegel revealed his vision of history as the out-working of a universal rationality, and of the state as the highest achievement of history, as 'objective mind', as 'divinity existing in and for itself', through which, and only through which, 'the individual has objectivity, reality and ethicality'.[1]

All these factors influenced German industrialization. In Germany as in Japan, what Günther Roth called ' "reactive nationalism" ' was 'a major non-economic motive', because 'bourgeoisie, land-owning aristocracy . . . the authoritarian state', and—it will be argued here—labour, 'shared an interest in making Germany strong enough to withstand military attacks'. Mid-nineteenth-century Germany therefore perceived industry as a fit field for governmental intervention and direction, and for subordination of personal and sectional concerns to promotion of the common welfare under state guidance.[2]

The great theorist of German industrialization was Friedrich List, whose *National System of Political Economy*, published in the early 1840s, was designed as a national riposte to what List disparaged as the abstract cosmopolitanism of Adam Smith. List saw England's industrial and commercial hegemony as the greatest challenge to Germany; and his aim was, he wrote, to show 'how by a national economic course Germany's welfare, culture and power might be furthered'. He remained sceptical

---

[1] Cf. T. M. Knox (ed. and transl.), *Hegel's Philosophy of Right*, Oxford, 1952, pp. 156–7.

[2] Günther Roth, *The Social Democrats in Imperial Germany, A Study in Working Class Isolation and National Integration*, Totowa, New Jersey, 1962, pp. 24–5.

of his success; feared the continued expansion of England, 'the predominant nation'; and indeed committed suicide at the end of 1846, shortly after, as he saw it, the repeal of the Corn Laws completed the structure of free trade and liberated England from the only obstacles to her permanent economic control of the world.[1]

In these circumstances List's *System* became his last testament to the German people: and what it has to say is perfectly plain. 'Individual liberty', List declared, 'is in general a good thing only so long as it does not run counter to the interests of society'; but in practice, he thought, individuals tend to exploit whatever liberty they get to pursue their own interests and to come into 'a condition of war' with each other, in the course of which 'the welfare of mankind sinks to its lowest level'. Moreover, since 'individuals draw the greatest part of their productive power from social institutions and the social environment', national unity 'is the fundamental condition for permanent national prosperity'; and only where 'private interest has been subordinated to national interest' have 'nations been led to harmonious development of their productive powers'. National unity must be based, List claimed, on the sufferings of individuals. 'The nation must sacrifice and forego material goods,' he warned, 'in order to obtain intellectual and social power; it must sacrifice present in order to secure future advantages.'[2]

Engels claimed in 1886 that 'the German working-class movement is the inheritor of German classical philosophy', a philosophy which, he believed, had been summed up 'in the most splendid fashion in Hegel'; and, if true, this was so not least in that movement's responsiveness to the collectivism and nationalism which informed the whole of Hegel's work, and was translated into economics by men like List. Certainly, German socialists and communists spoke sternly of expropriating landlord and capitalist: yet what would remain after the revolution would be, though socialist, first and foremost, *German*, and indeed nationalist. Hence, when Robert Ley, director of the Nazi Labour Front declared that, 'Socialism is not, in the final analysis, the concern for and the welfare of the individual, but

---

[1] Friedrich List, *Das nationale System der Politischen Ökonomie*, Jena, 1950, pp. 2, 213–14.

[2] Ibid., pp. 195, 210, 234, 254–5, 265.

the question: What is good for Germany? What is good for this nation?', he expressed a collectivist idea, which in an immediate, practical form had been seized on both by German manual workers and by their leaders and spokesmen.[1]

Marx himself affords evidence of this development, whether one turns to his proud boast, in 1843, that 'Germany alone can make a *fundamental* revolution. The *emancipation of the German* is the *emancipation of mankind*', or to his fervid insistence (after years of exile) that the English 'really stood far below the Germans, who had hitherto been prevented by miserable political and economic conditions from achieving any great practical work, but who would yet surpass all other nations.' Marx was an intellectual, a non-German and an outcast from German politics, and his utterances might seem untypical of the sentiments of organized German labour. Yet that this is very probably not so, can be seen from the views of native German labour leaders, such as August Bebel.[2]

Bebel was virtually the founder of the German Social Democratic Party which he dominated for nearly forty years. Praised by both Lenin and Stalin, he found perhaps his severest socialist critic in Jaurès, who, in a famous phrase, accused him of hiding his 'impotence' behind 'the intransigence' of his 'theoretical formulae'. Yet Bebel, who was imprisoned several times for speeches deemed seditious or treasonable by the German government, was no time-server but a man willing to stand by his convictions.[3]

These were more or less products of the era of Hegel and List. When Bebel denounced the German military, he did so very largely on the grounds that they exploited and ill-treated the German conscript: who, he claimed, would in any event be rendered warlike more efficiently by childhood training in martial arts (on what Bebel took to be the Japanese model) than by months of enforced service in the Reichswehr. And when Bebel threatened the German ruling class with expro-

---

[1] F. Engels, *Ludwig Feuerbach and the End of Classical German Philosophy*, Moscow, 1950, pp. 22, 91; Hilda Grebing, *The History of the German Labour Movement*, London, 1969, p. 140.

[2] Cf. Loyd D. Easton and Kurt H. Guddat (eds.), *Writings of the Young Marx on Philosophy and Society*, New York, 1967, p. 264; Wilhelm Liebknecht, *Karl Marx zum Gedächtniss, Ein Lebensabriss und Erinnerungen*, Nuremberg, 1896, pp. 83–4.

[3] Helmut Hirsch (ed.), *August Bebel*, Cologne, 1968, pp. 142–4; Roth, p. 168.

priation, he directed their attention towards a social commonwealth, one of the chief characteristics of which would be its
power to give Germany true predominance in Europe. He
aimed 'to transform . . . our fatherland into a country which has
no equal in perfection and beauty anywhere on earth'. Indeed,
he was certain that

> *Germany more than any other country will have the task of undertaking the*
> *leadership at the next stage of advance.* . . . Germany must take the
> lead in . . . the giant struggle of the future; her . . . development
> and her . . . position as the 'heart of Europe' have predestined
> it . . . It was no accident that the motive laws of modern society
> were discovered and socialism scientifically demonstrated to be
> the social form of the future by Germans. . . . It is no accident
> that German socialists are the pioneers who are spreading the
> socialist idea among the other nations of the world.

Bebel's idea of the socialist future was thus a highly nationalistic,
and in this sense a collectivist, vision. It was also a collectivist
vision in ways logically (though not necessarily in practice)
quite separable from his nationalism. For Bebel believed that
under capitalism, 'personal egotism and public welfare' contradicted each other; but that under socialism, 'these contra-
dictions are annulled' and—in a manner entirely consonant
with the most thorough-going collectivism of Rousseau or Hegel
—'personal egotism and public welfare become synonymous'.[1]

In short, the cultural development of both Japan and
Germany exemplifies the continuance, into and throughout the
period of industrialization, of collectivist doctrines that, for all
the many dissimilarities between these two nations, have certain
common characteristics. Both Japanese and Germans held, and
perhaps still hold, the notion of something other and higher than
the individual, something which by definition has authority
over the individual, and something by reference to which the
individual's true interests and needs may be better judged than
they could ever be judged by the individual himself alone. And
both in Japan and in Germany that higher something was
related to the nation, whether regarded as a primarily religious

---

[1] Carl E. Schorske, *German Social Democracy, 1905–1917, The Development of the
Great Schism*, New York, 1972, p. 76; Hirsch, pp. 173 ff.; Grebing, p. 91; cf. August
Bebel, *Woman in the Past, Present and Future*, London, 1893, pp. 185–6, 258, 262; and
see also the conclusion to August Bebel, *Die Frau und der Sozialismus*.

or as a primarily ethnic entity. Furthermore, while, both before and during the years of industrialization, Japanese and German intellectuals emphasized the individual's dependence on the nation for his health, welfare, and even existence, the particular circumstance of those years—the oppressive sense of dangers from without, and the widespread conviction that national destiny lay in adopting industrial techniques deemed unattainable except under governmental direction—caused such intellectuals also to affirm the individual's reciprocal duties to bend his efforts towards the health, welfare, and even existence of the nation.

The individual's liberty was, therefore, perceived in what has been called a 'positive' sense. It was 'in duty' that the individual gained his 'freedom', Hegel wrote, since any mere freedom from external constraints could only strengthen the individual's capriciousness and reinforce his personal inadequacies; while it was precisely in the individual's apparent self-abnegation in submission to the higher authority of the nation that he found true freedom to realize his full human potential. This concept of liberty must seem paradoxical to people educated in a culture which, as Arnold put it, teaches that the individual's 'best right' is 'to do as he likes'; but it will not seem so to those educated to think, with Hegel, that 'when we hear it said that freedom is above all that one can do what one likes, such an idea can only be treated as a complete misconception'.[1]

INDIVIDUALISM IN BRITAIN

Why not merely this concept of liberty, but the whole system of collectivist thought of which it is part, seems paradoxical to us, is a question that can only be answered from a study of the historical and cultural traditions that have shaped our ideas, and our social organizations. Among those traditions three seem peculiarly important. First, Britain's development, unlike Germany's, has been profoundly shaped by a radical reformation that reduced Catholicism, by the mid-eighteenth century, to so small an element in national life that religion could safely

[1] Matthew Arnold, *Culture and Anarchy* (ed. J. D. Wilson), London, 1932, p. 92; cf. *Philosophy of Right*, pp. 27, 107.

be dismissed as a great issue of state. Religious convictions were left to the individual; and the state tolerated any, all, or no religious opinions and convictions. Once the state thus ceased to direct men's religious affairs, those affairs tended to fall into desuetude; and the notion of the 'other' and the 'higher', a notion always reinforced in social life by popular religious fervour, was, to that extent, attenuated.

Secondly, neither in England, the paramount nation of the union of 1707, nor in Scotland, did any great number of men doubt or fear for their national identity. Tongues other than English died away; as between Protestants, ethnic origins lost their significance; and national minorities lived a life of *de facto* autonomy in virtual isolation from the chief centres of population. Moreover, though foreign wars persisted, the threat of invasion dwindled almost to nothing, and the British became increasingly ignorant of and indifferent to European culture. Had these circumstances not obtained, nationalism might perhaps have supplied religion's deficiency in conveying to the populace the authority and appeal of an easily understood notion of that which is 'other' and 'higher' than the immediacy of everyday life and individuals' personal concerns. In fact, however, nationalism, national identity, came to be taken almost as much for granted by the British as was their own, especially secularized, version of religion.

Lastly, while both religion and nationalism faded away in eighteenth-century Britain, a passionate interest in government did not. The seventeenth century had seen the collapse of monarchy; the execution of a king; the failure of a quasi-republican system; the restoration of monarchy; the flight of another king; and the appointment of a foreign king who was to remain in a sense on trial throughout his reign. Had religious or nationalist issues preserved their vitality, interest in government might have been elevated to a high plane of principle; but since they did not, it subsided to the plane of mere convenience and efficiency; and those two criteria came increasingly to determine British responses to political problems. The state, in short, lost its legitimacy, and came to stand or fall by its utility.

Bentham and his many admirers in Britain thus came to regard the notion of a social whole as a fantasy. 'The community is a fictitious *body*,' wrote Bentham, 'composed of the individual persons who are considered as constituting as it were its *members*. The interest of the community then is, what?— the sum of the interests of the several members who compose it.' Bentham, who was always eager to announce that, 'the season of fiction is now over', could find little substance in a 'body' of this sort. If indeed such a thing had any life of its own whatever (which was doubtful) its life must be derived, to use Locke's words, from 'the consent of the individuals to join into and make one society'; and the state's authority, supposing such a term were appropriate, must reside in the 'trust' conferred upon it to do the individuals' will; which 'trust', once broken, 'must necessarily be forfeited, and the power devolve into the hands of those that gave it, who may place it anew where they shall think best'.[1]

Once the state was seen in this light, the doctrine that individuals found their true selves in their duty to the greater whole, could only seem a fiction above fictions. 'That is my *duty* to do, which I am liable to be punished, according to law, if I do not do', was Bentham's disparaging view of obligation; while Adam Smith concluded that the idea of sacrificing private dealings and private profit 'to an idea of public utility, to a sort of reasons of state' was a doctrine to which men should resort 'only in cases of the most urgent necessity'. No 'positive' concept of liberty, according to which the constraint, the self-sacrifice, of the individual contained true freedom, could prosper in such a mental climate; and the British became committed to a 'negative' concept of liberty, according to which, freedom, in every sense and on every plane, consisted in the absence of constraint and the free activity of the empirical self.[2]

This 'negative' concept of liberty had been strongly affirmed by Hobbes. 'LIBERTY, or FREEDOM, signifieth (properly) the absence of Opposition', wrote Hobbes, who added, 'by Opposition, I mean external Impediments of Motion.' According to Hobbes, the individual is free only in the sense that Arnold identified, namely, to the degree that he does what he likes. 'A FREE-MAN, *is he*,' Hobbes concluded, '*that in those*

---

[1] Jeremy Bentham, *A Fragment on Government, and An Introduction to the Principles of Morals and Legislation* (ed. W. Harrison), Oxford, 1967, pp. 49, 127; John Locke, *The Second Treatise of Government* (ed. J. W. Gough), Oxford, 1966, pp. 54, 75.

[2] Bentham, p. 107; Adam Smith, *An Inquiry into the Nature and Causes of the Wealth of Nations* (ed. E. Cannan), London, 1904, vol. 2, p. 42.

things, which by his strength and wit he is able to do, is not hindered to do what he has a will to do.' Such a notion of freedom was reinforced during the eighteenth century by the authority of Locke, who argued, in the *Essay concerning Human Understanding*, that liberty is 'the power a man has to do or forbear doing any particular action . . . according as he himself wills it', since 'so far as a man has power to think or not to think, to move or not to move, according to the preference or direction of his own mind; so far a man is free'.[1]

Thus, while, in countries so diverse as Germany and Japan, great emphasis has been placed on collectivities, such as the nation, the race, the state, the community or society, almost all the emphasis of British social thought since the seventeenth century has been placed on the individual. Of the individual, the most influential British theorists have held that he is, and should be, motivated by considerations of immediate utility only. 'Nature has placed mankind under . . . two sovereign masters, *pain* and *pleasure*', wrote Bentham. 'It is for them alone to point out what we ought to do, as well as to determine what we shall do.' For Bentham, the notion, later so painstakingly built up by Mill, of qualitative differences between pains and pleasures was as fictional as the notions of state, authority and duty. 'Prejudice apart,' he observed, 'the game of push-pin is of equal value with the arts and sciences of music and poetry.'[2]

Bentham's view of the individual had the most far-reaching consequences. He held that 'pain' and 'pleasure' decided both what individuals did and what they ought to do. Now pain and pleasure cannot, in this sense, be taught to individuals, or even discussed by them: for, as Locke argued, 'pleasure or pain cannot be described, nor their names defined; the way of knowing them is . . . only by experience'. No individual, no group of individuals, no authority, can tell the individual what is, for him, pain or pleasure; and since, as can be seen from the equivalence of push-pin and poetry, no pleasure is better than any other pleasure, no one can do more to reprobate any man's pleasure than to point out what pains may follow from it—about which opinions will differ. The doctrine thus

[1] Thomas Hobbes, *Leviathan* (ed. A. D. Lindsay), London, 1914, pp. 66, 110; John Locke, *An Essay concerning Human Understanding*, II.21.8, 15.
[2] Bentham, p. 125; *The Rationale of Reward*, London, 1825, p. 206.

ineluctably flows to the conclusion that Mill, for all his unease about Bentham, enunciated as 'the great principle of political economy,' namely, 'that individuals are the best judge of their own interest.'[1]

Individuals so considered are of course self-interested, and self-interested especially in a materialistic sense. It was fundamental to Adam Smith's system that 'every man' should display a 'uniform, constant, and uninterrupted effort . . . to better his condition'; and that such betterment should be definable in the one word 'opulence'. These efforts, organized upon the principle of self-interest, must issue in conflict between individuals. Hobbes, who had identified as 'a general inclination of all mankind' the 'perpetual and restless desire of power after power', that is, of 'means to obtain some . . . Good', notoriously viewed the natural condition of man as 'war of every one against every one'. Smith not merely agreed with the doctrine—anathema to the most characteristic thinkers of countries with a strong and vital collectivist tradition, such as Germany and Japan—that man was by nature competitive; but he insisted that competition was the optimum rule of social organization.[2]

Smith argued that, even though 'free competition' might 'ruin' some individuals, it must nevertheless maximize 'exactness' or efficiency, and thus produce the 'lowest' prices. All things would be best used, all men put to their most valuable work, in a society ruled by free competition. Indeed, in such a society, individuals' pursuit of their self-interest (of which, of course, they are the best judge) becomes, through the activity of what Smith called 'an invisible hand', the pursuit of society's interest. Smith dismissed the claim that a man trades 'for the public good' as mere 'affectation'. But he believed that each individual's efforts to put his resources to the employment 'most advantageous' for himself would so optimize the use of those resources that 'the study of his own advantage naturally, or rather necessarily leads him to prefer that employment which is most advantageous to society'.[3]

This doctrine, castigated by Arnold as 'the specially British

---

[1] Locke, p. 351; John Stuart Mill, *Principles of Political Economy with some of their Applications to Social Philosophy*, London, 1848, p. 534.

[2] Smith, vol. 1, p. 325; Hobbes, pp. 43, 49, 67.

[3] Smith, vol. 1, pp. 63, 342, 419, 421; vol. 2, p. 249.

form of Quietism, or a devout, but excessive reliance on an over-ruling Providence', was enshrined in the attitudes and assumptions of the men who industrialized Britain. Mill expressed those men's ideas, with a moderation and a sensitivity of which perhaps not all of them were capable, in his *Political Economy*, where we learn that 'most persons take a juster and more intelligent view of their own interest, and of the means of promoting it, than can either be prescribed to them by a general enactment of the legislature, or pointed out in the particular case by a public functionary'. For this very reason,

> as a general rule, the business of life is better performed when those who have an immediate interest in it are left to take their own course, uncontrolled either by the mandate of the law or by the meddling of any public functionary. The persons . . . who do the work, are likely to be better judges than the government of the means of attaining the particular end at which they aim.

Thus, Mill concluded, '*laissez-faire*, in short, should be the general practice: every departure from it, unless required by some great good, is a certain evil'.[1]

The *laissez-faire* doctrine, evolved by Hobbes, Locke and Bentham, given special shape in the work of Adam Smith and other political economists, and argued in perhaps its most subtle form by Mill, dominated British thought till the end of the nineteenth century. During this period, few could look on the state as more than an instrument necessary to secure certain general conveniences, or on society as more than an aggregation of individuals, each perceiving and pursuing their own interests more efficiently than could any other person or agency. The optimum of social life was, therefore, a freedom in which men could seek their particular ends, either singly, or in voluntary association with each other, unchecked by any external disciplines and directions. No doubt men were greedy, ignorant, selfish and capricious, but they could not be otherwise; and their very faults were exploited by beneficent social and economic laws that derived out of purely and truly egotistic behaviour all the efficiencies of perfect competition.

Such was the radical intellectual system from which the

---

[1] Arnold, p. 124; Mill, pp. 515–16, 518, 524. For a general survey of *laissez-faire* in the nineteenth century, see Arthur J. Taylor, *Laissez-faire and State Intervention in Nineteenth Century Britain*, London, 1972.

British usually drew their ideas of themselves and their world during the period in which British trade unions evolved; and it would be curious if, while, say, German and Japanese labour organization was profoundly influenced by the collectivism of those countries, British labour organization were not profoundly influenced by individualism and *laissez-faire*.

2

Laissez-faire and Corporatism

> On the whole, in spite of certain opposing tendencies trade
> unionism is to be regarded rather as an expanded form of
> individualism than any thorough collectivism.
>
> ERNEST AVES in Charles Booth and Ernest Aves,
> *Life and Labour of the People in London,*
> second series, volume V.

> This congress and our movement generally suffers from the curse
> of individualism. We come here as a Trades Union Congress and
> talk about the solidarity of Labour, but a close study of the action
> generally of the various Trade Unions will let us see at once that
> we are merely a conglomeration of warring atoms which pursue
> our own individual road. . . .
>
> J. WALKER (Iron and Steel Trades Confederation)
> at the 1923 Trades Union Congress.

LABOUR'S LAISSEZ-FAIRE IDEOLOGY

The problem of working-class consciousness was stated simply,
if tendentiously, by Lenin, who wrote that, 'since there can be
no talk of an independent ideology being developed by the
masses of the workers themselves in the process of their movement, the *only* choice is: either the bourgeois or the socialist
ideology.' This antithesis must, of course, be broadened. The
only possible consciousness (or, in this sense, ideology) for any
organization is the consciousness of the society in which it has
its origin and in which it continues to exist. Organizations, and
even more individuals, may themselves modify the consciousness that they receive, at first quite passively, from the stock of
the common culture. But all such modifications are so exceed-

ingly slow that individuals scarcely ever, and organizations probably never, form for themselves 'an independent ideology'. They have, then, only the ideology or consciousness presented to them; the consciousness presented to the British working classes of the early nineteenth century was a 'bourgeois' consciousness; and the British bourgeoisie, unlike the German, or Russian, bourgeoisie, was profoundly committed to individualism.[1]

Thus both British capitalists and British labour accepted *laissez-faire* as the groundwork of their thought. Labour and capital believed that each individual could perceive his own interests; that each had no other, 'real' interests, which perhaps he could not perceive; and that, since there were no real interests, imperceptible to those whose interests they were, there was no room for a third party able to perceive and protect such real interests. Capitalists held (and labour agreed) that no central authority could or should determine any good, particular or general, to which individuals should submit. Labour held (and capitalists agreed) that no external authority had the right to direct or control the lives of working men, or to require their services. Of course the necessities of life obliged working men to seek employment, even at the price of obeying management, just as the necessities of the market obliged management to repay its debts to the owners of investment capital. But these were mere necessities, to which no right attached, and in which no virtue resided.

On the contrary, right consisted, as a long line of British theorists had argued, merely in the defence and furtherance of self; and, therefore, all that individuals could or should do was to discover their interests and pursue them, either alone, or in conjunction with others who shared those interests. As to which interests should prevail, *laissez-faire* theory was silent. For that theory denied the existence of 'real' interests (which, if they existed, should presumably prevail over 'apparent' interests); and admitted only an absolute equality both between interests, and also between those who perceive and pursue interests. Hence, according to the theory strictly construed, no demand can be preferred because its satisfaction is preferable to the

[1] V. I. Lenin, *What Is To Be Done? Burning Questions of Our Movement*, Moscow, n.d., p. 66.

satisfaction of any other demand, or because that demand is the demand of one individual rather than another.

In a *laissez-faire* world, therefore, only power settles conflicts between interests. Each individual must prefer his own interest, because it is his own; when his interest clashes with the interest of others, he must press his interest at the expense of others; and his interest does or does not prevail simply because it is the interest of him who has or has not the power to make it prevail. Such power has, in the abstract, no privileges other than those it can defend, and any given distribution of power, within a *laissez-faire* system, has only the merit of existence; and will no doubt at last succumb to some other distribution of power— even though the system itself persists. But each individual will of course seek to augment his power by whatever means: by acquisition of new resources; by combination with others; and by all manner of claims about his own moral worth: claims which must not, however, obscure the essential moral in-differentism, as between individuals, of *laissez-faire* doctrine.

A *laissez-faire* system is, for this reason, characterized by an intensely competitive spirit that arises from individuals' struggles to obtain those goods that will enable them in turn to obtain further goods; by much public discourse about 'rights', 'justice', 'fair play', and so forth, as individuals attempt to prove the morality of their own possessions, the immorality of others'; and by the very widespread development of those voluntary associations that enhance individuals' efforts to realize their own interests. Yet all these things can only occur in a highly individualistic fashion, in which even seemingly the most cohesive combinations of forces are always tending to break up into mere congeries of self-seeking individuals. Thus, for example, in a *laissez-faire* system, employers' organizations are always dissolving into a collection of rigorously self-involved firms; while the members of employees' unions are always arguing that they should be free not merely of any external authority but also from the authority of their own leaders.

Acquisition is the goal to be sought whenever individuals are free enough. No doubt material acquisitiveness has always directed the activities of capitalist entrepreneurs. That urban workers became so motivated may be attributed to three factors. First, the ever-increasing returns of industrial technology greatly stimulated both employers' and employees' hopes of higher rewards for their efforts. Secondly, factory production divided labour into an ever more elaborate structure of occupational grades, each so exciting the material envy or anxiety of adjacent grades as to make every man reckon his worth and happiness in terms of pay. And, thirdly, the transition from incomes in kind to money incomes made every man's pay readily objectified, analysed and compared with every other man's pay.

Money, indeed, becomes the symbol of interest in a *laissez-faire* system. Hence the emphasis on money in the works of critics of *laissez-faire*. The young Marx called money 'the visible divinity'. Money, he wrote, could secure 'the transformation of all human and natural properties into their opposites, the universal confounding and overturning of all things'. Money became 'independent in relation to both society and individuals', wrote Marx and Engels in *The German Ideology*; money was 'subversive in the economic and moral order of things', Marx reported in the first volume of *Capital*; ' "cash payment" ' the *Communist Manifesto* declared, was synonymous with 'naked self-interest'. Naturally, and especially in *Capital*, Marx sought to dismiss money as an economic irrelevance; yet such explanations do not reduce the force of money as an *idea* in Marx's work: and that idea is the idea of *laissez-faire* society.[1]

The influence exerted by *laissez-faire* society, and its 'bourgeois ideology' of the 'cash nexus', on the consciousness of British labour cannot readily be traced, given the very absence of indigenous labour social theory. Yet scattered observations by wage earners, and the precepts of those bourgeois theorists, right and left, who were popular among wage earners, do indicate the outlines of nineteenth-century labour's political and social notions. Into those notions, *laissez-faire* 'penetrated' deeply, as Perlman remarked. 'If workmen desire to know something about political economy, let them study Adam Smith and Mill', counselled the labour journalist Henry

[1] Karl Marx, *Economic and Philosophic Manuscripts of 1844*, Moscow, 1961, p. 139; *Capital*, vol. 1, Moscow, 1961, p. 132; Karl Marx and Friedrich Engels, *The German Ideology*, Moscow, 1968, p. 444; *Manifesto of the Communist Party*, London, 1938, p. 12.

Crompton in 1870—even as he warned against the 'immorality' of the political economic laws on which, however, 'modern industry unquestionably rests to a large extent'. George Howell, bricklayer and Liberal member of Parliament, writing in 1878, praised 'the clear insight and accurate knowledge of life' which Adam Smith 'so eminently possessed'.[1]

Most of British labour's ideas may be located from this orientation. Labour understood liberty, in strictly negative terms, as 'that power which belongs to a man of doing everything that does not infringe upon the rights of another', in the formula adopted by the National Union of Working Classes in 1831. No more than 'an aggregate of individuals compose a nation'; and (in the absence of any larger whole, any greater authority, than the self) 'every man has a right to do what he likes', reasoned J. F. Bray, author of *Labour's Wrongs and Labour's Remedy*, a work acclaimed as a pioneer text in the British socialist tradition. These doctrines determined labour's strictly economic opinions. Henry George was 'responsible', argued a leading British labour historian, 'for the early political education' of many of the 'leaders of the Socialist movement in this country'. But George deplored, in his *Progress and Poverty*, 'the substitution of governmental direction for the play of individual action', on the grounds that 'whatever savours of regulation and restriction is in itself bad.' And when such an unimpeachably *laissez-faire* attitude is so clearly enunciated by a radical like Henry George, it is not at all surprising to find a middle of the road labour leader, such as Howell, praising 'honourable competition' as 'beneficial to trade, commerce and industry', and even seeing a 'useful side' to what he called, by contrast, ' "unlimited competition" '.[2]

Labour thus necessarily perceived labour organization in *laissez-faire* terms. *The Pioneer*, published by the Owenite Operative Builders' Union, announced in 1834 that workers

[1] Selig Perlman, *A Theory of the Labor Movement*, New York, 1928, pp. 127–8; Henry Crompton, *Letters on Social and Political Subjects*, London, 1870, pp. 9, 10, 12; George Howell, *The Conflicts of Capital and Labour*, London, 1878, p. 209.

[2] Patricia Hollis (ed.), *Class and Conflict in Nineteenth-Century England, 1815–1850*, London, 1973, p. 129; J. F. Bray, *Labour's Wrongs and Labour's Remedy; or, the Age of Might and the Age of Right*, Leeds, 1839, pp. 32, 34; Henry Pelling, *The Origins of the Labour Party 1880–1900*, Oxford, 1965, p. 10; Henry George, *Progress and Poverty, An Inquiry into the Cause of Industrial Depressions and of Increase of Want with Increase of Wealth: The Remedy*, London, 1931, p. 228; Howell, pp. 210–11.

were 'practical men' who cared nothing for the 'mere theory' of republicanism, but wanted rather 'the management of . . . productive industry'. That goal could mean much or little. It meant little to the Amalgamated Society of Engineers, whose journal, *The Operative*, proclaimed the irrelevance of both socialism and communism. The 'objects' of the Society, it declared in 1852, were 'simply to sustain their members from poverty', to 'protect the interests of their trade, and generally to render such aid to their associated fellows as united members are capable of legitimately affording'. Such objects might indeed involve a share in 'management', but in no revolutionary indeed, no political spirit. Rather, labour organization was a business organization, pursuing business interests in a *laissez-faire* fashion. 'The Trade Unions', observed *The Poor Man's Guardian* in 1833, were 'seeking a revolution of comforts through a revolution of prices', especially prices for labour.[1]

A trade union was, in short, a device for getting more money for the same work; it was a joint-stock company for selling labour; and, like any similar undertaking, it hoped to make a handsome profit over and above the costs of supplying its product. Such an organization was forced to conceive of its world in the competitive terms of political economy, since it could only maximize its profit at the expense of other forms of labour (and indeed of other productive factors); yet, like most undertakings begun on *laissez-faire* presuppositions, it could scarcely object if its policies ultimately gave it a monopoly position, and all the price advantages inseparable from such a position.

By Howell's time, the entire doctrine was very well developed. Political economy, wrote Howell, 'practically says, love thyself; seek thine own advantage; promote thine own welfare . . . the welfare of others is not thy business, let them see to it for themselves.' 'Each union is its own best judge', he believed, since outsiders were not 'qualified' to identify a union's interest or assess its policies. Its interest was, however, plain. 'The great object of labour is pay,' declared Howell, who observed that, given political economy, 'no one need feel surprise' if the workman has but 'one aim—namely—screwing out of the employer the largest possible . . . wages for the least possible

---

[1] Hollis, pp. 67, 173; Torben Christensen, *Origin and History of Christian Socialism*, Aarhus, 1962, p. 245.

quantity of work.' Not surprisingly, either, Howell remarked
that trade unions 'do not profess to be associations for the regeneration of the human species'—rather 'they confine themselves to practicable questions and attainable objects', namely,
'the maintenance of trade privileges', and 'mutual assistance in
securing generally the most favourable conditions of labour.'[1]

Whatever socialist (or revolutionary) ideas were adopted by
labour during the early and middle years of the nineteenth
century could only be absorbed into this overwhelmingly
individualistic consciousness; and such ideas were indeed used
as instruments to achieve business ends rather than to overthrow the system and ethos of business. 'We have no wish to
hamper capital in any way,' declared the President of the 1880
Trades Union Congress, 'but we do wish . . . that our share . . .
of wealth shall not be the mite . . . which the capitalists seem
to think we are . . . entitled to.'[2]

Thus, socialist doctrines of fraternity were adopted by trade
unionists not in order to expedite the brotherhood of man but to
reinforce the solidarity of the sectional trade union in securing
its industrial objectives. When trade unionists seized on the
theme of 'productive' and 'unproductive' classes; insisted that
they, and they alone, were the 'workers'; and concurred in the
analysis of Robert Owen, for whom private property was
'useless', 'isolating', and stultifying of 'the finest and best
feelings of humanity': they had in mind not so much the new
heaven and the new earth as the next wage claim that these
moral appeals would serve to bolster. The famous labour theory
of value, developed by Adam Smith and David Ricardo, and
popularized by innumerable labour apologists, had precisely
the same tendency in labour's hands. 'It is labour alone which
bestows value', observed Bray, who concluded that therefore
'Every man has an undoubted right to all that his honest labour
can procure him.'[3]

---

[1] Howell, pp. 147, 196, 204; *Trade Unionism New and Old*, London, 1891, pp. 118, 120, 229.

[2] Trades Union Congress *Report*, 1880, p. 12.

[3] Cf. Patrick Colquhoun, *A Treatise on the Wealth, Power, and Resources of the British Empire*, London, 1814, and W. Thompson, *An Inquiry into the Principles of the Distribution of Wealth*, London, 1824, *passim*; Robert Owen, *The Revolution in the Mind and Practice of the Human Race, or, The Coming Change from Irrationality to Rationality*, London, 1849, pp. 65, 111; Bray, p. 33.

THE CHARACTER OF CLASSICAL TRADE UNIONISM

Some scholars have emphasized the solidarity created by common working conditions, and common working problems, as the mainspring of trade unionism; and have tended to see labour industrial organization as the product of a laudable desire to be master of one's own life and, in particular, of one's own job. But, whatever men's attitude to their employment, it is not so much the job as its money content, its utility as a source of income, that keeps them working. It is, far and above all else, because a job provides money that the employee seeks to protect his employment; and, whatever may be the other criteria by which he judges the success of any given method of controlling his employment, those criteria must be secondary to his evaluation of that method's efficacy in promoting a favourable ratio between his physical and mental effort on the one hand—and monetary reward on the other. Hence the relationship between trade unionism and the trade cycle. For, though the desire to be master of one's own life must be at least as prevalent in bad trade as in good, it is the opportunities that good trade affords for more money, and especially more money for the same work, that causes trade unions to expand almost solely during years of prosperity.

More money for the same work is labour organization's aim both because it is the chief common aim of all members, and because it is the one issue on which all can agree. This issue—and almost this issue alone—reconciles the members' extreme sectionalism, their individualism, with the demands (offensive to their *laissez-faire* beliefs) implicit in any such structure of common authority as is necessary to common action. Throughout the nineteenth, and during most of the twentieth century, labour industrial organization typically displays continual struggle between the members and their association. The members want more money but oppose, as intolerable incursions upon their freedom, most forms of organization designed to secure this end. The association tries to get the members more money but finds that the members refuse it most of the necessary means.

Modern labour industrial organization began in small local trade clubs meeting in public houses. These clubs recruited the most skilled manual workers who, unlike men less fortunately placed, enjoyed industrial power and the ability to exploit it. Belief in what the Webbs were to call 'the "freedom" of the corporation'—that is, the right to negative liberty of the employees thus associated—animated the local clubs, some of which long excluded and opposed even fellow tradesmen from clubs in other districts. The breakdown of this exclusivism produced small 'unions' of clubs such as the Operative Stone Masons, formed in 1831, and the Boilermakers, formed in 1832. The clubs so united now called themselves 'branches', but in no sense depended on the central organization of their 'union' which often· lacked offices and, quite frequently, full-time officials too. Some unions formed in the late 1820s and 1830s later re-formed themselves into yet larger groupings, such as the Miners' Association of Great Britain and Ireland of 1842, and the Amalgamated Society of Engineers in 1851. But the club-branches remained the pillars of the edifice, and the leaders of these clubs the perhaps defeated Samsons still not averse to giving the pillars a shake from time to time.[1]

The chief links between branches long remained the visits of artisans tramping in search of work; and indeed the major difference between club and branch was perhaps that a club excluded, but a branch assisted, such travelling workmen. The Mutual Association of Coopers found itself so well sustained in this way that it let the nineteenth century pass before it established a central executive to co-ordinate its club-branches. No doubt, however, the Association was deterred from this step by principle as well as expediency. For a central executive might mean central authority, constraint of members, a claim to judge individuals' interests better than those individuals could themselves: all of which would be an affront to *laissez-faire* doctrine. That danger would be the greater if the central executive was composed of officers elected from and by the members as a whole, and thus presumed in some sense to have received a mandate from the whole. Many unions therefore directed one branch, or group of branches, to form an executive among themselves, and then periodically rotated this obligation from district to district. The Boilermakers sent their executive from town to town until 1880; and the General Union of

---

[1] S. and B. Webb, *Industrial Democracy*, London, 1920, p. 73.

Carpenters and Joiners last rotated their central administration in 1919, when they moved it from London to Warrington. Most trade unionists despised their executive, and considered administrative office 'a cushy job', as George Barnes, Secretary of the Amalgamated Society of Engineers, put it. Indeed, during the 1830s some Stone Masons thought so little of their general secretaryship that they proposed to put it out to the lowest tender.[1]

But however an executive was constituted, control of union funds might still enable it to direct the whole organization; and for this reason most unions resisted central control, and even central location, of funds. The Papermakers distributed their moneys among five leading branches or 'grand divisions'. The districts of the Miners' Association gave their national executive some financial powers but tried to conceal from it the balances held in district treasuries. The Engineers hit on the ingenious device of the so-called equalization of funds. *Laissez-faire* Engineers could not accept that their society should have power over its cash; but they did want stronger sections of the Society to give to weaker sections that minimal degree of assistance without which membership of the Society would be meaning-less. The Engineers decided that the branches, not the executive, must hold the funds; but that these funds must, at fixed intervals, be equalized proportionately between the branches, as if there were a common authority that could help all alike from common moneys. The arduous book-keeping of this curious exercise fell upon the executive which, as a bonus for liberty, was thus inhibited from meddling in union affairs.[2]

Trade unions formed in this way sought to replace the clubs' geographical exclusivism with the caste-consciousness implicit in the concept of 'craft'. The essence of craft is the claim to skill, to all-round ability and to self-direction. The craft idea interacts with *laissez-faire* doctrines because it presumes an omnicompetent individual who knows what he wants and can get it. Craft is an inegalitarian notion when referred to those that the craftsman deems below himself, such as 'semi-skilled', 'unskilled', or, in a later dispensation, 'white-collar' workers. Yet craft is also a highly egalitarian notion when referred to

---

[1] George Barnes, *From Workshop to War Cabinet*, London, 1924, p. 36.
[2] S. and B. Webb, *The History of Trade Unionism*, London, 1920, p. 220.

those nominally set in authority over the craftsman. For, according to craft principles, the craftsman receives his skill either from heredity or on the job from another craftsman; and nineteenth-century craftsmen denied that either managerial interference or formal education entered into this 'apprenticeship'. Of course apprenticeship itself implies an infringement of negative liberty, and is accordingly spoken of in feudal or almost penal terms as 'serving one's time'; while a craftsman out of his apprenticeship is known as a 'time-served man'.

Craft claims rest on insecure foundations. The demarcation of one 'craft' from another is always artificial, and can always be changed by some modification either of methods or of materials. Hence the recurrent 'demarcation disputes' that have characterized especially those industries, such as ship-building, where the work has often been reorganized by changes in productive technique. Many craftsmen are, furthermore, peculiarly vulnerable to 'de-skilling'. Wherever technical change is unregulated by considerations of individual convenience—as in a system such as *laissez-faire* capitalism—new machinery must be forever making difficult work easy: indeed, this is the essence of industrialization. What this year can only be done by a time-served man will be done next year by dozens of upgraded labourers. The craftsman is, therefore, technologically speaking, a reactionary. He is also a man naturally disposed towards solidarity; for, in a world where his job is always being made obsolete, he is unlikely ever to get more money for the same work without his trade union. And in all these respects the craftsman is the employee writ large.

Both employers and employees attributed the price of labour to natural rather than social forces, to the operation of the 'laws' that governed human behaviour, rather than to the application of 'rules' that men could make and remake at will. From time to time in the nineteenth century employers and employees spoke of their 'rights' in regard to wages, or of a 'just' or an 'unjust' price of labour. But these notions were introduced almost as afterthoughts by those who, first and foremost, looked on remuneration for work as a matter, like so many others, to be determined by self-interested manipulations of the machinery of supply and demand, rather than by free rational choice among several possibilities that could be ranked according to various moral criteria.

A bourgeois critic of trade unionism argued in 1869 that 'nature awards' those who labour only a certain (if changing) proportion of the economic product; and that this proportion or 'wage-fund' seeks a 'natural level', or a 'natural equilibrium', to which all divergences towards an unnaturally high or low price for labour in general, or for any class of labour, must ultimately return. 'In the long run, God's laws will overwhelm all human obstructions', concluded this writer; and in that opinion trade unionists concurred. 'I may say,' replied the secretary of the Amalgamated Society of Engineers when asked in 1867 about wages, 'that we are very little engaged indeed in regulating these points, they regulate themselves, if I may use the expression.'[1]

But such theories of wages must not be construed in too formalist a sense. In practice, both employers and employees recognized three factors which determined the price of labour from time to time. In the first place, the accumulation of capital inversely controlled the cost of production, the greater the accumulation the lower being the cost. Secondly, the demand for, and the supply of, the product controlled the price of the product, excess demand producing a high price, excess supply producing a low price. And thirdly, the difference between the cost of the product and its going price was divisible between the owners of capital and the suppliers of labour in almost any proportions, depending on the size of this difference, current expectations of future profitability, the relationship between the demand for labour and the supply of it, and so forth.

Employers and employees disputed the distribution of the difference between cost and price so conceived; and of course neither were willing to accept rules (other than those of their own devising) to order this distribution. Both parties therefore resorted to industrial action; and both viewed such action as experimental investigations into the operation of 'natural' economic laws. Since men must disagree not merely about their deserts but also about the degree to which, at any point in

---

[1] James Stirling, *Trade Unionism, with Remarks on the Report of the Commissioners on Trade Unions*, Glasgow, 1869, pp. 26–9; *Organisation and Rules of Trade Unions and Other Associations*, London, 1867, p. 36.

time, trade did or did not suffice their deserts to be met, strikes and lock-outs must be resorted to, in a fundamentally empirical frame of mind. If trade was good, then the employer's desire to continue production in order to maximize profit would weaken his power and resolve to keep wages low by enduring a strike or by locking-out his employees. If trade was bad, the threat of unemployment would weaken the employee's power and resolve to get higher wages by enduring a lock-out or by striking against his employer. The notion of any authority, or any principles, relevant to wages was, in short, repudiated; and individual or sectional power to pursue individual or sectional interests was the only admissible criterion.

Craftsmen tried to pursue their interest in high wages by controlling the availability of labour, a method specially, though not uniquely, attractive to apprenticed workers who always tended, largely because of the length of their training, to be in short supply. While labour was relatively immobile, and where employers could not adapt the job fast enough, unions now and then enjoyed a monopoly of labour competent to perform certain productive functions. Moreover, when all the craftsmen in the shop, and their foremen, were members of or sympathizers with the union, the foreman would seek the names of new workmen either from the union men already in the shop or from the union club in the nearby public house. In these conditions, whenever the union men judged the time right for wages to rise, they could, in theory, withdraw their members in ones or twos until the employer, unable to replace them because of the union's monopoly, and unable to continue production without them, would increase wages—probably without a formal demand having been made. Such was the 'strike in detail', in which the craftsmen did not acknowledge the existence, let alone the authority, of the employer even to the extent of negotiating with him.[1]

Employers shared the presuppositions of the craftsmen's policy, and were not at all unhappy to shun negotiations themselves. Management hated but used unions, just as unions hated but used management: because each thought the other merely an external agency, useful if exploited, but unacceptable if it obliged them to consider interests other than their own.

[1] Webbs, pp. 46, 199–200.

Nevertheless employers hoped, and not without reason, to win their encounters with trade unions, and, when that hope got the better of them, strikes in detail turned into prolonged battles sometimes lasting months, in which each side, rigidly faithful to their *laissez-faire* doctrines, refused to negotiate with each other, and usually met only in the correspondence-columns of newspapers, or through the activities of self-appointed mediators. By the twentieth century such practices had been sanctified by tradition: 'you present your petitions to the bosses, and if they refuse it, you strike . . . they present a petition to you, which you refuse, and they lock you out', observed Will Thorne in 1918. The pattern could become drearily monotonous. As Baldwin remarked in 1926:

> The recurring crises have always had certain common symptoms. Either the Mining Association gives notice of a reduction or the Federation demands an advance. They do not negotiate; each side refuses to take less than it asks and ties itself up in a complete deadlock.

In the end either the employers won (as in the engineering lock-out of 1852), or the unions won (as in the 'nine hours' movement' of 1871); but whatever the outcome, the subsequent complaints of the defeated could not disguise most men's complacency that 'God's laws' had again triumphed, things had again 'regulated themselves', and the free competitive market of *laissez-faire* ideology stood firm.[1]

COLLABORATION AND CO-OPERATION

That ideology directed labour, not merely towards doctrines of individualism and negative liberty, but also towards a general acquiescence in the emergent order of industrial capitalism. The approximation of this acquiescence to collaboration with employers, can be seen in much of the politics of early nineteenth-century wage earners. These politics did sometimes contain a certain revolutionary element. J. F. Bray's *Labour's Wrongs and Labour's Remedy* appeared in 1839 with the slogan, 'THE PRESENT ARRANGEMENTS OF SOCIETY MUST BE TOTALLY SUBVERTED', while Ernest Jones's *Notes to*

[1] Trades Union Congress *Report*, 1918, p. 194; *House of Commons Debates*, vol. 195, col. 58.

the People of 1851 declared that the capitalists 'will be our foes as long as they exist'. 'Therefore,' Jones concluded, 'they must BE PUT DOWN. Therefore we MUST have class against class . . . CLASS AGAINST CLASS—all other mode of proceeding is mere moonshine.' Yet Bray and Jones appear neither to have convinced many wage earners nor to have secured a permanent organized following among them.[1]

This should not be surprising, since even if class were set against class, *and* the present arrangements totally subverted, some new order must ensue: and, given most employees' attitudes, this order could scarcely be based on any principles other than the *laissez-faire* doctrines that sustained the existing order. The case of Robert Owen is highly instructive in this respect. G. D. H. Cole noted that 'working-class Owenism' developed in the physical 'absence of its inspirer', who was living in North America during the mid-1820s, when his ideas first took hold on a significant section of the British wage-earning population. Yet Owen, who had been reviled as a paternalist by *The Black Dwarf* as early as 1817, was absent from 'working-class Owenism' even more in the spirit than in the flesh. For Owen, unlike his ostensible disciples, was a thorough-going collectivist, who deplored the notion that humanity should be given over to a 'mass of contending interests', and favoured nothing less than 'a refined parental democracy' with a national 'system for the formation of character, and general amelioration of the lower orders'. Nothing could be farther removed from J. S. Mill's great *laissez-faire* belief that 'individuality should assert itself': and in general J. S. Mill has prevailed in Britain, both with capital and with labour.[2]

Indeed, it was the *solidarity*, rather than the conflict, between capital and labour, which labour politics expressed during

[1] Bray, p. 17; Hollis, pp. 82–3.

[2] G. D. H. Cole, *A Short History of the British Working-Class Movement 1789–1947*, London, 1948, p. 55; Hollis, p. 31; Robert Owen, *The Book of the New Moral World containing the Rational System of Society, founded on Demonstrable Facts, developing the Constitution and Laws of Human Nature and of Society*, London, 1836, pp. 6, 86; *A New View of Society: or, Essays on the Formation of the Human Character preparatory to the Development of a Plan for gradually Ameliorating the Condition of Mankind*, 3rd edn., London, 1817, p. 65; *The Revolution in the Mind and Practice of the Human Race*, p. 77; J. S. Mill, *Utilitarianism; Liberty; Representative Government*, London, 1968, p. 115.

much of the nineteenth century: that is to say, these politics were specifically industrial politics, arising from the concerns and concepts of an industrial and, in particular, a manu-facturing milieu. This milieu was characterized first, by the intense utilitarian egocentricism explicit in the political economists' notion of economic man, secondly, by strong hostility to the pre-industrial (or non-industrial) order. True, certain labour political leaders vigorously attacked capital, and demanded 'the full proceeds' of labour's work (as O'Brien put it in *The Operative* in 1839), even though such a demand could only lead to internecine warfare of industrialists. But to a very great extent, labour's political ambitions—parliamentary reform, extension of the franchise, and land nationalization—were aims to which capital could in the last resort assent, since they threatened the agrarian, aristocratic world with which capital conflicted at least as much as did labour. Hence the ability of many owners of capital and the great majority of manual workers to combine in support of the Liberal Party right up to the outbreak of the First World War.[1]

In any event, large political objectives were on the whole foreign to organized labour which (however far-seeing any individual labourer might have been) preferred to devote its collective force towards securing narrow and immediate objectives, and preferably objectives with a cash value. 'The great and ultimate object' of the Grand National Consolidated Trades Union was 'to establish the paramount rights of Industry and Humanity'—itself an instructive sequence—but 'the design of the Union' was 'in the first instance, to raise the wages of the workmen, or to prevent any further reduction therein, and to diminish the hours of labour'. These priorities determined the famous political 'neutralism' of labour, expressed, as late as 1885, by the President of the Trades Union Congress, who declared that, 'it has been the boast of trade-unionists that they belong to no political party; I hope they never will as it is now understood.' Such 'neutralism' did not signify non-partisanship: for most trade unionists were Liberals, and the rest were Tories. Rather, it indicated labour leaders' desire to shun the 'ultimate', whether in its political or any other form, and to cleave to the immediate industrial concerns

[1] Hollis, p. 216.

that absorbed them in what they alleged to be 'the first instance'.[1]

The all-pervading force of liberal individualism, the ambiguity of large political goals that seem always to resolve themselves into simple industrial objectives, can also be seen in the various schemes of co-operation, planned and executed, that took up so much of organized labour's energy in the Victorian era. By 1880 the debate about co-operation was over: it was hailed as 'the logical consequence' of trade unionism, the 'true solution' to labour's problems. From then on, many have come to speak only of the Co-operative Movement, as if there were some great unified league going forward to realize in practice a scientific truth of social and ethical theory. But the shops and factories that formed the 'Movement' were not particularly unified even by 1880, while its allegedly far-reaching aims fell well short of those bolder schemes of co-operation that succumbed to fate on the road to the essentially bourgeois orthodoxy of the late nineteenth century.[2]

This orthodoxy originated, like so much in labour organization, in the benefit society. Early trade unions took money from their members, saved it, and returned it to them in the form of unemployment, funeral and other benefits. Goose clubs, and similar institutions, took money from their members, saved it and returned it, say at Christmas, in the form of a lump sum for the purchase of goods. The shops that together came to constitute the Co-operative Movement were rather more ambitious. These shops bought goods and sold them to their members on such terms that part of the price was returned, after a time, in the form of a 'dividend' which members were encouraged to leave, as an interest-bearing loan, with the shop. In theory, the goods sold were cheaper than those available elsewhere, although, since in 1900 only about 8 per cent of the population aged twenty and over belonged to co-operative societies of this type, that theory does not seem to have been widely perceived as a reality.

Nevertheless, the members both filled their shopping

[1] *Rules and Regulations of the Grand National Consolidated Trades' Union of Great Britain and Ireland: Instituted for the Purpose of the more effectually Enabling the Working Classes to Secure, Protect, and Establish the Rights of Industry*, London, 1834, p. 22; Trades Union Congress *Report*, 1885, p. 17.

[2] Trades Union Congress *Report*, 1880, pp. 32–3.

baskets and got small lump sums to spend; and this benefit, tricked out with a curiously capitalistic terminology of 'dividends', 'share capital', 'interest', and so forth, had perhaps a similar appeal to that of 'gift' or 'trading' stamps today. 'As soon as is practicable', resolved some of the first managers of co-operative shops, the Equitable Pioneers of Toad Lane, Rochdale, 'this society shall proceed to arrange the powers of production, distribution, education and government.' This project did not prove immediately practicable; but the Rochdale men and others meanwhile built up, on quite straightforward managerial lines, a network of shops and warehouses and, eventually, a number of factories engaged in the production of consumer goods, whose rules of procedure and remuneration were sufficiently objectionable to many trade unionists to rouse severe criticism at successive Trades Union Congresses. Indeed, in 1890 the spokesman of the Co-operative Movement only succeeded in addressing the Congress through the President's casting vote.[1]

The *other* co-operative organizations, so to speak, the organizations that disappeared so completely while the Co-operative Movement consolidated itself, arose not from friendly societies and goose clubs but from the ideal of the sovereign individual implicit in the concept of craft. This type of co-operation was designed, as *The Operative* put it in 1851, to 'preserve the independence of the workers'; and this notion must cast some doubt upon the same paper's proposal, in the same year, to achieve through the same agency 'a great and absolute change in the system of society'. For the principle of this type of co-operation was the organization of self-governing workshops in which, on quite novel lines, free and independent craftsmen would associate together in emancipation from all undemocratic forms of oversight and direction; and though such a principle might, if triumphant, modify property relationships in certain respects, it could only do so by realizing in drastic form the inner logic of liberal individualism, in which each man strove (and was taught to strive) to be his own master.[2]

[1] Cole, pp. 155–6; Trades Union Congress *Report*, 1880, p. 32; 1890, p. 46; 1909, p. 156.
[2] Christensen, pp. 245–6.

Just as the co-operative shops expressed their practical commitment to *laissez-faire* capitalism by their choice of terminology, so the co-operative workshops confessed their loyalty to the same system in the overt aims that they set themselves. Co-operating craftsmen would 'become their own Employers', believed *The Operative*, for which paper 'the only remedy' was 'that the labourer should become a capitalist'. Yet no man is a capitalist entire of himself but is rather joined to all men, and subordinated to some, in the larger social enterprise: so that even though he became his own employer the employee must still remain under some species of the external direction so irksome to *laissez-faire* doctrine. Indeed, within the co-operative workshop, each new advance of production would tend to require new rules, new authority, and, in short, new management.[1]

'Co-operation' of this sort, unlike 'co-operation' in the goose club tradition, was doomed to defeat itself. Unless the co-operative workshops succeeded, they must fail; but if they succeeded, they must cease to be co-operative. In practice, these co-operative ventures—such as the National Building Guild of 1833 and the Christian Socialist schemes of 1850–2, which involved, among others, carpenters, cabinet makers, printers and engineers—tended to fail for lack of capital and expertise. Yet these purely commercial pressures vied for destructive effect with the paradox of the attempt to escape management by creating one's own management. The workers, Perlman concluded, 'will mistrust and obstruct their union leaders who have become shop-bosses under whatever scheme of "workers' control".'[2]

THE CHALLENGE OF COLLECTIVISM

By the later years of the nineteenth century, therefore, labour had to show for its activities the trade unions and the Co-operative Movement, both of which expressed labour's fidelity to *laissez-faire* ideology. Yet new ideas were already being forced not merely on labour but on the whole of British society. Certain deficiencies of *laissez-faire* theory had long been con-

---

[1] Ibid., pp. 257, 267.
[2] Perlman, p. 246.

cealed only by British manufacturing hegemony and the world
vacuum of power after 1815. During these years Britain had
dominated the world's markets for finished goods, both by technical and commercial skill. Meanwhile, France was removed as
a power of the first order; Germany was disunited; Russia was
remote from British interests; and the United States were in their
infancy. In these circumstances, British naval power and
laissez-faire industrial capitalism proved more than adequate
to the requirements of the most ambitious policy then
devised.

During the next sixty years that followed the downfall of
Napoleon, these circumstances were entirely altered. The
United States began to develop an industrial technology soon
second to none; Germany moved at even greater speed towards
her European predominance in application of scientific research to industrial production; and both Americans and
Germans took the first steps towards displacing Britain as the
workshop of the world. The American Civil War, the Austro-
Prussian War, and, above all, the Franco-Prussian War,
demonstrated to Britain the possibilities of an industrial war
machine working on a principle of mass, conscript armies quite
unacceptable to *laissez-faire*. The 1870s therefore introduced a
period of crisis from which Britain has not yet escaped.

At the onset of this objective crisis, various theorists were
ready with criticisms of the older *laissez-faire* notions, arising
from a subjective perception not merely of the deficiencies of
those notions and the system built upon them, but of the
challenge of other ideas developed in continental Europe and
especially in Germany. Carlyle and Arnold were foremost
among such critics: the former through his translations from
and studies of the German romantics, and through his social
criticism, especially *Chartism*, which appeared in 1838, *Past and
Present*, which was first published in 1843, and 'Shooting
Niagara: and After?', which came out in 1867; the latter
through his researches into the German education system,
summarized in his *Higher Schools and Universities in Germany* of
1868, and through *Culture and Anarchy*, first published as a series
of articles in 1867–8.

'Shooting Niagara' and *Culture and Anarchy* coincided with the
introduction of Hegel to England, beginning with J. H.

Stirling's *The Secret of Hegel*, published in 1865, and continuing through the work of William Wallace, F. H. Bradley and others, and the translation of Hegel's works, from the *Logic of Hegel* which appeared in English in 1873, to the *Phenomenology of Mind*, translated or paraphrased in 1910. It was in this context that T. H. Green produced in 1879 a series of lectures with the ominously un-English title 'Lectures on the Principles of Political Obligation', from which stemmed various Hegelian and Rousseauesque studies, culminating in Bernard Bosanquet's *The Philosophical Theory of the State* of 1899.

E. E. Williams, lamenting the ground England had lost to Germany, called, in his famous book '*Made in Germany*', for a 'revolution in the English State or in the English mind and habit'. *That*, Williams feared, was impossible; but Carlyle, Arnold and their successors nevertheless devoted themselves to it. These critics repudiated liberal individualism and hoped to see, in Arnold's words, 'the State' become 'the appointed frame and prepared vessel of our best self', and 'our best self's powerful, beneficent and sacred expression and organ'. A great new goal had opened up for men like Arnold, an end that superseded the individualist and sectional ends of *laissez-faire*. 'That end is what I call freedom in the positive sense:' Green told a Liberal party meeting in 1880, 'in other words, the liberation of the powers of all men equally for contributions to a common good. No one has a right to do what he will with his own in such a way as to contravene this end.' And this doctrine slowly crept into practical politics, so that even a man like Asquith could warn the public in 1902 that, 'Liberty (in a political sense) is not only a negative but a positive conception.'[1]

The most significant response to these ideas was 'social imperialism'. Social imperialists first looked to the British empire as a source of strength with which to combat the new challenges to Britain. Britain, wrote J. A. Froude in 1869, might 'sink, as Holland has sunk, into a community of harmless traders, and leave to others the place which once we held and

---

[1] Ernest Edwin Williams, '*Made in Germany*', London, 1896, p. 164; Matthew Arnold, *Culture and Anarchy*, Cambridge, 1960, p. 205; Melvin Richter, *The Politics of Conscience, T. H. Green and his Age*, London, 1964; H. C. G. Matthew, *The Liberal Imperialists: The Ideas and Politics of a Post-Gladstonian Elite*, London, 1973, p. 140.

have lost the energy to keep'; or, on the contrary, might 'become the metropolis of an enormous and coherent Empire'. Schemes of imperial federation were debated; Gladstonian 'Little Englandism' was rejected, even by sections of the Liberal Party; and the British government now took a new and active directing role in the development of empire, notably in the acquisition of the Suez Canal and in the 'scramble for Africa'. Social imperialists then sought to concentrate national energies on the creation of what Rosebery called 'an Imperial race', whose social efficiency should enable both the harmonious development of all, and the extension and maintenance of British influence throughout the world.[1]

The project received its definitive form in the work of the so-called 'National Efficiency' party of the years about 1900. But its outlines were already present in Disraeli's government of 1874–80, which carried various welfare measures that, though of little practical significance, did embody this new collectivist doctrine of positive liberty. Indeed, as early as 1869, Sir Stafford Northcote, later Chancellor of the Exchequer under Disraeli, told the Social Science Congress that though 'individual freedom and fair competition are the very breath of our nostrils', social questions were 'assuming such large dimensions' that they could only be dealt with 'by the employment of the central administrative machinery'. Politicians thus began to give notice to the nation both that *laissez-faire* had in part been abandoned, and that policy at home and abroad would be established on new principles: namely, that some general good, outside the competence of separate individuals and sections, could be discerned by the organs of the state; and that citizens could be required to assist in the achievement of this good. In other words, a new type of citizenship was envisaged, a citizenship founded on what Bosanquet called 'Freedom in the greater Self'.[2]

Whether or not this doctrine of collectivism and social

---

[1] C. A. Bodelson, *Studies in Mid-Victorian Imperialism*, Copenhagen, 1924, pp. 106, 109; Matthew, p. 236; cf. Bernard Semmel, *Imperialism and Social Reform, English Social-Imperial Thought, 1885–1914*, London, 1960, *passim*; and G. R. Searle, *The Quest for National Efficiency, A Study in British Politics and Political Thought 1899–1914*, Oxford, 1971, *passim*.

[2] Paul Smith, *Disraelian Conservatism and Social Reform*, London, 1967, p. 131; Bernard Bosanquet, *The Philosophical Theory of the State*, London, 1965, p. x.

direction was necessary to Britain in the new world situation, it was certainly unpopular with the British people. Joseph Chamberlain's theory of the 'ransom' shows the difficulties of the new doctrine. Chamberlain was closely associated with the growth of social imperialism through various schemes culminating in his tariff reform programme. Yet Chamberlain was, if a collectivist at all, a collectivist of a very special sort. The essence of the idea to which social imperialism was itself a response was the transcendence of a society, deemed to be no more than an aggregate of bargaining, fighting individuals, in a state whose harmony would bring all men into one co-operative whole, able to order itself single-mindedly. The essence of the 'ransom' theory, on the contrary, was an order in which individuals were combined into a small number of corporate entities, whose relative fewness merely simplified and rationalized the bargaining and fighting, and whose power was sufficient to quell whatever dissidents might remain in their own ranks.

Men's common rights to the earth had been abrogated, delared Chamberlain in his speech of 5 January 1885. 'What ransom will property pay for the security which it enjoys?' he asked. 'What substitute will it find for the natural rights which have ceased to be recognized?' On 28 April, returning to the myth of a primeval universal natural right to the earth now reserved to the rich, Chamberlain was more explicit. 'Society owes a compensation to the poorer classes of this country', he announced. If such 'compensation' was to be paid in orderly fashion, the country would need to be grouped into sections— such as 'property' on the one hand and 'the poorer classes' on the other—able to formulate demands and come to a rational, enforceable agreement about their settlement. The era of *laissez-faire* in which individuals (or possibly certain petty sections of individuals) were best judges and best executors of their interests, and pursuit of those interests was the high road to the good of all, was dead. But this era was to be succeeded simply by a higher sectionalism, a corporatism, in which—as a compromise between the full collectivism which the world crisis seemed to some to demand, and the *laissez-faire* fragmentation of pure Gladstonian democracy—separate individuals would be grouped, organized and set to bargain. That compromise was the farthest *laissez-faire* Britain would go towards E. E. Williams's revolution of 'mind and habit'.[1]

THE CORPORATIST COMPROMISE

News of the corporatist compromise between discredited *laissez-faire* and over-radical collectivism was brought to trade unionists not so much by Chamberlain as by the Fabian movement, and above all by the chief spokesmen of Fabianism, Sidney and Beatrice Webb, whose influence on the intellectual development of British labour can scarcely be overstated. The Webbs were, to a certain extent, collectivists. 'We ourselves', they wrote at the end of their *Industrial Democracy*, 'understand by the words "Liberty" or "Freedom" ' not 'natural or inalienable rights', but such conditions as result in 'the utmost possible development of . . . the individual human being.' The 'Perfect City was something different from any number of good individuals', argued Sidney Webb, in his book *Socialism in England*. Rather, it was a structured organism in which each 'cell', including the 'cell' of the expert governing class, had its own special work to do. Hence his faith in paternalistic notions such as compulsory arbitration of industrial disputes, a scientific 'apportionment of income', and a legal National Minimum of welfare to be determined by the state.[2]

Yet 'English Socialists' were, Sidney Webb claimed, 'by no means blind worshippers of Karl Marx': on the contrary, the 'economic influence most potent' among them was 'still that of John Stuart Mill'. It was in the spirit of Mill that the Webbs, and other Fabians, looked with disfavour on the somewhat commonplace collectivist notion that the economic activity of the community should be carried on by the whole community, through the organs of the whole community. Socialism certainly did not mean 'a rigidly centralised national administration of all the details of life', claimed Sidney Webb, whose preference for 'municipalization', rather than 'nationalization' led him to advocate 'gas and water' socialism: that is, the

[1] Peter Fraser, *Joseph Chamberlain, Radicalism and Empire 1868–1914*, London, 1966, pp. 50–1.

[2] Webbs, *Industrial Democracy*, pp. 598, 766 ff., 813–14, 816–17, 847; A. M. McBriar, *Fabian Socialism and English Politics, 1884–1918*, Cambridge, 1962; Sidney Webb, *Socialism in England*, London, 1890, p. 83.

public control of those utilities that lent themselves most obviously to municipal rather than national administration.[1]

The Webbs approached trade unionism in the same spirit. For nearly a century the unions, dedicated to *laissez-faire*, had tried to further the interests, and especially the monetary interests, of their members—and no more. The Webbs now summoned the unions to expand till they were coterminous with society, to represent the principles of a new era, and to exemplify, by their inner workings and by the practice of 'collective bargaining' (a phrase Beatrice Webb claimed to have invented), a system of corporatist 'industrial democracy'. 'Each class of producers', whether by hand or brain, should be organized in 'a wisely directed Trade Unionism'; and these great sections, once established, should devote themselves to the improvement of their own corporation, and the making of 'national agreements' with other sections. True, administration and use of national resources must be conducted by reference to 'the scientifically ascertained conditions of efficiency'; but, in the Webbs' version of collectivism, 'the "established expectation" and the "fighting force" of all the classes' must bear heavily upon these matters. For sectionalism would remain, as would the self-interested struggles beloved of *laissez-faire* theorists: even if, in the Webbian utopia, these struggles would be rather fewer in number and distinctly more rational in tone.[2]

Once more corporatism must be seen precisely as a compromise between Marx and Mill, between a collectivism perceived as an alien, disquieting, yet finally foreign doctrine, and an individualism, recognized, with whatever regretful reservations, as British commonsense. Even so, corporatism seemed daring enough to trade unionists who, though flattered by the Webbs' attentions, cared little for their novel ideas. Trade unionists did not understand the municipalization of industry, which they interpreted solely as a means to restrict unemployment by transforming private into public employers, less able to sack their employees. And trade union leaders disliked the Webbs' more generous ideas for the future of labour because they feared that assumption of corporate responsibilities of whatever kind would merely further complicate the

[1] Webbs, pp. 85, 109–10.
[2] Webbs, *Industrial Democracy*, pp. 173, 599, 809, 825.

already exceedingly difficult task of satisfying their members.

The 'new unionism' of the years about 1890 might be thought to go some way to fit trade unions for the role that the Webbs planned for them. Before 1889 unions were self-avowedly sectional societies, usually of higher paid workers, pursuing sectional ends, and little given to edifying rhetoric. After 1889 some unions appealed to 'labour', rather than a specific 'trade'; tried to recruit all workers, sometimes adopted the vocabulary of socialism; and professed to represent or aspire to 'the brotherhood of man'. Before 1889 unions organized about 4 per cent of all workers; but in the 1890s they organized about 10 per cent. The 'new unionism', as people began to call it, thus made trade unions seem more worthy of the corporatist doctrine. But new unionism left trade unionists openly divided among themselves. Those older unions that did not grow so rapidly as other older unions more favourably placed to exploit the new recruiting opportunities, or were simply ejected from their accustomed pre-eminence by the new organizations, resented these innovations and were displeased by the aggressive methods and large social claims of the new unions. 'I for one', declared a leader of the Boot and Shoe Operatives in 1890, 'am not going to follow the new trades unionism of dragging men through the gutter with flags and big drums.'[1]

The older unionists' scepticism was expressed most thoroughly in George Howell's *Trade Unionism New and Old*, published in 1891. 'Continental workmen believe in the State, at least theoretically', observed Howell: but those new unionists who demanded a socialist state and socialist laws were the first to 'set at naught' the laws already 'in existence'. Such demands fared ill at both the 1890 and 1891 Trades Union Congresses. Thomas Burt, Lib.-Lab. M.P., and Northumberland Miners' leader, warned the 1891 Congress, over which he presided, that 'the great dividing line among us is as to the proper functions of the State'. 'My own leaning, he declared, 'is in the direction of self-help, rather than that of State compulsion'. The call for a statutory eight-hours day, much favoured by new unionists, was carried, by just under 60 per cent, in a thin vote in 1891.

[1] Alan Fox, *A History of the National Union of Boot and Shoe Operatives*, Oxford, 1958, p. 114.

But the new unionists won favour for their 'militancy' rather than their 'socialism'. As Tom Walker of the Cabinet Makers put it, 'Unite labour, and then the workers could snap their fingers at everyone. . . . Workers should bind themselves into strong unions, and then they could force up the price of labour.'[1]

So long as these sentiments persisted, neither the socialist new unions' example nor their persuasion could bring the old unionism to collectivism or even corporatism. Indeed, few unions would have treated either collectivist or corporatist notions as anything more than utopian theorization, of an excessively dangerous kind, had not employers eventually been willing and able to force on unions a new structure of industrial relations that realized, at least in part, some of the corporatists' theories. During most of the nineteenth century most employers tried either to ignore or to destroy labour organization since, like trade unionists, they held to an absolute *laissez-faire* doctrine which required them to resist all external interference and to seek to order industry unilaterally. But after 1870 a few employers adopted new policies. In the Durham and Northumberland coalfield, the north of England ironworking districts, and the South Wales coalfield, employers seized the opportunity afforded by the severe downturn in trade of the mid-1870s to bring trade unions into a system of unitary corporatism.[2]

According to the ideas that sustained this type of corporatism, each productive sector formed an 'industry' in promotion of whose affairs employers and employees should unite, above all in joint settlement of wages by reference to the selling price of the product. Labour would thus surrender all claim to a special or separate interest in the determination of earnings. 'Sliding scales' and other devices created to control wages very largely precluded the possibility of independent trade unions, and put the broadest direction of production almost entirely in the employers' hands. In the South Wales coalfield, management came almost to run the employees' organization, which was maintained very largely by deductions from the men's wages,

---

[1] Howell, pp. 119, 190; Trades Union Congress *Report*, 1890, pp. 44–5; 1891, p. 34.

[2] H. A. Clegg, Alan Fox, and A. F. Thompson, *A History of British Trade Unions Since 1889*, vol. 1, 1889–1910, Oxford, 1964, pp. 18–23.

made by the employers, and handed over to the union's leaders. Such a system—collectivism in one industry, so to speak—was moving, Sidney Webb observed, towards 'a gigantic coal-trust governed by a joint committee of capitalists and workmen, regulating output, prices, and rates of wages': though in practice the employer could and would dominate any such 'joint committee'. This was not lost on the unions; and, as trade recovered, they rejected the 'sliding scale' agreements, most of which had been terminated by 1900.[1]

As the failure of unitary corporatism became apparent, some employers favoured the more modest schemes of bipartite corporatism advocated by the majority of the Royal Commission on Labour of 1891–4. According to this doctrine, 'industries' did not possess a unitary existence; and employers and employees were agreed to have separate and sometimes conflicting interests. But both were expected to compromise and even, on certain occasions, to surrender some of those interests in order to achieve negotiated settlements through the machinery of some form of 'collective bargaining'. Eight commissioners did indeed recommend optional legal incorporation of the parties to any bipartite corporatist system: but this was the boldest proposal put forward in 1894.

The shift towards a system of 'collective bargaining', including one or more joint committees, formulating their agreements by reference both to the demands and concessions of the disputing parties, and to some rules of procedure already settled between them, affected several industries, coalmining among them. In the 1870s one such system gained popularity in the boot and shoe industry, but, the Webbs noted, caused 'endless friction . . . among workmen and employers alike' before it collapsed in 1894. Another major step towards collective bargaining of this type was taken in the cotton industry while the Royal Commission sat. The Federation of Master Cotton Spinners' Associations, dominated by new joint-stock companies, and influenced by the advanced views of Sir Charles Macara, locked-out the spinning operatives in 1892–3, and in March 1893 negotiated with the operatives the 'Brooklands Agreement' which contained rules for wages negotiation and joint settlement of other disputes. The Agreement was established by the

---

[1] Webbs, *Industrial Democracy*, pp. 210–11, 576–7.

employers and on their terms; but included concessions by them, and was not entirely unacceptable to the spinning operatives' leaders who were no longer quite so loyal to pure *laissez-faire* and a *laissez-faire* system of industrial relationships as were some of their followers.[1]

Yet the bipartite corporatism of collective bargaining, the system that has had so decisive an effect on twentieth-century industry and politics, owed its origins not so much to the mine owners or the boot and shoe or cotton manufacturers as to the organized engineering employers. Engineering employers, like many others, long favoured *laissez-faire* and condemned anything that suggested collectivism. They had associated together in 1851–2 to attack the newly formed Amalgamated Society of Engineers, but they had done so reluctantly and, after their victory, soon separated from each other. Indeed, the lock-out of 1852 was quite free of *doctrinal* controversy between employers and trade union, since both agreed that *laissez-faire* should prevail, and struggled merely over the division of the spoils of a *laissez-faire* system. Both employers and employees in the engineering industry desired, in the mid-nineteenth century, to deny each other's existence, and to refuse each other any share in and claim upon the conduct of their own affairs, affairs that they interpreted in the widest possible sense.

By the end of the nineteenth century these ideas had begun to lose their persuasive force among engineering employers who saw themselves threatened by both Germans and Americans. German industry was now applying the results of scientific research to the manufacture, with newly-built machine tools in newly-built factories, of goods designed for British markets; and the United States was rapidly progressing from its well-established dominance of machine tool technology to the position of a leading exporter of finished engineering goods. Engineering employers therefore wished to cut their costs by retooling their factories and by employing the less skilled and cheaper labour required by a new generation of metal-working machines. And to do this they needed, they believed, not to 'outlaw' trade unions, as they had done in 1852, but to integrate those organizations into a new industrial system able to meet the new world situation.

[1] Ibid., p. 187; Clegg, Fox, and Thompson, pp. 114–17.

Engineering employers found the theory of such a system in the thinking of men like H. C. S. Dyer, manager of Armstrong's Elswick works in Newcastle. Dyer rejected the *laissez-faire* doctrine that underlay the lock-out of 1852. He reasoned that employers must create a new type of common or bilateral authority better equipped to formulate general policy for the engineering industry than had been the old, free, unregulated organizations of employers and employees alike. Since Dyer believed that management should predominate, and that the unions had excessive power, he expected the employers to exert their will against the unions at least as decisively as they had done in 1852. But he did not hold either that employers could subsume and speak for unions, as in unitary corporatism, or that they should abolish unions.

'Don't think for one moment that I am objecting to your Society in any way', he told the Engineers' leaders in April 1897.—'I hope to see the day when every workman shall belong to some Trade Society, and when every employer shall also belong to an Employers' Trade Society. We shall then . . . be able to discuss questions on a broad and sensible basis.' In other words, employers and employees should be organized, in the characteristic manner of corporatism, into large, rationally ordered sections, and set to bargain. Unlike the more drastic form of corporatism which saw each industry as a unified section, all decisions in and for which should be taken by those that commanded the decision-making machinery of the productive process, Dyer's corporatism conceded the existence, within the industrial section, of separate interests whose disputes must be settled by mutual bargains: bargains which, of course, would be shaped by the common need of all to resist the pressures from other and rival sections.[1]

A prolonged lock-out ended, in 1898, with 'Terms of Settlement', by which, in return for recognition of unions' 'proper functions', the unions had to acknowledge the employers' right to unimpeded 'management of their business'. The unions' proper functions remained unspecified, but clearly included negotiation with the employers both at local and national level, since rules about such negotiations were written

[1] *Conference between the Employers' Federation of Engineering Associations and the Amalgamated Society of Engineers . . . April 1897*, pp. 52, 84.

into the Terms. From the employers' point of view, the chief appeal of these rules, the 'Provisions for Avoiding Disputes', lay in the prohibition of industrial action in any dispute until the possibilities of the negotiating machinery had been entirely exhausted. That prohibition clearly attacked the notion of a 'right to strike' so important to the *laissez-faire* doctrine that each man could judge his own interest, which he was or should be free to pursue by whatever means he thought appropriate. For this reason, the 'Provisions for Avoiding Disputes' were never acceptable to the Engineers who repudiated them *de facto* as soon as they were able, though that opportunity did not arise till many years later.[1]

By about 1900, nevertheless, the concept of negative freedom implicit in *laissez-faire* had given way in industrial relations to something rather nearer the concept of positive freedom. No longer did all men believe that individual or sectional interest should be pursued regardless of all else; but, rather, at least some men thought they perceived a general good, if only in the affairs of a particular industry, to which individuals should surrender some of their own goods. Conflict between employers and employees continued; but conflict was now modified to a remarkable degree by collective bargaining between parties organized to represent divided interests in the formation of a single set of policy decisions. In due course, and with various adaptations, the engineering industry's example was followed in almost every other section of employment. Liberal individualism and market economics were abandoned only in part and with regret; but bipartite corporatism now gave British industry and British society a basic shape that was largely retained over seven decades.

---

[1] Arthur Marsh, *Industrial Relations in Engineering*, Oxford, 1965, p. 20.

3

Syndicalism *versus* Labour Politics

What is a Trade Union? It is a combination of workers to defend their own interests from the encroachments of the employers.

Well, a Labour Party is a combination of workers to defend their own interests from the encroachments of the employers or their representatives in Parliament and on Municipal bodies.

ROBERT BLATCHFORD, *Britain for the British*

many of those who but yesterday were shouting against the strike, and in favour of fighting the battle on the floor of the House of Commons, are now telling us that legislation is too slow, and what is required is 'the general strike'.

W. BRODIE (Amalgamated Society of Engineers) Election Address, 1910.

THE REACTION TO CORPORATISM

When engineering employers tried to introduce drilling, grinding, and sawing machinery in the 1890s, they were responding to pressures—of foreign competition and technological change—which reshaped, not merely engineering, but much of British industry between 1890 and 1920. The industrial innovations of these years would have been startling enough if, as was the case in America, they had followed a period of continuous technical development. But the resistance to change that characterized mid- and late-Victorian manufacturing made the sudden surrender to 'new machines' the more alarming to a workforce long used to materials and methods often fundamentally unaltered since the industrial revolution. About 1900, wood-working machines operable by men who had never undergone an apprenticeship were introduced on certain jobs hitherto the preserve of craftsmen carpenters and joiners; metal moulding machines, worked by upgraded labourers, began to do the work of the skilled moulder; and turret and capstan metal working lathes ousted the centre lathe and the craftsman turner who alone could use it. In all these cases the new methods threatened existing levels of wages. Workers outside manufacturing also suffered. Tramwaymen were obliged to convert from steam to electric trams; cab drivers had to reckon with the replacement of horse-drawn vehicles by motor cars; and metropolitan railway men had to face the advent of the electric train. In these cases, jobs as well as wages were threatened; but in no instance did such transitions prove easy for labour.[1]

Even where management did not bring in new machines, it modified the older machines so that they ran faster and produced more. Many factories tried to 'speed up' not only the time in which work was processed on the machine, but also the pace at which work was brought on and off machines, and moved between one shop and another. The 'speed up' was achieved by employing more, and more active, foremen to watch over production; and by introducing systems of piecework designed to control effort within precise limits. Under timework, an employee was paid for the hours he worked, regardless of what he produced; under traditional piecework systems, he was paid for what he produced, regardless of how long he worked. The former system prevented employers from securing extra effort from their employees, because employers had to pay employees for the hours they were in the shop, however little they produced; and the latter system prevented employers from controlling their wages bill, because they had to pay employees for what they produced, however little time it took them.

The employers' first response to this problem was to study their employees' capacities closely enough to find out how much work they could do: and, then to fix piecerates accordingly. In this way, they hoped to avoid the 'loose' piece price, that is, a price that so underestimated the employee's capacities as to allow him to make high wages, whether by redoubling his

---

[1] H. A. Clegg, Alan Fox, and A. F. Thompson, *A History of British Trade Unions Since 1889*, vol. 1, 1889–1910, Oxford, 1964, pp. 332, 424.

efforts or by deceiving the rate fixer. The employers' second
response was to devise methods of payment such as the 'premium
bonus system', whereby employees received both a time rate
and a 'bonus' so calculated that it could never exceed the time
rate itself however fast the job was done. In this way, the
workforce either raised its effort to (but not beyond) a level
determined by the employers, or it surpassed that level purely
at its own expense. A manager 'always urges you to get bonus',
wrote a machinist working in Rugby in 1911, one year after
unions affiliated to the Trades Union Congress had voted 91
per cent against the system. 'He knows perfectly well that . . .
you will never be outrageously overpaid. That if he gives you
ten thousand hours to do a job and you did it in the ten-
thousandth part of a second you would just about double
your wages.'[1]

In fact real wages did decline after the turn of the century,
since earnings rose 6 per cent and the cost of living 12 per cent
between 1900 and 1913. This development hardened attitudes
within the factory, men accusing management of 'hustle', and
management accusing men of 'ca'canny', or slow working.
Some trade unionists had heard of, and feared, the methods of
'scientific management' pioneered by the American metallurgist
F. W. Taylor, who was held to have devised a system that far
surpassed premium bonus in its power to control effort, output
and remuneration. Still more trade unionists had heard of the
American trusts, whose 'tyranny', frequently condemned by
the Trades Union Congress, was said to include wage-cutting,
strike-breaking and large-scale dismissals. Few British employers wanted to 'smash the unions', but the new productive
methods, and the fall in real wages, left many workers sceptical.
When the British Federation of Master Printers, or the National
Federation of Building Trade Employers, sought to follow the
example of the Engineering Employers' Federation by introducing methods of collective bargaining based on the principles
of bipartite corporatism, they raised grave doubts in trade
unionists' minds.[2]

[1] *Amalgamated Engineers' Monthly Journal*, August 1911, p. 26.
[2] A. H. Halsey (ed.), *Trends in British Society Since 1900, A Guide to the Changing
Social Structure of Britain*, London, 1972, pp. 121–2; Trades Union Congress *Report*,
1901, p. 55.

In any event, unions had difficulties quite apart from those of their relationships with employers. Inter-union disagreements over demarcation of jobs continued (and indeed were increased by new productive techniques), especially in shipbuilding, but also elsewhere: for example, in building, where bricklayers and stonemasons disputed the laying of breeze blocks. But, as the number of trade unionists rapidly increased from 1889 onwards, unions became more conscious of their own and their rivals' opportunities; and demarcation disputes became less significant than disputes about unions' jurisdiction over different groups of workers. Jurisdictional quarrels grew steadily in number up to 1914; and multiplied thereafter until, by 1918, the President of the Trades Union Congress could speak of 'the innumerable cases that are constantly coming before us of complaints of societies overlapping in their members and activities.' During the years 1890–1920, among many other conflicts, the Amalgamated Society of Railway Servants sought to recruit footplate men organized by the Associated Society of Locomotive Engineers and Firemen, and indeed to become the one union recognized by railway employers; the largely provincial Typographical Association and the London printers' societies disputed the organization of printing machine men; and the Steel Smelters' Amalgamated Association and the Associated Iron and Steel Workers fought a particularly bitter struggle to recruit the day-wage workers at John Summers' factory at Hawarden Bridge.[1]

The Trades Union Congress's authority did not suffice to allay, resolve or even mitigate these conflicts. In fact, for *laissez-faire* trade unionists, that authority did not exist. When Congress decided in favour of the Co-operative Smiths against the Amalgamated Society of Engineers in 1899, and in favour of the Iron and Steel Workers against the Smelters in 1910, the disappointed party merely disaffiliated from the Congress. Congress could not, therefore, secure any such unity as might meet the new-found unity of employers bent on realizing their newfangled corporatist policies. Indeed the General Federation of Trade Unions, established by Congress in 1899 to assist affiliated unions, was so hampered by its own and its constituents' weaknesses that it devoted almost all its efforts to

[1] Trades Union Congress *Report*, 1918, pp. 53–4.

discouraging industrial stoppages. 'Caution was the characteristic of the Federation', write the historians of modern trade
unionism.[1]

So long as unions clung to their *laissez-faire* orthodoxies, they
stood alone. Labour industrial organization's traditional concept of itself was simply that it serviced its members' sectional
trade activities: and this concept survived substantially un-
damaged into the twentieth century. Each union executive was
constituted under a rigid, closely detailed and highly restrictive
rule book, and did little more than administer benefits and
tender rarely-sought and rarely-welcome advice. The union's
real life lay in the club-branch, that is, as close to the individual
member as was compatible with preservation of the minimum
advantages of unified organization. The chief doctrine of corporatism was that this fragmentation and particularism should
be transcended in the life and work of a larger whole, first
the national, 'industry'-wide union or federation of unions;
then the 'industry' itself, whose goals were to be determined
through negotiations between employers' and employees'
leaders.

Some, and especially weak, unions did demand official
recognition by employers, creation of machinery of collective
bargaining, and arbitration or conciliation boards with or
without government representatives. But such demands reflected the tactical situation of particular organizations and
indicated little if any change in those organizations' basic
attitudes, values and convictions. The Amalgamated Society of
Railway Servants was a larger and weaker union than the
Associated Society of Locomotive Engineers and Firemen; and
while the former sought to secure a system of formal recognition
and negotiation—a system partly realized in the conciliation
boards set up by almost all railway companies during the
years 1907-9—the latter wished to give this machinery a
'wide berth', partly because they did not need it, partly
because they feared the Railway Servants' desire to become
the sole (or 'all grades') railway union. The locomotive men's
circumstances led them to shun and distrust collective bargaining, the railway men's circumstances led them to seek it: and
had the two groups' circumstances been reversed, their views of

[1] Clegg, Fox, and Thompson, p. 356.

collective bargaining would also have been reversed—without any fundamental change in their common dislike of corporatist principles.[1]

Many unions were deeply disturbed by the changes forced upon them by the partisans of corporatism. A *de facto* revision of union constitutions was inseparable from such changes, because union leaders, and national union leaders in particular, ceased to represent only the members (who alone still paid their salaries, however) and began to represent the broader interests of their 'industry', as determined in negotiations with employers. These leaders, who now became both national and indeed leaders in quite a new sense, soon demonstrated a perhaps surprising loyalty to a system that nevertheless continued to offend members still devoted to a practical out-working of the doctrines of *laissez-faire*. This very loyalty irked many trade unionists. Collective bargaining, argued the authors of *The Miners' Next Step*, in 1912, gave 'the real power of the men into the hands of a few leaders' who 'become "gentlemen" ' and get 'corrupt, in spite of their own good intentions'. For 'in order to be effective, the leader *must* keep the men in order, or he forfeits the respect of the employers and the "public".'[2]

Collective bargaining aroused a controversy nowhere fiercer than in engineering. On the one hand, the executive council of the Amalgamated Society of Engineers affirmed their confidence in the new system and accepted a 'moral obligation' to honour the collective agreements they made. On the other hand, many members despised the new system and intended to accept no such obligation. Activists who hoped for seats on the executive council took up such members' causes; and made a series of almost annual attacks on the elected leaders of the Society. These attacks culminated in the 1908 north-eastern wages strike, in which even some of the executive council's most severe critics supported its case against the local dissidents, who called for 'freedom', 'democracy' and power to 'work out their own destiny'. George Barnes, the Engineers' General Secretary, claimed that, through this revolt against national leaders, 'the effectiveness of Trade Unionism, as an agent for

---

[1] Ibid., pp. 235, 238, 423–8.

[2] *The Miners' Next Step, Being a Suggested Scheme for the Reorganisation of the Federation Issued by the Unofficial Reform Committee*, Tonypandy, 1912, pp. 8, 13–14.

Labour will be weakened, and collective bargaining under-
mined'; and the Boilermakers' executive warned their own
north-eastern rebels that 'no true advance or good can come
without true and complete executive control.'[1]

New methods and machines, falling real wages, inter-union
conflict and the encroachments of collective bargaining on the
autonomy of labour, induced in trade unionists an unease as
intense as that experienced by employers a decade or two
earlier. But just as 'made in Germany' summarized the
employers' fears in the 1890s, so 'Taff Vale' summarized the
fears of labour in the first years of the new century; and thus
the challenge of corporatism was represented in trade unionists'
minds, not by the development of collective bargaining, which
constituted the true danger to their traditional way of life, but
by the now somewhat archaic policies of the Taff Vale Railway
Company. Ammon Beasley, general manager of that undertaking, had no sympathy with the novel corporatist ideas of
men like Henry Dyer, and repudiated all notion of a common
interest within the company. On the contrary, Beasley proposed
to treat any association of the company's employees as he would
any rival railway company: namely, as a competing organization legitimately open to attack by all the conventional
weapons of the *laissez-faire* struggle: and Beasley's views were
the mirror-image of those that James Holmes, the railwaymen's local organizer, held regarding the Taff Vale Railway
Company. Holmes and Beasley brought the Company and
the Amalgamated Society of Railway Servants into a conflict which the Company won in a month. Beasley then
secured, ultimately with the approval of the House of Lords,
costs and damages against the Society amounting in all to
£42,000.

Before, and after, the Lords' judgement on the Taff Vale
case, most trade unionists believed that the supply, and the
withholding, of labour, together with the terms on which labour
was supplied or withheld, were matters entirely and solely
analogous to non-contractual commercial dealings in, say, tea,
sugar or coffee. *If* industrial capitalism made labour into a
commodity like any other, that transformation was welcomed

---

[1] *Amalgamated Engineers' Report*, April 1908, pp. 7–9, 13; *United Society of Boilermakers' and Iron and Steel Shipbuilders' Monthly Report*, May 1908, p. 21.

nowhere more heartily than among British wage earners. Labour, like any other commodity, was to be sold, as dear as could be, to the highest bidder, whoever he might be; and was to be removed from the market whenever it suited the proprietors of labour. The buyer's sole resource was to beware how he bought—and to do without when he could not buy. The notion that a supplier of labour could incur a legal liability through any injury to private (let alone public) interest by withholding his labour seemed to organized labour as ridiculous as the notion that a grocer could incur just such a liability by withholding any tea, sugar or coffee he might have on his shelves but be unable to sell at what he thought was the right price. This attitude was strengthened by the fiction, characteristic of *laissez-faire* doctrine, that, provided a free market remained, an organization was no more than a big individual: or rather, a collection of individuals, perhaps like-thinking but still essentially free and independent agents. For if so, an organization should enjoy, necessarily on a larger scale, all an individual's 'rights' to do as he pleased—as long as, in Mill's phrase he did no 'harm to others', which he was deemed unable to do by the merely negative act of shutting up shop, or withholding labour. And these rights were freely conceded, by common law, not least to owners of capital engaged in business.[1]

But by the late nineteenth century practical necessity had caused Parliament and the law courts to distinguish between organizations and individuals, including the individuals of which those organizations were composed. In particular, organizations were permitted, and sometimes required, to take on a corporate status with an express legal liability *as a corporation*. This liability was certainly, in the case of limited companies, more or less separated from the liability of the individuals who nevertheless directed the organization, and without whom it would not exist; but even in this case the corporation could be required to meet, from its resources *as a corporation*, legal charges in respect of damages arising from its acts and from those of its agents. Such corporate legal liability, limited or unlimited, was unacceptable to trade unionists, who sought

---

[1] J. S. Mill, *Utilitarianism; On Liberty; Representative Government*, London, 1968, p. 73.

(and got, from the Conspiracy and Protection of Property Act of 1875, and the Trade Union Amendment Act of 1876) what appeared to be a statutory rule that a trade union was to be treated, in the exercise of all its characteristic functions, *as a collection of individuals*, none of whom were liable for the others' acts. Above all, if a union caused its members to withhold their labour, that act was to have the same legal status as an individual's withholding of his own labour, and would therefore incur no legal liability where no contract was broken. Actions committed by union officials, on behalf of the union, to secure a withdrawal of labour would be illegal, and their authors liable to prosecution, if and only if these actions were such that they would be illegal when committed by the same men, acting as individuals and on their own behalf.

But when Beasley took the Amalgamated Society of Railway Servants to the House of Lords, Lord Mcnaghten rejected the doctrine that there could be 'numerous bodies of men, capable of owning great wealth and of acting by agents, with absolutely no responsibility for the wrongs they may do other persons by the use of that wealth and the employment of those agents'. No longer was a union to be treated in law as if it were merely a number of grocers severally unwilling to sell their groceries. On the contrary, a union could be treated as if it were a monopoly of grocers withholding food and drink, in breach of a contract, either from consumers thereof or from businessmen whose trade and livelihood consisted in resale of such commodities to third parties. A union could not, Lord Mcnaghten held, use its corporate resources to organize a strike and require persons to join the strike, and then, when sued for damages, claim to be only a number of individuals, not under contract, coincidentally withholding a commodity in their rightful possession.[1]

Such a claim nevertheless still seemed entirely persuasive to most trade unionists, partly because their intense individualism led them to dislike and distrust even their own trade organization, and partly because repudiation of their claim must expose their contributions to trade union funds to legal action from the victims of industrial action. Some supporters of trade unions held other views. Asquith and Haldane were, like many Liberals, highly sympathetic to the Railway Servants' com-

[1] Clegg, Fox, and Thompson, p. 315.

plaints against the Taff Vale Railway Company: indeed, Haldane briefed the Railway Servants on the Taff Vale case. Yet both men agreed, Asquith said, that 'the common sense of the community would not be easily convinced that an association of persons—whether technically incorporated or not made not the slightest difference—wielding great powers, controlling considerable funds, should not be answerable for the conduct of agents acting under their authority.'[1]

'Common sense' did not prevail. Asquith and Haldane were overruled in cabinet; and the Campbell-Bannerman government passed, through a profoundly *laissez-faire* Parliament, a statute based on the Labour Party's own proposals and designed, not to meet Lord Mcnaghten's complaints, but to render them ineffectual. This statute, the Trade Disputes Act of 1906, held that any action legal (or even tortious) if committed by an individual was legal if 'done in pursuance of an agreement or combination', and if 'done in contemplation or furtherance of a trade dispute'. A trade dispute, the statute declared, was 'a dispute' between any or 'all persons employed in trade or industry' and any other such persons, or any employers, regarding 'the employment or non-employment, or the terms of employment' or 'the conditions of labour of any person'. Campbell-Bannerman and those who thought with him wished to please the trade unions, whose parliamentary representatives had just been increased from two to thirty. This, Liberals believed, could best be done by a quick bill designed to prohibit the corporatist heresy that had persuaded the House of Lords to find for the Taff Vale Railway Company. The resultant measure, which the Webbs thought 'monstrous', sharply reduced the civil liabilities of certain citizens of the United Kingdom.[2]

In consequence of this 'anomalous immunity', as E. H. Phelps Brown put it, organized labour suddenly acquired, in the midst of a corporatist era, a negative liberty greater than that enjoyed by any group of men since the abolition of benefit of clergy. This 'anomaly', however 'monstrous', fossilized

---

[1] H. C. G. Matthew, *The Liberal Imperialists. The Ideas and Politics of a Post-Gladstonian Elite*, London, 1973, p. 247.

[2] 6 Edward VII, cap 47, sects. 1, 3–5; Sidney and Beatrice Webb, *The History of Trade Unionism*, London 1920, p. 606.

laissez-faire, in the interest of that section whose intellectual and practical commitment to *laissez-faire* was itself most thoroughly petrified; and the principle—which might have pleased J. S. Mill, and has certainly baffled twentieth-century Britain—that trade unions shall be corporations in their powers, but mere aggregated individuals in their liabilities, survives as a strange but apparently indestructible relic in contemporary conscious-ness.[1]

LABOUR POLITICS AND BRITISH SOCIALISM

'Taff Vale' is thus the title of a story with an exceedingly happy ending for the old-fashioned ways of liberal individualism. By 1906 trade unions had their indisputable liberties, like the barons and clerics of feudal society, and could enjoy to the full, under statutory protection, the very real advantages which these liberties would secure to them. But before the happy ending of Taff Vale had been seen, and whenever trade union-ists reflected on the fate of the Railway Servants' £42,000, they tended to think of 'Taff Vale' solely as the slogan of an all-out employers' attack upon what little, trade unionists believed, remained to organized labour in the modern world. Such reflections quite often stimulated the view that, while industrial action might no longer be feasible or profitable, 'political action' might have new potentialities, not least in restoring feasibility and profitability to industrial action; and, about 1900, an increasing number of trade unionists sought an active part in local or national politics. This development aroused new interest in the notion, or rather notions, of 'labour repre-sentation'. For 'labour representation' signified manual workers' participation in the political system, either as private individuals nevertheless able to express views common among the socio-economic group to which they belonged, or as formally appointed spokesmen of a particular organized section of that group: and these two significances indicated two quite different theories of representation.

The idea that all kinds of men, regardless of origin, status or peculiarity, might, or indeed should, make their voices heard

[1] E. H. Phelps-Brown, *The Growth of British Industrial Relations*, London, 1959, p. xxviii.

in the nation's political deliberations was easily reconciled with the principles of Gladstonian individualism, according to which every man had a moral (or human) right to share in the political process, each counting for one and no more than one. Those who held such principles noted that Gladstone had given many manual workers the vote; and they sometimes argued that the moment had come for manual workers not merely to choose, but also to be chosen as, representatives of the people. This was not an exclusive claim that manual workers should have a special right to vote at elections, stand for parliament, and so on. On the contrary those who supported labour representation on grounds such as these rejected the view that *any* man should enjoy class privilege, or endure class disability, in politics or elsewhere. 'Real political democracy cannot be organized on the basis of class interest', wrote Arthur Henderson who, indeed, wished to create a political movement of 'all classes'—and hence of none.[1]

But some men inside and outside trade unions disliked this essentially *laissez-faire* concept of politics and of political representation. These men did not see labour representation as the simple extension to individuals, debarred by historical accident from enjoyment of their due, of a right to participate in politics on equal terms with all the other individuals that composed the atomistic aggregation with which *laissez-faire* theorists equated society. On the contrary, these men favoured labour representation as a means by which organized labour would obtain formally appointed responsible political spokesmen or delegates; and in adopting this policy they had, at least to a certain extent, followed the lead of corporatist thinkers. For while such union leaders usually denied that an 'industry' —employers and employees together—constituted a corporate entity, they believed that employees alone, organized in a trade union, did form such an entity and should enjoy, even at the expense of others, certain privileges that appertained to corporations. Among those privileges, they claimed, was the tenure of public offices and representative positions; but such tenure was, they asserted, the monopoly of certain corporate entities only, 'the ruling classes', who should be required to share their privileges with other corporate entities, such as

[1] Arthur Henderson, *The Aims of Labour*, London, n.d., pp. 21, 76.

trade unions, which at present received no share in conventional party politics. This *corporatist* notion of labour representation was expressed in Robert Blatchford's demand for 'a
working-class party' acting to ensure that 'the interests of the
working-class' were 'attended to'. Such a party would be, in
the terminology of the time, 'independent': that is, free from
the need to co-operate with other social groups.[1]

The former, individualist notion of labour representation
could not greatly commend itself to the institutions of organized
labour, simply because it allowed those institutions no role in a
system of politics which would consist in the representation of
individuals by individuals, freely exercising their own judgement. The latter, more corporatist, notion of labour representation did find some favour with the institutions of organized
labour, if only because it indicated an extension of those
institutions' power by the formation of political structures
designed to promote labour interests. But what were labour
interests? Individual trade unions had interests, yet these often
conflicted with the interests of other unions; every new
machine that displaced a skilled worker recruited by a craft
union, for example, upgraded a less skilled worker recruited by
a general union. And partisan political disagreements divided
labour no less than industrial disagreements. Thus the chairman
of the Labour Representation Committee conference of 1904
told the assembled delegates, 'there is no single Trade Union
represented today, but within whose ranks there are almost
equal numbers of members professing the Liberal and the Tory
faith.'[2]

Were labour to seek some common political representation,
these differences would have to be concealed if not removed: and
the simplest method of achieving this was to deny any partisan
(or even political) character to the representation sought. 'They
had fixed upon a common denominator', declared Keir Hardie
in 1903, 'that, when acting in the House of Commons, they
should be neither Socialists, Liberals, nor Tories, but a Labour
party.' The Boilermakers' executive committee went further.
Let members support the Labour Representation Committee,
they urged, and let them adopt this course 'without political

---

[1] Robert Blatchford, *Britain for the British*, London, 1902, p. 148.
[2] Labour Representation Committee *Report*, 1904, p. 31.

feeling'. Labour representation in this sense was not more than interest-group representation, of the type the Miners had long practised, in co-operation with the Liberals, in the Midlands and in north-eastern England; and the Miners' example had considerable influence on the champions of labour representation, partly because almost all the most advanced thinkers in the trade unions were Liberals.[1]

Had a new large 'Lib.-Lab.' grouping been formed in Parliament, not on the basis of absolute 'independence', but after the model of the Miners' scheme, Conservative trade unionists would no doubt have been aggrieved. But the first scheme for an alliance between labour and the Liberal Party failed before anyone could take umbrage at it. Certainly labour representation needed the Liberals: to provide money, political enterprise, and some sort of overall political shape to a venture into what was undeniably the world of politics, however non-political was labour's approach thereto. But though national leaders of the Liberal Party welcomed the chance of consolidating their links with labour, they could not find money to support labour's parliamentary ambition. Nor could they persuade local Liberal leaders to adopt as parliamentary candidates, not wealthy members of their own bourgeois world, but impecunious wage earners, apparently unable to pay either for the electoral campaign or for their own keep and expenses should they ever get to Parliament. 'Liberalism, and more particularly local Liberal Associations, have definitely declared against Labour', wrote Ramsay MacDonald to Keir Hardie in 1894.[2]

Those in the trade unions who favoured labour representation were then left with the problem of how to raise money for, and where to find the political direction necessary to, their project. They eventually solved the first problem by levying trade unionists for political purposes, more or less regardless of the political views of the members so levied; and they solved the second problem by turning at once from the Liberals to the Socialists, and above all to those Socialists who were trying to establish an Independent Labour Party in Parliament. That

---

[1] Ibid., 1903, p. 31; J. E. Mortimer, *History of the Boilermakers' Society*, vol. 1, 1834–1906, London, 1973, p. 146.
[2] Henry Pelling, *The Origins of the Labour Party 1880–1900*, Oxford, 1965, p. 165.

Party was then the closest approximation to a British mass socialist party. At its height, in 1895, it recruited almost 11,000 dues-paying members, or rather less than one in every 2,000 Britons aged fifteen or over. The Party was an electoral failure which, by 1900, seemed unlikely to secure significant political power: indeed, according to Henry Pelling, it then 'had so little support in the country that it was on the verge of utter bankruptcy'. But the leading figures in the Independent Labour Party dominated the intelligentsia of organized labour in Britain, and represented, to that intelligentsia, the chief doctrines of British socialism.[1]

The most distinctive of these doctrines was, and is, not the reconstruction of society on collectivist principles but the redistribution of wealth within a *laissez-faire* society changed no more than would be necessary to maximize redistribution. As G. D. H. Cole and William Mellor put it in 1918, 'in Great Britain, where men have been . . . constitutionally averse from idealism. . . . Socialism . . . has been almost purely a doctrine of distribution of income.' Hence both Blatchford's claim that 'industrial emancipation' meant getting 'the fruits of labour for those who produce them', and his appeal to the 'robust commonsense' of the 'hard-headed, practical', Englishman who 'would rather be well off than badly off'. Hence, too, Tom Mann's identification of 'conducting the class war' with 'obtaining anything worth getting towards mitigating the poverty of the workers'. Given this concept of socialism, the criterion by which any present or future society had to be judged was not its ability to do great things or to make better or finer men but its power to raise wages. Indeed, Snowden argued that, 'if under a system of private land-owning and private capitalism, the condition of every individual in the community was all that could be desired, there would be no argument for a change of the system.' For this reason, most British socialists began their case for 'socialism' by arguing— like most trade unionists negotiating a wage increase—that those for whom they spoke were impoverished by comparison with those from whom they demanded money. While the masses were in a 'serious and baleful condition', so ran the classic formulation of this case, capitalists were indulging

[1] Ibid., pp. 226, 229.

'ostentatious displays of wealth at race meetings and social functions'.[1]

But British socialist thought was characterized, not only by an individualistic notion of economic redistribution, but by a strong emphasis on the apparently collectivist notion of public ownership of economic power. Most British socialists, whatever their partisan allegiance, would assent to H. M. Hyndman's claim that a socialist Britain would mean 'universal co-operation, where each shall work for all and all for each'; and the Labour Party's programme *Labour and the New Social Order*, drafted in 1917, spoke of 'deliberately planned co-operation in production and distribution'. Such co-operative production and distribution was to be 'controlled by a democratic State', the Labour Party conference of 1908 resolved. Publicly owned and operated (or 'nationalized') undertakings were to be subject to what Snowden called 'joint control by representatives of the State and the workers and consumers'. But British socialists were unclear whether the executive power of such management was to reside in a 'managerial' class, more or less in continuity with the management of the period before nationalization, or in new organs of 'workers' control'. Men as diverse as Ramsay MacDonald and Harry Quelch spoke of nationalized management as 'salaried managers' or 'paid officials of the community': and these phrases strongly suggested the preservation of the managerial class into and beyond nationalization. Yet MacDonald also argued that 'the producers' must 'control the means of production'; the Labour Party favoured a 'steadily increasing participation of the organized workers in management'; and the Trades Union Congress advocated 'steadily increasing democratic control' by 'employees' and 'representatives of the working classes', in nationalized undertakings: and these phrases just as strongly suggested the supersession of the managerial class by new employee or trade union managers.[2]

---

[1] G. D. H. Cole and W. Mellor, *The Meaning of Industrial Freedom*, London, 1918, p. 6; Nunquam, *Merrie England*, n.d., pp. 1, 3, 91; Arthur D. Lewis, *Syndicalism and the General Strike, An Explanation*, London, 1912, p. 190; Philip Snowden, *Socialism and Syndicalism*, London, n.d., p. 17; *Debate on Socialism between Henry Labouchere . . . and H. M. Hyndman . . . 8 February 1894*, London, n.d., p. 2; Philip Snowden, *Socialism Made Plain*, London, 1920, p. 6.

[2] *Debate on Socialism*, p. 5; Henderson, pp. 92, 100; Labour Party *Conference*

Uncertainty about the structure of nationalized undertakings reflected British socialists' uncertainty about the principles on which they were advocating nationalization. A co-operative system of production and distribution, owned and directed by the community, is a highly collectivist concept which can be realized most consistently on the basis of thoroughly collectivist principles. Such principles were entertained by certain but by no means all British socialists, notably MacDonald himself: who was later to be accused by Jimmy Maxton of treating J. S. Mill 'with a scurviness . . . not . . . usual in the Labour Party'; and whose *Socialism and Government*, published in 1909, is perhaps the most collectivist document ever written by a leading British politician. In this book, MacDonald, probably under the influence of advanced 'New Liberals', such as L. T. Hobhouse, rejected the liberal individualist notion of society as a 'collection of separate and free individuals', who were 'for all political purposes, to be regarded as the same as every other individual'. On the contrary, MacDonald sought 'a higher organic unity' directed by the 'superior will and intelligence' of the State, which he described as 'the embodiment of the general will' and the expression of 'the political personality of the whole'. Such a state would bring true 'liberty' and true 'realization' to the individual (whose 'quality' it would thereby 'improve') because it would be founded on his 'real will', the voice of his true 'moral self', and not upon his 'expressed will' which could indicate only 'shortsighted self-interest'.[1]

If members of trade unions, of the Labour Party, or of the Independent Labour Party (under whose auspices this book appeared), had assented to the principles propounded by MacDonald, nationalization would have developed as one element in a coherent transformation of British politics and society. But such principles were, at best, unfamiliar and, at worst, abhorrent to almost every member of these organizations.

Report, 1908, p. 76; Snowden, 1907, p. 14; J. Ramsay MacDonald, *Socialism*, London, 1907, p. 82; J. Ramsay MacDonald, *Syndicalism, A Critical Explanation*, London, 1918, p. 3; *State Socialism: Is It Just and Reasonable?*, London, 1893, p. 6; Trades Union Congress *Report*, 1913, p. 198.

[1] Labour Party *Conference Report*, 1930, p. 190; J. Ramsay MacDonald, *Socialism and Government*, London, 1909, vol. 1, pp. xvii, xx, xxix, 8–10, 17, 41, 78–9; vol. 2, pp. 117, 119.

When Keir Hardie wrote that 'Socialism represents the same principle in industry which Radicalism represented in politics', he accurately identified the tradition in which, despite MacDonald's collectivism, British socialism developed. Like the nineteenth-century Radicals or like less advanced Liberals, the Labour Party and the Trades Union Congress could, for example, find free trade 'beneficial to industry', and could condemn protection as a system for 'impoverishing the workers' and 'bleeding consumers', even though protection is an economic system much more readily reconciled with a collectivist doctrine such as the 'socialism' these bodies professed.[1]

Following the liberal individualist tradition which maintained these orthodoxies, most British socialists saw the national will, in strictly majoritarian terms, as the will of 'the greater number', or the expression of 'the greatest common measure'. Society was, therefore, an aggregate without a 'general will' in the sense of the term as used by Rousseau, or in MacDonald's *Socialism and Government*. Moreover, the individuals that composed the social aggregate were deemed in British socialism, as in trade unionism and in liberal individualism, to be the best judge of their own interest: that is to say, their 'expressed will' *was* their 'real will'. Since individuals were the best judge of their own interest, the Labour Party favoured individual or sectional self-help. In this respect it expressed the fundamental assumptions and attitudes of the trade unionists who financed and voted for it. 'If there was one thing more abominable than another, it was that working men were prepared to draw everything from the State, and do nothing for themselves', the 1885 Trades Union Congress was told by a printers' delegate: who perhaps heard a Miners' delegate lay down, at the Congress of 1904, the more succinct formula, 'commit not to the hands of others that which we could do better for ourselves.'[2]

Despite the trades unions' and the Labour Party's increasing overt enthusiasm for 'nationalization', and the collectivism implied in that notion, labour spokesmen rejected collectivism again and again in the years after 1890. It was not just W. V.

---

[1] J. Keir Hardie, *From Serfdom to Socialism*, London, 1907, p. 28; Labour Representation Committee *Report*, 1904, pp. 40–2; Trades Union Congress *Report*, 1917, pp. 297–8.

[2] Blatchford, p. 84; Henderson, p. 80; Trades Union Congress *Report*, 1885, p. 34; 1904, p. 89.

Osborne, the Labour Party's most notorious trade union opponent, who held that 'socializing all the means of production, distribution and exchange' was 'fundamentally opposed to the whole principle of Trade Unionism'. For many others saw that the sectionalism and individualism implicit in labour organization was inimical to any extension of state power, whether capitalist or socialist. 'If a compulsory Arbitration Court were set up,' a Miners' delegate told the 1902 Trades Union Congress, 'the Trade Unions would wither and die.' For such a Court would use the state's regulatory power to settle industrial disputes; and unions would no longer be able to claim to facilitate their members' self-help. 'The principle of arbitration, both voluntary and compulsory . . .' another Miner warned the 1909 Congress, 'would prevent strikes.'[1]

If labour opposed even voluntary arbitration in industrial disputes, it could scarcely welcome the social possibilities suggested by the slogan of 'nationalization'. From time to time outspoken delegates to the Trades Union Congress or the Labour Party Conference condemned nationalization as 'slavery' or 'bureaucratic control of the workers'. More often than not, however, resolutions for nationalization passed on the nod: yet this did not necessarily indicate either emotional commitments or intellectual loyalties. A favourite labour term for a stereotyped or platitudinous resolution, so impracticable as to be above discussion, and so popular with a certain fraction as to be reintroduced year after year, is *a hardy annual*. Nationalization resolutions were growths of this type, as indeed their supporters sometimes admitted during the few minutes allotted to such resolutions. Trade unionists who favoured nationalization did so, not because it would realize the general will, raise a higher race of men, or make a new Britain, but quite simply because it would aid economic redistribution. 'It will be useless to nationalize' undertakings 'unless the workers . . . have control of the authority which is to settle the conditions under which the men are to work', declared the President of the South Wales Miners' Federation in 1913. In this respect, he anticipated the Labour Party's manifesto *Labour and the New Social Order* which called for an 'equitable sharing of the

---

[1] W. V. Osborne, *Sane Trade-Unionism*, London, n.d., p. 65; Trades Union Congress *Report*, 1902, p. 68; 1909, p. 178.

proceeds' of each nationalized industry 'among all who participate in any capacity' in that industry 'and only among these'.[1]

Thus when trade unions turned to socialist members of the Independent Labour Party, and of similar organizations, to promote 'labour representation', they did not thereby affirm their assent to socialist, or any other collectivist doctrines. In any event, few members of the Independent Labour Party were conversant with, or sympathetic to, such doctrines. On the contrary, their 'socialist' phraseology, their talk of 'nationalization', concealed a strong commitment to a Gladstonian liberalism sometimes tinged by the corporatist notions entertained rather more whole-heartedly by radical Liberals like Hobhouse or Lloyd George. The Independent Labour Party spoke of socialism, but meant sectionalism: and this example was readily followed by trade unionists, who regarded their new understanding with the Party as the means to a new and apparently persuasive legitimation of the age-old function of trade unionism, namely, more money for the same work. As J. R. Clynes told the 1909 Labour Party Conference, in his presidential address, the Labour Party was an alliance between trade unionists and socialists, in which, while 'The Trade Unionist asks for but a share of the wealth he creates, the Socialist tells him to claim the full product of his labour'.[2]

It can of course be argued that this attitude to politics was merely a further stage, or a new variant on, nineteenth-century Liberal movements for the redistribution of political power, movements which brought into existence the parliamentary system completed during the years before the Second World War. But liberal redistributionism was political in character: that is, it was concerned with alterations in large, universal rules appertaining to the conduct of polity and society; whereas labour redistributionism was almost entirely concerned with economics. In this sense, the Labour Party 'industrialized' British politics, both by replacing a political debate with a debate about money; and by converting almost all political institutions into quasi-trade unions, or groups of trade unions, which treated all issues as if they were wages negotiations. The

---

[1] Ibid., 1913, pp. 199, 203, 320–1; Henderson, p. 99.
[2] Labour Party *Conference Report*, 1909, p. 57.

notion of 'Labour politics' is thus something of a paradox.

The Labour Party's determined innocence of political partisanship, which would jeopardize the project of labour representation, can be seen in its leaders' refusal to offer electors a programme. Proposals to draft a Labour programme were rejected or passed over every year from 1900 to 1917. In 1908 Will Thorne complained that 'the Tory Party had a programme. . . . The Liberal Party had a programme. . . . But when it came to the Working Class Party, they had got absolutely no programme at all.' Any such document would have at least to reckon both with labour's attitude towards the political principles of individualism and collectivism and with the purpose of labour representation itself; and Thorne's complaint was prudently ignored. When socialist enthusiasts tried to coax the Labour Party into a commitment to some political principles, if only by a declaration of 'ultimate objects', they were forcefully opposed. 'We were not out, as a matter of fact, for ultimate objects . . . we were out for immediate . . . legislation', declared Clynes. So it went on until the closing months of the First World War; and even then preparation for what was to become the manifesto *Labour and the New Social Order* caused many misgivings. The Labour Party had 'steadily, and, in my opinion wisely, always declined to be bound by any programme, to subscribe to any dogma, or to lay down any creed', observed the Railway Servants' leader in his presidential address to the Labour Party Conference of 1917.[1]

What was left of the Labour Party, when politics had thus been eliminated from it, was a sort of parliamentary trade union, a type of labour representation that found favour with many inside the Party. Advocates of the Labour Party justified it to fellow trade unionists not as the vehicle of sound political doctrine but as 'a good investment', as a 'cheap' means to secure industrial ends without industrial action. Do not, it was argued, forego your pay from time to time in order to increase it by striking against your employer; instead contribute a few pence a week to the installation and upkeep of a member of Parliament who, without further cost, will increase your pay for you. 'I venture to say' remarked W. E. Harvey, the Derbyshire Miners' agent, at the 1913 Trades Union Congress,

[1] Ibid., 1908, pp. 58, 64; 1917, p. 82.

'—and I think I am now voicing the opinion of the Miners' Federation as a whole—that we have found the money spent upon political action the best investment we ever made'.[1]

The concept of labour representation as a non-political party, or as a parliamentary substitute for strike action, was rather too subtle for most trade unionists. Union executives impressed by the case for labour representation tried to persuade their members to vote first to affiliate to the Labour Representation Committee, then to pay a subscription for affiliation, the so-called 'political levy'. But there was little enthusiasm for either of these courses. The executive council of the United Association of Operative Plumbers remarked of the political levy, in 1905, that 'the apathy and want of interest by the members' seemed 'almost incredible'. Fewer than 500 of the Stonemasons' 14,000 members voted to affiliate to the Labour Representation Committee; and, until the Engineers' executive council put heavy pressure on the branches, only between 3,000 and 7,000 of the 85,000 members of the union took part in ballots on either affiliation or levy. Some trade unionists tried to prevent affiliation to the Labour Representation Committee, the most important of these being W. V. Osborne of the Railway Servants who financed his legal campaign against the political levy by a highly successful appeal to 'individual working men and trade union branches'.[2]

The Taff Vale affair of course enabled executive councils to strengthen their case for affiliation to the Labour Representation Committee. The House of Lords' judgement directly threatened strike action, and it seemed plausible to argue that this judgement could only be overturned by a new trade union law, the passage of which would be substantially eased by the presence of more labour representatives in the Commons. Thus the Boilermakers, who had a membership of about 48,000, failed to affiliate to the Committee in 1900 because only 3,157 members could be found to support affiliation, while 6,880 opposed it. But the executive council issued a 'strong appeal' immediately after the Taff Vale judgement and, in the ballot

---

[1] Trades Union Congress *Report*, 1913, p. 227

[2] J. O. French, *Plumbers in Unity, 1865–1965*, Manchester, n.d., p. 79; *Amalgamated Engineers' Journal*, February 1902, p. 65; July 1903, p. 67; Clegg, Fox, and Thompson, p. 416.

which followed, 26,478 members voted for, and 8,905 against, affiliation. In this way the number of trade unionists affiliated to the Committee nearly trebled between February 1901 and February 1904, from 353,000 to 956,000, even though the introduction of a compulsory political levy caused a drop of 100,000 affiliated trade unionists between February 1904 and February 1905.[1]

The 1906 Trade Disputes Act could be regarded as the reward for these efforts, but after 1906, it became decreasingly clear what else was to be gained by labour representation. Though no doubt some Labour voters were not trade unionists, the Labour Party was a party organized and paid for by trade unionists, composed of trade unionists, and designed to promote the interests of trade unionists. Indeed the Party was so exclusive that no one could formally join it except as a member either of an affiliated trade union or of one of the few other organizations approved by affiliated trade unions. Moreover, since the leaders and admirers of the Labour Party commended it to trade unionists as a 'good investment', trade unionists naturally wanted to know what *their* party was providing in return for *their* subscription. Some Labour apologists pointed to the Workmen's Compensation and Old Age Pensions legislation as examples of what could be done through the House of Commons: but these were Liberal measures carried out by a Liberal government and had no direct effect on what most concerned trade unions, namely, wages and hours of work. The Labour Party could not influence such matters even in sectors like coal-mines and railways, where governments had traditionally intervened; while in other sectors, such as mechanical engineering, the government seemed very unlikely to intervene on these or any other issues.

Doubts about the Labour Party increased during the trade depression of 1908–9. Unemployment rose between 1907 and 1908 from 3·7 to 7·8 per cent of the members of all unions making unemployment returns; while the carpenters, and engineering and shipbuilding unions, reported that 11·6 and 12·5 per cent of their members respectively were out of work in 1908. Some trade unionists accused the Labour Members of Parliament of failing to secure from the government measures

[1] Ibid., p. 375; Mortimer, loc. cit.

to alleviate the depression; and in subsequent months and years, as the Labour Party's electoral appeal waned, so too, trade union support for the Party declined. At the 1913 Labour Party conference the Electricians put forward a resolution condemning the 'inactivity displayed by the Labour Members in the House of Commons on behalf of Labour'; and, though this resolution was overwhelmingly defeated, it was vigorously debated. The Labour Members had 'received their social revolution', claimed the Electricians' spokesman, who meant by this phrase, significantly enough, the £400 annual allowance paid to all Members of Parliament since 1911. *Post* or *propter hoc*, he believed, 'they forgot the men on a pound a week'. In short, he declared that 'he did not give a twopenny toss for the whole of the Labour Party.'[1]

THE SYNDICALISTS

After 1909, therefore, the entire enterprise of labour politics was challenged by critics within the trade unions themselves. Some of these critics feared subordination of 'industrial action' to 'political action'; others alleged that labour's new political leaders were corrupt; others distrusted the collectivism they thought they saw in those leaders' attitudes. Many such critics were attracted to the set of ideas summarized as 'syndicalism', even though many who favoured syndicalism would not call themselves syndicalists. Syndicalism developed in Britain from two main sources. Between 1900 and 1910 the semi-Marxist notions of Daniel De Leon's Socialist Labour Party crossed the Atlantic from North America and began to influence both the Clydeside trade unionists who formed the British Socialist Party in 1903, and those militants, especially from the Miners' and railwaymen's unions, who caused the great ideological controversy at Ruskin College, Oxford, in 1908–9. De Leon's ideas, as propagated by his trade union, the Industrial Workers of the World, also entered Britain via Australia, whence the Engineer Tom Mann returned in 1910. About the same time, Mann and others became aware of the doctrines of the French revolutionary syndicalists, especially as laid down in the

[1] B. R. Mitchell and Phyllis Deane, *Abstract of British Historical Statistics*, Cambridge, 1971, p. 65; Labour Party *Conference Report*, 1913, pp. 112–14.

Charter of Amiens, drafted by the General Confederation of Labour in 1906.

The French syndicalists, like the De Leonists, were in greater or lesser measure collectivists; but their collectivism, as re-interpreted by British syndicalists soon acquired a character-istically *laissez-faire* flavour. Most varieties of British syndicalism developed as reactions to corporatist or collectivist forces. Thus syndicalism proved most popular among railwaymen, whose employers maintained a unitary corporatism so extreme as to deny their employees any autonomous existence whatsoever; among the South Wales Miners, struggling to liquidate the last remnants of the unitary corporatism embodied in the sliding scale system; and among Engineers, who had felt the full force of the new bipartite corporatism implicit in 'collective bargaining'. When the Ruskin College dissidents determined, with railwaymen's and Miners' support, to promote their own pedagogical doctrine, their ideal was a system of intellectual *laissez-faire*, free from the constraints of the national educational tradition as exemplified by institutions both public and private: 'ruling-class culture' with its 'fetters' and 'blinkers' was to be replaced in its entirety by the 'independent working-class education' supplied by a trade-union run Central Labour College. Finally, the syndicalists condemned some Labour leaders' approval of 'nationalization' which syndicalists viewed as the embodiment of the iniquities of 'state socialism'.

This attack proceeded from the conviction that, as a leader of the British Socialist Party put it, the state was and always would be 'the executive committee of an order of property owners'. Were the Labour Party to obtain supreme power, syndicalists believed, it would merely convert itself into a new propertied ruling class and use the instrumentalities of the state to oppress the workers no less rigorously than the capitalists had done. Hence the only alternative to oppression was the workers' own control of all social and economic functions: the goal of 'nationalization' must be superseded by that of 'socialization', that is, by pure workers' control, undisturbed by the operation of state power, or indeed of any external influence.[1]

The syndicalists proposed to achieve a syndicalist society by dispossessing the employer class through a 'GENERAL

[1] J. T. Walton Newbold, *Marx and Modern Capitalism*, London, 1918, pp. 18–20.

STRIKE of national proportions', which would, Mann held, constitute 'the actual . . . Revolution'. What would be left, given the abolition of labour politics, would not be the collectivist state, which syndicalists dreaded, but rule by trade unions. Speaking at Battersea in January 1912, Mann declared that he 'believed in each union controlling the conditions of its own trade and distributing the products in conjunction with all the other trades'. Now, though not fully collectivist, there is something exceedingly corporatist about the vision of a society divided into 'industries' each run by a trade union, wielding absolute power in its own sphere, and settling all other affairs, not by reference to a common authority, but by fraternal negotiations with other unions. Such a notion is in effect a version of unitary corporatism, in which labour organizations and not employers possess the corporate authority; and MacDonald had some right to claim that 'the Syndicalist State is but an evolution of trust capitalism'. Even before 'the Syndicalist State' was fully realized, its corporatist tendencies would manifest themselves. For if each 'industry' was to be run by a trade union, then existing trade unions would have to be amalgamated into groupings such that each 'industrial' sector, however defined, would have one union and one union only.[1]

Yet the syndicalists' corporatism was largely superficial. They did seek to remove the external authority of management; but their seeming desire to internalize this authority within what would appear to be immensely strengthened industrial organizations of labour was in fact somewhat deceptive. For syndicalists believed that unions could only be fitted for the extended functions required of them in a syndicalist society by removal of 'bureaucratic' leadership and transfer of power to the 'rank and file'. 'The time has really gone by', declared Mann, 'when reactionary officials are to be allowed to impede working-class advance; it is really a case of "get on and lead", or "get out and follow" ': and Mann's notion of 'leading' was, in this instance, not far off his notion of 'following'. The authors of *The Miners' Next Step* put the matter briefly if elliptically when they wrote, 'workmen the "bosses", "leaders" the servants'. Leaders were to be 'excluded from all

---

[1] Webbs, *History of Trade Unionism*, p. 658; Lewis, p. 202; J. Ramsay MacDonald, *Syndicalism*, p. 58.

power' in truly reformed, syndicalist unions: they were to constitute at most 'a purely administrative body', and 'the rank and file' were to have 'control of the organization'. In short, the employee was not to be absorbed into a new dominant, corporatist labour organization, but rather all—employers and union leaders included—were to be absorbed in a new individualist, hegemonic employee. There must be 'real democracy in real life', claimed *The Miners' Next Step*, which described the first great move towards this end as 'continual agitation' until 'we have extracted the whole of the employers' profits.'[1]

The years immediately before the First World War were indeed characterized by 'continual agitation', as the decline in real wages, discontent with collective bargaining, distrust of elected leaders, and disillusionment with labour politics, all made themselves felt. But pre-war conditions gave syndicalists little assistance in realizing their objectives. Two major disputes alone showed any signs, however uncertain, of a syndicalist influence designed to extend a relatively narrow conflict into a broad struggle to expropriate the employers.

In September 1910 the Cambrian Combine locked-out the miners of Tonypandy who refused to accept the company's rates for work on a new coal seam then being opened up. Almost all the Combine's manual employees struck, and remained out of work, in an atmosphere of bitterness that led to riots before the men returned to work on the original terms in August 1911. The strike was perhaps partly influenced by syndicalists and their sympathizers, who, the secretary of the Miners' Federation of Great Britain complained, had 'only one weapon to fight with, that of 'force', which alone means anarchy'. The original dispute was rather unreal, since most men made good money at the new seam after the resumption of work; and the length and violence of the stoppage depended chiefly on the men's general hostility to the Cambrian management. Syndicalists may have hoped to use this hostility to destroy the Combine and to turn the conflict into a national coal strike. But the Cambrian Combine survived; the Miners' Federation refused a general stoppage; and syndicalist policy finally collapsed.[2]

---

[1] Lewis, p. 196; *The Miners' Next Step*, pp. 16–17, 23, 26, 30.
[2] R. Page Arnot, *The Miners, Years of Struggle*, London, 1953, p. 73.

The second major pre-war dispute in which syndicalists were apparently involved was the lock-out of James Larkin's Irish Transport and General Workers' Union, from August 1913 to February 1914, by W. B. Murphy, the dominant figure among Dublin's nationalist employers. Larkin was a noisy advocate of syndicalism and allied causes, who once declared, 'If we were the men we think we are, the employing class would be wiped out within the hour'. Murphy intended to break Larkin's power; and this, aided by the British Trades Union Congress's hostility to Larkin's syndicalism, he did—at least for the time being. Murphy's victory was perhaps brief, for by 1920 the Irish Transport and General Workers' Union claimed, albeit in very different circumstances, to organize half Ireland's trade unionists. But the Irish employing class remained unshaken, and the Ireland of the 1920s bore no resemblance to the syndicalist society.

Even if syndicalists had come closer to engineering the expropriatory general strike for which they strove, they would still have had difficulty in establishing such a society, the fundamental principle of which was a system of 'industrial unionism' which the syndicalists entirely failed to achieve. Industrial unionism of the syndicalist type meant division and amalgamation of existing unions to form units each coterminous with, and psychologically and practically prepared to control, the rationally defined 'industries' into which, in theory, all social productive and distributive activity could be distributed. The industrial unionists' major success was the formation, during the building trade lock-out of 1914, of the Building Workers' Industrial Union, an alliance of syndicalists and craftsmen bricklayers fearful for their jobs in a period of changing building techniques. The Building Workers called for '*associations of workers for overpowering the octopus of capitalism*' and for '*securing the complete control of industry in the interests of the whole community*'. But the established building unions rejected these proposals; the bricklayers' enthusiasm declined in the circumstances of wartime full employment; and by the end of 1917 the Building Workers' Industrial Union had collapsed.[1]

The syndicalists were not much more effective at reforming existing unions from within than they were at constructing new

[1] R. W. Postgate, *The Builders' History*, London, n.d., p. 403.

organizations like the Building Worker's Industrial Union. The syndicalists' vision of a free, general-less army of the trade union 'rank and file' inspired a 'Reform Committee' movement that developed particularly in mining and engineering. An Unofficial Reform Committee, set up by a group of South Wales Miners, led by Noah Ablett, and including some syndicalists, published *The Miners' Next Step*; and that pamphlet's proposals for a purge of corrupt union officials seemed to take on some substance when several syndicalists were elected to office in South Wales. Yet the results of those elections scarcely show anything much more significant than a spread of syndicalist rhetoric; for the social structure of mining, both in Wales and elsewhere, remained largely unchanged, and, if the South Wales Miners displayed a suitably syndicalist 'militancy' after 1912, they were not lacking in militancy before the syndicalists gained power among them.

Meanwhile, however, the example of the Unofficial Reform Committee was followed by certain Engineers who established Reform Committees in Cardiff and in London. These committees proposed to remove bureaucracy from the Amalgamated Society of Engineers through devices such as control of the executive council by an annual convention of plenipotentiary representatives; short tenure and frequent election of councilmen; and recall of councilmen before the expiry of their term if they failed to satisfy the members' demands. Any of these measures would in part realize syndicalist ideas of union reform and would, at the same time, express the democratic egalitarianism of the *laissez-faire* tradition to which syndicalists, for all their corporatist notions, responded.

Syndicalists and sympathizers seem to have dominated the Engineers' delegate meeting of 1912, where they strongly advocated their proposals for a plenipotentiary annual convention, and for short tenure of executive office. Under rules drafted by syndicalists, the sitting executive councilmen, most of whom had just been elected to office, were obliged to submit to immediate re-election and, in some cases, to a further re-election eighteen months later. 'I'm all out for all up for election and nothing less will suit me', declared the syndicalists' spokesman Henry Hisee. The executive councilmen resisted this scheme to the extent of barricading themselves in the

Society's general office whence they were evicted by a non-elective provisional executive, appointed by the delegate meeting, and led by syndicalists. But the syndicalists could neither consolidate their hold on the union nor justify their theories of reform. The old executive were debarred from the subsequent election, in which at least two syndicalists were appointed to the new executive council. The new councilmen achieved no appreciable reform of the Engineers' society; and since they held office on average three years longer than had their predecessors, they scarcely practised the principle of a non-bureaucratic short-tenure leadership.[1]

Syndicalism was, then, very much an anticlimax in the pre-war years. But the leaders of the Labour Party nevertheless deplored and feared this new development, which was plainly antagonistic to the whole project of labour politics: partly because, if the Labour Party retreated from collectivism towards corporatism, syndicalism retreated still further back towards individualism; and partly because syndicalism rejected every aspect of the Party's parliamentary activities. If the syndicalists had succeeded in expropriating the employers and forming a syndicalist society, the Labour Party would have become superfluous; both the Lords and the Commons would have been abolished; and trade union leaders, as well as Labour parliamentarians would have been reduced to a clerical role in the administrative offices of the producers' syndicates. So much was common ground in the party. And those few that accepted at least part of the collectivist principles which go to form socialism properly so called also saw the syndicalist society for the negation of socialism that it was. As MacDonald put it, 'the workman is just as incapable as the capitalist of keeping national interests and concerns in front of him when he is working under conditions which make exploitation in his own interests easy.'[2]

Many leaders of the labour intelligentsia therefore condemned syndicalism. But they recognized the appeal of syndicalist notions to trade unionists who were delighted to sweep away, apparently under the very banner of corporatism

---

[1] *Amalgamated Society of Engineers. Executive Council Statement to Members*, 16 January 1913.
[2] MacDonald, *Syndicalism*, p. 58.

or even collectivism, the national political order, the employer and managerial class, and even their own trade union leadership; and this recognition coloured the non-syndicalists' reply to syndicalism, namely, the doctrine known as guild socialism. Guild socialism was, in principle, a disarmingly simple compromise between the two antagonistic positions of the immediate pre-war years. MacDonald observed that, 'Syndicalism is largely a revolt against socialism'. Cole and Mellor, however, claimed that guild socialism 'may be called Syndicalism on a Socialist basis'. This combination was above all the work of S. G. Hobson and A. R. Orage, who collaborated in a series of articles that appeared in Orage's periodical *The New Age* in 1912–13; and these two men, together with Cole, were to have a considerable influence on the development of Labour Party thought.[1]

The avowed syncretism of guild socialism meant that its doctrines were necessarily somewhat mixed. On one hand, guild socialists condemned collectivism. In 1920 Hobson dismissed the notion that 'every national activity' must serve one 'great end' as a heretical germanism that could only create an 'impotent mass of servile workers' ruled by an autocratic state. Cole regarded 'state socialism' as 'state capitalism'; and all guild socialists interpreted the 'nationalization' tradition within Fabianism and the Independent Labour Party as an attempt to create 'a universal civil service' consisting of 'an army of wage-paid workers'. On the other hand, guild socialists disliked trade unionists for their 'sectionalism'; and accused trade unions of 'tacitly accepting the capitalist system' by 'aiming at higher wages'—even though guild socialists simultaneously adjured organized labour to absorb 'every shilling of surplus value'.[2]

Guild socialism drew much of its inspiration from the notion of enlightened self-interest, a concept of course well within the purview of *laissez-faire* theory. The relentless pursuit of short-term material interest was to be subordinated to a larger aim: Cole, for example, liked to speak of mankind throwing off its spiritual bondage. But this larger aim was certainly not to be

---

[1] Cole and Mellor, p. 40; MacDonald, *Syndicalism*, p. 6.
[2] Ibid., p. 40; S. G. Hobson, *National Guilds and the State*, London, 1920, pp. 81, 114; A. R. Orage (ed.), *National Guilds, An Inquiry into the Wage System and the Way Out*, London, 1914, pp. 5, 8–9, 103.

found in the highly collectivist idea of the state or society beloved of the theorists of positive freedom. There was a great deal of talk of 'self-government', and of 'industrial democracy', among guild socialists; and in this respect they came rather closer to the syndicalists than to the Labour politicians. Moreover, guild socialists had no doubt that labour politics was a mistake. 'Labour's adventure into politics' had been an 'appalling waste of time' which had destroyed the trade unions' 'economic power', the *New Age* group argued. 'The struggle for social democracy must be fought out in the economic and not the political province', they declared; and they even proposed complex schemes whereby the Co-operative Wholesale Society would provide the 'commissariat' for the 'industrial strife' which was to be conducted by the trade unions.[1]

But the guild socialists' vision of the future, amorphous as this was, differed fundamentally from that of the syndicalists. Like syndicalists, guild socialists could speak of 'producers' control of Industry'; and what Cole and Mellor meant by this was that 'the normal direction of industry' would be 'in the hands of the unions', duly constituted as industrial 'guilds'. These would act through 'officers' elected by the 'workers engaged in' each separate industry, who would have in their hands therefore 'the task of actually conducting the business'. But unlike the syndicalists, guild socialists insisted on what Hobson and Orage called 'the indispensability of the state'. In the guild-socialist new order the state would have the task of 'representing the general public'. It would therefore meet the need for what MacDonald described as a 'civic authority' although, whereas MacDonald expected such an authority to be indeed authoritative, guild socialists seemed unclear about the precise relationship of the productive guilds and the state.[2]

Cole and Mellor claimed that each guild 'would carry on production without interference from politicians'; yet they also conceded to the state the right to 'occasional and external' intervention in guild affairs. Hobson and Orage held that the guilds would manage their 'own affairs', and 'protect their corporate interests': if necessary, against the state. These authors favoured 'an equipoise between State policy and

---

[1] Cole and Mellor, p. 1; Orage, pp. 5, 50, 104, 106, 132.
[2] Cole and Mellor, pp. 8, 22–3; Orage, p. vi; MacDonald, *Syndicalism*, p. 6.

Guild interests', which they hoped to find in guild-state 'co-management' subject to 'the principle of industrial democracy'. They declared that the state must remain 'certainly independent; probably supreme': and this dictum appears to summarize the guild socialists' position. In later years Hobson emphasized the *supremacy* of the state through parliamentary government. Guild socialism, he wrote in 1936, meant 'an industrial Parliament' of guildsmen, 'subject', however, to the Commons 'on large issues of public policy'. Yet in earlier years the state's *independence* had received greater emphasis. In 1920, for instance, Hobson urged 'Guild representation in Parliament', where the guilds' 'spokesmen and official heads' were to be seated. Since the 'supremacy' of such a parliament would, in effect, be only the supremacy of the guilds themselves, the legislature would presumably be no more than a forum 'independent' of the guilds solely because it represented not merely the guilds but 'the general public' also.—Yet even a parliament 'independent' simply in this sense would differentiate the guild socialist order from the syndicalist.[1]

The obscurity of guild socialists' statements about the future that they planned may well be due not so much to confusion of thought as to the tergiversation inescapable from the task that the guild socialists set themselves. Guild socialism was to be 'a politico-economic *tertium quid*' between syndicalism and socialism, in Hobson's words. It was designed to reconcile syndicalists to the virtues of what Cole called 'a reorganized State', and to convince labour politicians that 'the whole responsibility for the conduct of industrial affairs' could be given to the trade unions. Both 'industrial action' and 'political action', both a 'political' sphere and an 'industrial' sphere, were to be preserved; and, despite Hobson's talk of industrial parliaments and guild representation, there was to be a distinctness, even a certain distance, between the two. 'At a Trade Union Conference we want to have a boilermaker, not a politician; in Parliament we want to have a politician, not a boilermaker', concluded Orage's symposium *National Guilds*.[2]

[1] Cole and Mellor, pp. 26–7; Hobson, pp. 139, 140; S. G. Hobson, *Functional Socialism*, London, 1936, p. 13; Orage, pp. 132, 233–4, 263.

[2] Hobson, *Functional Socialism*, p. 142; G. D. H. Cole, *A Short History of the British Working-Class Movement, 1789–1947*, London, 1947, p. 325; Orage, p. 356.

By 1914, therefore, the political and social thought of organized labour and its advisers (both official and self-appointed) may be said to have developed along three, or perhaps two-and-a-half lines. Labour politics had been firmly established on the principle that labour representation would secure such executive and legislative acts of government as could redistribute wealth by raising incomes, by lowering profits, and in certain cases, by substituting some form of corporatist state-ownership for private ownership of economic undertakings. Syndicalists agreed that incomes must be raised; but they altogether repudiated profits, Parliament and labour politics; and proposed to give ownership, control and management of all undertakings into the hands of those undertakings' employees, who would then be free to fix their incomes as they chose. Guild socialists insisted that incomes should be raised; but while, like syndicalists, they wished to abolish employers, unlike syndicalists, they did not wish to leave the conduct of the community's affairs purely to the separate and joint decisions of the employees of expropriated undertakings: and hence they wished to preserve at least some of the institutions of the state.

On the outbreak of the First World War, organized labour's attention was, in short, focused on economic redistribution. That goal need not be in any sense collectivist and, if to be achieved more or less within the framework of British society, must be very largely individualist in character. Moreover, even labour's proposals for major changes in British society had a strongly individualistic cast. Under the regimes projected by the Labour Party, the syndicalists, and the guild socialists, trade unions would lose none of their powers over against the outside world, and would gain no new powers over against their members, whose concerns they would still be required to further in the manner traditional to the world of British labour. Indeed, the syndicalists (and possibly some guild socialists) proposed to destroy 'bureaucratic' leadership in the trade unions and give all power to the 'rank and file', that is, to the members. Individuals pursuing their own self-assessed interests would then entirely predominate and *laissez-faire* would be virtually completed, whatever the superficial details of the social order.

LAISSEZ-FAIRE AND WORLD WAR

Since labour remained loyal to *laissez-faire*, it could only regard the First World War as a most serious threat not merely to men's bodies but to their ideas also. For that conflict posed, in the clearest and most direct fashion, questions that had been put in Britain in various ways ever since the 1870s. Above all, the military challenge of centralist, collectivist Germany obliged Britain to adopt economic and military counter-measures, all of which demanded a substantial shift towards collectivism. Social and political principles that once seemed to some to be useful for the nation's prosperity now seemed to many more to be necessary for the nation's survival. The Liberals, who had been part-converted from *laissez-faire* to corporatism during their long period of government from 1905 onwards, constructed new social and economic forms, first alone and later in coalition with the Conservatives who, since their acceptance of imperialist and protectionist doctrines, had developed a distinct bias towards collectivism. These new social and economic forms both strengthened the war effort and hastened the movement of Britain towards—and, indeed, beyond—corporatism.

The most obvious wartime innovation inimical to *laissez-faire* principles was the introduction of conscription at the beginning of 1916, following the failure of high-pressure voluntary recruitment in 1914–15. Conscription divided the Liberals, the more old-fashioned of whom, led by Asquith, would only accept conscription as a disastrous evil in a situation of direst necessity such as had not, they felt, arrived by 1916. The Asquithite position was shared by extreme labour militants. David Kirkwood, one of the most notorious of these, told the Labour Party conference of 1919 that 'all the liberties they had always boasted as Britons' were 'stopped the moment conscription was on the Statute Book'. Conscription was objectionable to anyone who favoured liberty in the strictly negative sense in which it was understood by liberal individualism, since the conscript lost almost all his liberty (so defined), and quite probably his life, as the mere slave of a social aggregate which represented no more than a quantitative superiority over the individual: and Kirkwood was unable to entertain any other concept of freedom.[1]

Conscription is a thoroughly collectivist social instrumentality. Methods corresponding to a perhaps more limited collectivism were introduced into the production of munitions and other war materials. Undertakings engaged on such work were classified as 'controlled establishments', and were subjected to state direction through legislation, through close official surveillance and through the substantive details of government contracts. Thus these establishments' product was generally recognized to serve the good of the whole community, and their affairs were in a sense controlled by the central authority of the whole community, as was demonstrated both by the state's limitation of profit in these establishments, and by the government's active intervention after the employers' failure to satisfy their employees' grievances in 1917. Government intervention in munitions production, and in other sectors such as mining, often favoured organized labour; but trade unionists did not like state lawyers, as a Boilermakers' leader put it in 1917, telling them 'how to dig coal, or weave cotton, or build ships'.[2]

Nor did trade unionists like the shape taken by the government's ventures into manufacturing; for once the state determined to reorganize production on collectivist principles, it naturally adopted what it thought the most advanced case of collectivism among the examples familiar to it: and in Britain that case could be none other than unitary corporatism. Pre-war collective bargaining had, in the main, developed as a system of bipartite corporatism that acknowledged the conflict of sectional interests within an industry by allowing either side to take industrial action against the other after the exhaustion of negotiating procedure. But the system devised for war work denied the possibility of conflict of interests and vested overall industrial control, within each establishment, in the hands of the employers. Unions were forbidden to strike. Employers were permitted to keep a man in his job against his will by refusing him the 'leaving certificate' without which he could not get a job for six weeks after quitting his old employment.

---

[1] Labour Party *Conference Report*, 1919, pp. 166–7.
[2] Trades Union Congress *Report*, 1917, p. 55.

Comprehensive and often stringent regulations, drafted by employers and enforced if necessary by tribunals, strengthened discipline, and required increased effort from the workers. 'Mr. Lloyd George . . . would apparently like to see the rules of the army applied to the workshop', complained the chairman of the 1916 Labour Party conference.[1]

Meanwhile, stage by stage, employers won the power to 'dilute' labour, by introducing new machines and adapting old: so that work hitherto done only by skilled craftsmen could be given to upgraded non-craftsmen (and even women) 'dilutees'. Production rapidly increased, but the craftsmen's monopoly was at least temporarily broken. When 'it is realized that skill is a quality peculiar to no one set of persons alone', wrote an Engineer in 1916, 'the craft idea is completely destroyed'. At the same time, wages were largely removed from the sphere of industrial action and were determined by periodic national arbitration awards, a development as unacceptable as ever to those many trade unionists who preferred to be judge of their own interests and to defend those interests by pitting their strength against the employers'. Moreover, arbitral awards were chiefly based on the government's newly introduced cost-of-living index, an arrangement indeed 'scientific' beyond the Fabians' boldest dreams, but nevertheless highly unpopular with trade union leaders whose negotiating skills became virtually superfluous once an arbitrator could settle a claim simply by referring to a statistical series.[2]

Trade unionists' discontent with their national leaders came to a head in the May strikes of 1917. These stoppages were very largely organized by unofficial committees of syndicalists and sympathizers, who were able to appeal to a widespread suspicion that wages and working conditions were being sacrificed to the war effort, with the secret assent of complaisant union executives. 'As leaders we were appointed to lay down the hammer or the trowel, and stand on the ramparts to warn our members of danger,' declared the President of the 1917 Trades Union Congress, 'and in their opinion we had either fallen asleep at our posts, or we have sold their birthright for a mess of pottage.' As in pre-war years, therefore, syndicalists could argue that

[1] Labour Party *Conference Report*, 1916, p. 96.
[2] *Amalgamated Engineers' Monthly Journal and Report*, April 1916, p. 59.

union leaders had betrayed their followers, and should be turned out of office as a necessary first step to justice for the workers.[1]

Unlike the pre-war years, however, the war period did afford syndicalists a means of obtaining power in trade unions without securing national or district elective office. About 1890 craft unions began to appoint shop stewards to protect members' interests against managements' attempts to replace skilled by less skilled labour. These stewards, chosen by the men in the shop, soon turned their attention to piecework; and, though few in number by 1914, they had acquired sufficient expertise in piecework negotiations to convince most craft workers that they too must appoint shop stewards if they were to reckon with the rapid spread of payment-by-results on war work. When dilution was introduced, craftsmen found further uses for shop stewards; and even the dilutees themselves felt the need of directly appointed delegates able to cope with the problems thrown up by the complexities of wartime production. Many shop stewards, especially on the Clyde, were syndicalists; and those that were not came under syndicalist influence through the creation, outside the factories, of 'workers' committees', led by syndicalist stewards.

In 1917 the workers committees were loosely co-ordinated into the National Shop Stewards' and Workers' Committees Movement, a paradigm of syndicalist organization which repudiated 'leadership' and sought to reveal the possibilities of 'rank and file' government. Because the Movement particularly interested itself in 'unofficial' stewards—that is, stewards chosen by the men in the shop but not authorized by the trade union outside the shop—it asserted the syndicalist aim of 'reforming' labour organization, in preparation for an extended future role, by removal of undemocratic bureaucracy. Indeed, the Movement could even claim to have pioneered the general strike, through the work of leading syndicalist activists and sympathetic stewards in the various wartime stoppages on the Clyde, the strikes of 1917 and, above all, the shorter hours strike of January 1919, which was described by the Secretary of State for Scotland as a 'Bolshevist rising'. These stoppages all had something of the insurrectionary character of a general

---

[1] Trades Union Congress *Report*, loc. cit.

strike, not least if a general strike is to free unions from bureaucracy at the same time as it frees industry from employers. The
organizers of these 'unofficial', large, and enthusiastic strikes,
and probably many participants, expected a withdrawal of
labour to introduce radical changes; and governments, influenced above all by the urgency of the war effort, met what they
regarded as major threats to national security with considered
conciliation.[1]

These stoppages tested the meaning of the 1906 Trade
Disputes Act. Almost the only incontestable elements in that
statute were its conferment of legal immunities on parties to
trade disputes; and its definition of trade disputes as disputes
between persons who had something to do with, and were in
disagreement about, 'employment' or 'labour'. Persons employed or employing in 'trade and industry' could engage in
trade disputes: and they would engage in such disputes whenever they disputed an issue or issues regarding 'the employment
or non-employment or the terms of employment' or 'the
conditions of labour of any person'. Two problems at once arose
from these provisions. First, the Act gave no clear rule about
the power of persons not employed or employing in trade and
industry—such as full-time employees of trade unions or
employers' associations—to engage in a trade dispute: but this
problem was virtually ignored, since the statute extended its
legal immunities to acts 'done in pursuance of an agreement or
combination'; and in modern industrial conditions, agreements,
let alone combinations, very often involved, and were widely
accepted to involve, persons not in a strict sense employed or
employing in trade and industry. Secondly, the Act gave no
clear rule about the substance of a trade dispute. A dispute
about hiring and firing, wage increases or wage cuts, would be
a trade dispute, since these were matters that affected employment, non-employment, terms of employment or conditions of
labour; but it was not clear whether, say, a dispute about
expropriation of capital, introduction of socialism, or establishment of workers' control, all of which would certainly appear
to affect conditions of labour (at the very least), would in law
be a trade dispute.

---

[1] Arno J. Mayer, *Politics and Diplomacy of Peace-making, Containment and Counter-
revolution at Versailles, 1918–19*, London, 1968, p. 609.

The wartime stoppages that syndicalists and their sympath-izers influenced were relevant to the first problem, because of the not inconspicuous activity in those stoppages of persons not employed in trade and industry; but they were relevant to the second problem in a much more instructive fashion. The 1919 strike for shorter hours, and the May 1917 strike against dilution, were undeniably stoppages arising from disputes about 'terms of employment' or 'conditions of labour'. The November 1917 strike about recognition of shop stewards was less evidently covered by these phrases; and the 1915 Clyde Rent Strike was not so covered at all, unless the rent of an employee's private dwelling be a condition of labour. Never-theless both stoppages were sanctioned by the government, to the extent that the November 1917 strike was followed by direct government intervention in favour of recognition of shop stewards, while the 1915 strike was followed by the Rent Restriction Act: and in neither case did the government so much as suggest that these disputes were not trade disputes within the meaning of the statute of 1906. The government's conduct thus afforded practical support for the view that a trade dispute, in the 1906 sense, was very probably any dispute, on any issue, that involved employees acting in concert. In the long term this both encouraged trade unions to withdraw labour for ends such as expropriation of capital, introduction of socialism or establishment of workers' control; and also assisted trade unions to assimilate such ends to those simpler economic goals sought by withdrawal of labour: in other words, to industrialize politics.

In the short term, however, the flexibility of both govern-ments and employers robbed the great wartime strikes of any insurrectionary significance; so that, by the onset of the post-war slump, syndicalists had few concrete changes in industrial structure to show for all their efforts. Their one apparent achievement, the recognition of works committees, gave them little of the power they sought in the factories. In 1917 stewards, including syndicalists, had tried to secure from employers, especially in Birmingham and Coventry, formal recognition of 'works committees' of shop stewards, who would in turn be linked with more explicitly syndicalist 'workers' committees' set up outside the factories. Employers feared that recognition of works committees would yield some of management's powers to the employees, while union leaders interpreted works committees as a syndicalist bid to supplant national leadership and liberate the 'rank and file', or rather its spokesmen. Some employers argued that works committees must be recognized because those who demanded them could, if not satisfied, disrupt production; others argued that, unless employers co-operated with national union leaders to recognize works committees on terms which would contain them within a 'constitutional' framework, the trade unions themselves would collapse under syndicalist and stewards' pressures. Works committees were recognized in 1919, by which time, with little left of the war period's prosperity, most such committees had about two years' active life ahead of them; and so successfully were they contained by employers and union leaders that they achieved next to nothing in those two years.

Nevertheless, wartime syndicalism had laid something of the foundations of the later shop stewards' organization, and it had acquainted many trade union members with notions of 'workers' control' of which they had hitherto been ignorant. Syndicalists had also played some part in the wartime expansion of trade unions. British trade unions numbered 2·6 and 8·3 million members in 1910 and 1920 respectively; and these totals represent 14·6 and 45·2 per cent of the male and female labour force at these dates. The magnitude of this expansion is indicated by the fact that trade unions did not surpass their total membership of 1920 until 1946, and they did not equal the percentage of the labour force they had recruited by 1920 until 1948. If syndicalists had gained more power in the trade unions, the growth of labour industrial organization in the 1910s would have given them by 1920 a highly significant position in British society as a whole. However, the chief beneficiaries of trade union growth in this period were not the syndicalists but labour politicians. In December 1910 the Labour Party had polled 371,000 out of a total of 5·2 million votes, or 7·1 per cent. In November 1918, on a much enlarged franchise, the Party and its allies polled 2·4 million out of a total of 10·8 million votes, or 22·2 per cent, and formed for the first time the largest opposition group.[1]

[1] Halsey, op. cit., pp. 123–4, 235–6.

THE PROBLEM OF NATIONALIZATION

The Labour Party of 1918 differed somewhat from that of the pre-war years. Some members still favoured the concept of 'a Labour Party which shall be used exclusively by Trade Unionists for the furtherance of their own work and objects', as one speaker put it to the 1918 Trades Union Congress. But the Party's executive did not share certain trade unionists' antipathy to 'brains' and 'brilliant middle-class speakers' who 'have never been in a factory in their lives'. On the contrary, the executive proposed that full and formal membership of the Party should at last be opened to both those who 'have neither the necessity nor the opportunity of joining Trade Unions', and those 'who are not prepared to associate with the Socialist organizations already affiliated with the Party': that is, more or less, to join the Independent Labour Party. In this way, the Party's leaders hoped to widen the Party's socio-economic spread, while preserving all existing links between the Party and the unions. The proposal was carried, amid complaints that it was 'unfair to Trade Unionists', on a card vote by a margin of only 0·8 per cent of the votes cast.[1]

At the same time as the Party adopted direct individual membership, it also accepted the 'programme' it had so long evaded, by approving, not only the manifesto *Labour and the New Social Order*, but a new constitution containing in clause 3(d)—later, in slightly modified form, clause 4—the resolution 'To secure for the producers by hand or by brain the full fruits of their industry, and the most equitable distribution thereof that may be possible, upon the basis of the common ownership of the means of production and the best obtainable system of popular administration and control of each industry or service.' This formula, probably the work of Sidney Webb, was the 'definite' or 'ultimate object' for which socialists in the Labour Party had so long striven. Yet the significance of the clause is not easy to determine, especially since, though it speaks of 'common ownership of the means of production', it was expected to be acceptable to persons 'not prepared to associate'

[1] Trades Union Congress *Report*, 1918, pp. 251–3; Labour Party *Conference Report*, 1918, pp. 103–5.

with 'Socialist organizations already affiliated with the Party'. Indeed, despite Labour's sudden new emphasis on nationalization at the end of the First World War, there was still very little discussion of the meaning of 'common ownership'. Though Arthur Henderson spent much time and effort defending the new constitution to the unions, he concentrated on the sensitive issue of the admission of non-trade unionists to the trade unionists' party; and virtually ignored the small question of that party's proposed new socialist doctrines. That was not because trade unionists were already so conversant with and enthusiastic about socialism. The 1919 Trades Union Congress, for example, which was told by Robert Smillie, speaking for the Miners' Federation, that 'it is not necessary to go very deeply into the question of the nationalization of the mines', devoted to a debate on free trade more than twice the time it spent on debating 'industrial control'.[1]

The Party's apparent assumption that one could object to joining a 'Socialist organization' yet be willing to assent to clause 3(d), and the absence of any serious consideration of the significance and consequences of adopting that clause, reinforce the evidence which seems to show that the Party included clause 3(d) in its new constitution for no better reason than the desire to differentiate itself from those outside the Party, whose political persuasions Labour in fact shared: in other words, the Liberals. At the 1922 Party Conference, the miners' leader Frank Hodges observed that,

> It was this question of Nationalization which distinguished the Labour Party's practical programme from the practical programme of any of the other Parties. There had been a danger, within the last year or so, of the language of the other Parties approximating to that used by the Labour Party, until it had required, oftimes, a very careful analysis to distinguish in the written statements the difference of fundamentals in an election programme.

The Labour Party was largely led by Liberals, chiefly worked with Liberals, mainly appealed to Liberals; and was indeed, in

---

[1] Labour Party *Conference Report*, 1918, p. 140; Trades Union Congress *Report*, 1919, p. 260; Ross McKibbin, *The Evolution of the Labour Party, 1910–1924*, London, 1974, pp. 98–9.

the general tone of its life and language, probably in the gravest danger of 'approximating' to the Liberals. So long as the Labour Party was a trade union party pure and simple, that did not greatly matter; but once the Party started recruiting individual members it had both to remain sufficiently like the Liberals to be able to poach Liberal supporters, and to become sufficiently unlike the Liberals to enable Liberal supporters to distinguish some point that could warrant abandoning their old allegiances for the new Party. MacDonald, not surprisingly, dismissed the new 'socialist' constitution as 'in spirit and grasp just an election agent's document'.[1]

Yet nationalization was an issue that would have repaid much more than the highly perfunctory discussion devoted to it by Labour in 1918. The crux of the problem was, of course, power. Once the employers had been expropriated, who was to control and administer their undertakings? The Fabians and their followers had required control and administration to be given to public authorities, local and perhaps national, subject to existing local and national representative bodies; and as late as 1918 the Miners' Federation could propose simply that 'the mines . . . should be owned and controlled by the State'. But by this date the Labour Party had already advocated 'participation of the organized workers in the management' of nationalized industries; and, no doubt with such notions in mind, the Miners agreed to a General Workers' Union amendment that the mines should not 'be . . . controlled by the State' but 'be . . . democratically controlled by the State'. 'Democratic' control, or 'popular' control were nevertheless vague concepts which, despite syndicalist pressure, few trade unionists or labour politicians seemed anxious to define in detail. Since the Labour Party now spoke of 'producers by hand or by brain', it might seem that some control would be given to the managerial class of the pre-nationalization era (that is to say, to the 'producers by brain'). A number of labour spokesmen expected there to be Ministers for nationalized undertakings, and 'representatives of the State' in nationalized managements; and if nationalized industries were to be managed, largely, if not exclusively, by a Minister, representatives of the State, and other producers by brain, manual employees might seem likely to get little more

[1] Labour Party *Conference Report*, 1922, p. 222.

share in the 'popular administration and control' of industries than they had in the days of unadulterated capitalism.[1]

Certain trade unionists did make detailed proposals for the management of nationalized industries, and these proposals gave most power to elected district or national trade union leaders, and a little power to shop stewards. Clynes told the 1917 Trades Union Congress that, under nationalization, he favoured giving 'the average man of the rank and file' a share in determining 'his daily conditions', 'the question of super-intendence', and other 'little matters' arising in the workplace: 'while leaving to the Trade Unions those bigger questions which they have to define and defend', and which would be dealt with by a system of joint district and national councils. Clynes's scheme showed the way in which socialist and syndicalist demands were likely to be realized; and the structure that he outlined gave full force to the impulse that lay behind those demands, namely, the impulse towards economic re-distribution. It was in response to that impulse that the Labour Party committed itself in 1918 to the view that what could be secured 'upon the basis of . . . common ownership . . . and . . . popular administration and control' was precisely 'the full fruits' of employees' labour, 'and the most equitable distribu-tion thereof'.[2]

Since labour's interest (such as it was) in nationalization at the end of the First World War arose from a concern not with the intrinsic merits of different social and economic structures, or the effects of those structures on men as men, or *as citizens*, but with the cash rewards to be obtained from those structures, the entire movement for nationalization had, at least up to that period, an 'industrial' or economic, not a political cast. The test of a good nationalization scheme, like the test of a good strike, was fundamentally what it paid. Yet because manage-ment, consumers, the proprietors of capital (whether public or private), and indeed the community, all had claims on an industry, even nationalized undertakings could never pay out what manual workers called the 'full fruits of their labour', namely, the total return on the sale of products at the highest

---

[1] Henderson, p. 100; McKibbin, loc. cit.; Trades Union Congress *Report*, 1917, p. 345; 1918, pp. 176–7; 1919, pp. 58–9.

[2] Ibid., 1917, pp. 230–1; Labour Party *Conference Report*, loc. cit.; 1919, p. 118.

available price, minus the funds required for necessary re-investment. Indeed, even nationalized undertakings would be subject to those economic fluctuations which would oblige them to pay out less in some years than in others.

Given the intense sectionalism and individualism of most trade unionists, the low level of their commitment to the undertakings in which they were employed, their strong *laissez-faire* faith in selling their own labour dear, and using the proceeds solely as they thought best, any situation in which they received less pay than in the past, or in which they saw the income from the sale of their products going elsewhere than into their pay packets, was unacceptable to them. In the days before collective bargaining, trade unionists could either resist such developments, by strike action, or acquiesce in them. Under collective bargaining and negotiated agreements, how-ever, trade union leaders at all levels had to compromise them-selves by accepting the existing system of distribution of industrial undertakings' income; by agreeing on fixed wage increases (which by definition fell short of what their members regarded as the 'full fruits of their labour'); and even by con-senting to wage cuts. Under nationalization, the scope for such compromises would be still greater, and the effects on trade unions still more damaging. Had trade unionists or their leaders a genuine collectivist faith in nationalized under-takings, or in a state constructed only from such undertakings, this problem would have been at least less severe. But they had no such faith, which indeed, from the standpoint of their liberal individualism, they despised.

The issue was put to the 1917 Trades Union Congress by H. Dubery, of the Post Office Sorters' Association, who said:

We think that if you had a [managerial] body composed of an equal number of views of both sides, with a chairman satisfactory to both sides, and you came out . . . round certain concessions, and your members were dissatisfied with what you had got, although you had gone in on fair terms and thrashed the matter out, you would have no right to go outside afterwards and use the old weapon of the strike . . . there is just a risk that once you got upon this method of settling disputes, public opinion as well as your own sense of fairness might cause you to drift further and further away from the particular kind of agitation which you have been so fond of using in the past.

The strike, that great symbol of self-interest and self-help, had, in short, little part in the corporatist, if not collectivist, world of nationalization: and with the strike would die *laissez-faire* trade unionism. This problem was to beset all later debate on workers' control.[1]

[1] Trades Union Congress *Report*, 1917, p. 231.

4

The Failure of Workers' Control

How to control industry; that is a question above all others—that is the concern of the organised workers of this country.

TOM MANN at the 1920 Trades Union Congress

'Anarchy', exclaim some; the 'Social Democratic Revolution', shout others; meaningless words even by the lips of those who use them; more meaningless still to the poor struggling workman who wants to know, at once, where he can get the wherewithal to purchase a dinner.

GEORGE HOWELL, *Trade Unionism New and Old*

THE COMMUNISTS' LOST OPPORTUNITY

Syndicalism, though still diffuse in thought and deficient in leadership, seemed to offer, even after the end of the First World War and the brief boom that succeeded it, the political concepts most acceptable to organized labour, despite, or perhaps because of, these concepts' rapid dissolution into simple, traditional industrial notions. 'The only difference . . . between us,' said Lenin in 1920, after he had listened to the speeches of the British syndicalists who attended the second congress of the Comintern, 'is the sort of mistrust which the British comrades entertain towards political parties. They cannot imagine political parties as being anything else than parties . . . of parliamentary fakers and traitors to the working class.'[1]

The 'difference' between syndicalists and Bolsheviks certainly included, but nevertheless went beyond, this issue. When Lenin

---

[1] V. I. Lenin, *British Labour and British Imperialism, A Compilation of Writings by Lenin on Britain*, London, 1969, p. 265.

spoke of the 'proletariat', for example, he meant something closely akin, but not merely equal to manual wage earners; and when he spoke of 'revolution', he meant a broad political conflict in which trade unions' wage claims were but one part, and a small part at that. British syndicalists, on the other hand, equated the 'proletariat' solely with manual wage earners and, though they had to make room for working-class autodidacts like themselves, intended to have no truck with the progressive 'middle-class intellectuals' who formed so significant an element of the embattled vanguard of the oppressed as perceived by Marxists and Leninists. Nor did British syndicalists propose to minimize the revolutionary force of trade unions' wage claims. Indeed, they were loth to admit the existence of any other revolutionary force; since they tended to regard even that great expropriatory general strike, which would eliminate capitalism and usher in the syndicalist society, as one gigantic wages dispute. In this respect they could only concur in the sentiments of a delegate to the 1944 Trades Union Congress who extolled strike action by saying that, 'he was one of the primitive trade unionists' who 'believed there was only one way in which this class issue could be really decided, and that was for the parties on either side to take their chances in a good wrestling match.'[1]

Not merely syndicalists but British trade unionists in general feared and distrusted Communism and Communists after the First World War. Frank Hodges, opposing Communists' demands to be affiliated to the Labour Party, warned his liberal-individualist audience at the 1923 Labour Party conference that 'they in the Labour Party abhorred the very element of dictation.' A year earlier he told the same audience that the Communist Party of Great Britain consisted of 'intellectual slaves of Moscow', who lacked the decency even to follow the thinking of 'the plain Russian people' but preferred to trust the 'type of intellectuals despised in this country'— that is, despised by trade unionists. Trade unionists, at least of the 'primitive' type, therefore doubted the virtues of communist theory as an aid to the kind of class-consciousness they favoured. 'On the industrial field', declared Ernest Bevin in 1927, 'Tories were as class-conscious as the most advanced Com-

---

[1] Trades Union Congress *Report*, 1944, p. 227.

munist' who, after all, in England at least, could boast little more than 'a very mixed idea of what Karl Marx said.'[1]

Nevertheless by the mid-1920s organized syndicalism had largely collapsed; and the Communist Party of Great Britain which attempted to annex the syndicalist tradition, and which drew members and leaders from the syndicalists' ranks, had taken its place. 'The Shop Stewards' Movement had been liquidated into the Communist Party of England', wrote a hostile critic of communism in 1922. This development was secured partly by the post-war slump, which destroyed the syndicalists' power in the mines and the workshops; partly by the Bolsheviks' prestige; and partly by the flow of funds from Moscow to the nascent Communist Party of Great Britain and its ancillary institutions. For just as the Labour Party might be said to be the product of 'trade union gold' (plus a secret deal with the Liberal Party), the Communist Party might be viewed as the product of 'Moscow gold' (plus a secret deal among certain left-wingers to concentrate their efforts where they would be financed).[2]

A recent historian of twentieth-century extremist politics has described the British Communist Party as 'an almost wholly artificial creation which wrenched the whole course' of the left-wing 'out of direction'. Now, not merely is the phrase 'an almost wholly artificial creation' as appropriate to the Labour as to the Communist Party, but it would be more precise to describe the pre-Communist labour left and the trade unions as the force that 'wrenched' the 'whole course' of the Communist Party 'out of direction'. Had that Party retained its own 'direction', interpreted fairly broadly, it might have formed at the very least a new type of syndicalism, in which the syndicalists' tentative corporatism was strengthened and developed by the much fuller collectivism of revolutionary Marxist doctrine. Such a syndicalist-Marxist synthesis could have raised trade-union politics to a new height; it could have elevated the manual wage earners' narrowly industrial concerns to the plane of political activity properly so called; and, if the transition from individualism to collectivism is progress, it could, by facilitating

---

[1] Labour Party *Conference Report*, 1922, p. 198; 1923, p. 188; 1927, pp. 185–6.
[2] Roderick Martin, *Communism and the British Trade Unions 1924–1933, A Study of the National Minority Movement*, Oxford, 1969, p. 22.

that transition, have merited its claim to be the truly progressive element in British society.[1]

There were, however, no precedents for such a synthesis, since the Russian Communists had merely suppressed the syndicalist movement in the Petrograd and Moscow factories, and had taken their practical model of industrial organization very largely from the exceedingly anti-syndicalist example of the German war economy of 1914–18. Furthermore, British Communists were infinitely weaker than Russian Communists, both in political power and in Marxist theory. In practice, therefore, the Communist Party of Great Britain subordinated its state-socialist aspirations to the dictates of the syndicalist tradition, and of trade-union industrial 'militancy'; and during most of the 1920s British Communists were rather less collectivist than the Lloyd George Liberals of the pre-war years.

In order to exploit the support of various syndicalists and pro-syndicalist labour activists, the Communist Party established the National Minority Movement, a special labour agitation-group, which endeavoured to recruit followers and contest union elections in those industrial sectors where the syndicalists had formerly prospered. As if to get on the record its unease at this manner of proceeding, the Communist Party did warn that 'only a revolutionary Communist struggle' could achieve the proper objectives of the 'active workers who participate' in the National Minority Movement. Yet the Communists' everyday activities belied this revolutionary rectitude. Just like Labour left-wingers before them, they relegated socialist and collectivist notions to the sphere of 'ultimate' goals in order to devote themselves the more happily to the sphere of the 'immediate' programme. 'Bread and butter problems first, high politics later, that is the method to adopt', the Party counselled, as it directed its members to involve themselves with 'the immediate struggles of the workers'. Such a policy could only mean the abdication of all efforts to politicize manual wage earners, in favour of a surrender to those workers' determination to industrialize all around them.[2]

---

[1] Walter Kendall, *The Revolutionary Movement in Britain 1900–1921. The Origins of British Communism*, London, 1969, p. xii.

[2] Martin, pp. 36–7.

Communism is Commonsense, a Party statement issued just after the General Strike, did speak bravely of 'the destruction of the capitalist imperialist State, and the building up of a workers' State', based on nationalization 'with workers' control', which would 'carry us through' until 'full Communism has been achieved.' But the document chiefly emphasized the handiness of Communism in shop-floor disputes. 'There is no difference', the statement declared, 'between Communist principles during a Revolution or when the question of the day is how to stop a foreman's bullying or squeeze another penny an hour out of the boss. We are the Party of working-class common-sense.' And since, in Britain at least, 'working-class common-sense' means one or other variant of liberal individualism, British Communism had to mean liberal individualism too. The Communists could not politicize labour, except in the sense of reinforcing its already well-formed political notions; their self-appointed task was merely to serve trade unionism as hewers of industrial wood and drawers of industrial water.[1]

THE SOCIALIST COMMONWEALTH AND WORKERS' CONTROL

Since the Communist Party thus failed to educate trade union opinion during the 1920s, the chief agency whereby labour might at least consolidate its wartime notions of workers' control, if not perhaps move towards some more collectivist ideas, was the Labour Party itself, which was devoted, throughout this period, to what Sidney Webb, in a famous phrase, called 'the inevitable gradualness of our scheme of change'. Between 1918 and 1929 the number of Labour voters rose from 2·4 million (or 11 per cent of the electorate) to 8·4 million (or 29 per cent of the electorate). In 1929, the number of Labour voters for the first time exceeded the number of trade unionists, and in that year, as in 1924, the Parliamentary Labour Party formed a minority government under Ramsay MacDonald. But neither government did much to change the thinking of organized labour, at least during the 1920s. MacDonald had retreated from much (though by no means all)

---

[1] *Communism is Commonsense, A Statement of Aims and Policy published by the Communist Party of Great Britain*, London, 1926, pp. 3–4, 11, 18.

of his collectivism; and by the 1920s he proved to be little more than 'a magnificent substitute for a leader', in the words of Beatrice Webb: whose remark was, in a sense, more damaging to the Labour Party's reputation than to MacDonald's. Meanwhile the Labour left showed itself to be scarcely more effective than MacDonald, with the exception, it is generally held, of John Wheatley, whose monument was a Housing Act that raised Neville Chamberlain's building subsidy of £6 per house to £9 per house.[1]

Had the Parliamentary Labour Party commanded a majority in 1924 or 1929, it would nevertheless probably have done relatively little to alter the character of political discourse in Britain. The 1920 Labour Party conference had indeed 'almost unanimously' reaffirmed its support for 'the principle of public ownership'; and *Labour and the Nation* (the policy statement submitted to the 1928 conference as a replacement for the wartime document *Labour and the New Social Order*) declared that, since men were all 'members of one another', they should devote themselves not to competition but to 'co-operative effort'. Moreover, there is some evidence of collectivist convictions underlying these formulas, at least in certain sections of the Labour Party. In April 1921, R. H. Tawney, a fellow of Balliol, and for many years an adviser to Labour leaders, published his book *The Acquisitive Society*, which was to run through annual editions for most of the 1920s. Tawney's doctrine was a collectivism almost as thoroughgoing as that of MacDonald's *Socialism and Government*. Tawney argued that contemporary society was founded, not on the 'mutual obligations arising from' individuals' 'relation to a common end' (as, according to Tawney, it should be), but on 'private rights and private interests', and on 'the contracts of individual with individual'. The 'social war' of such a society, devoted as it was to individuals' 'acquisition of wealth', should be replaced by the harmony of a 'functional' society 'organized primarily for the performance of *duties*', not 'the maintenance of *rights*'. The functional society would be founded on 'service'; and would be characterized by the 'subordination', 'authority',

---

[1] M. I. Cole (ed.), *Beatrice Webb's Diaries 1924–1932*, London, 1956, p. 112; Labour Party *Conference Report*, 1923, p. 178; Charles Loch Mowat, *Britain Between the Wars 1918–1940*, London, 1955, pp. 164–5, 176.

and 'discipline' that spring from the 'necessity' of pursuing a 'common end'.[1]

If widely held by trade unionists and labour politicians, views such as these would have formed a theoretical basis for the most far-reaching transformation of British liberal individualism: a transformation in which 'workers' control' (or indeed schemes of a larger collectivism) would have acquired an urgency they lacked during the First World War. On the contrary, however, both trade unionists and labour politicians held principles so close to *laissez-faire* that workers' control, or any other variant on socialist themes, could signify, in their mouths, little more than a partisan reformation of old liberal themes. 'I look forward to a future in which there will be less law-making, less governing, fewer restrictions on individual liberty', declared Maxton. And this libertarian, but certainly not specifically socialist paradise, was to be qualified only by special powers for organized labour. 'I do not need any one to tell me about the general principles of Socialism,' he announced at the 1928 Labour Party conference, 'I know them—absolute equality and the workers controlling and directing the destinies of the nation.'[2]

What labour politicians stated thus vaguely, Labour Party theorists openly and explicitly admitted. The Webbs' *Constitution for the Socialist Commonwealth*, which appeared in 1920, a document of unparalleled influence on the detail of Labour thinking about a future state, contains a remarkable labour version of Mill's famous principle 'that the sole end for which mankind are warranted, individually or collectively, in interfering with the liberty of action of any of their number, is self-protection'. Wrote the Webbs: 'The freedom that the Socialist Commonwealth will seek to maximize can be no other than an individual freedom' for each 'vocational organization', that is, trade union, 'to protect and develop so long as this freedom does not conflict with a like freedom of other vocations or with the welfare of the community as a whole.' Such welfare was, in

[1] Labour Party *Conference Report*, 1920, p. 181; G. D. H. Cole, *A History of the Labour Party from 1914*, London, 1948, pp. 205 ff.; R. H. Tawney, *The Acquisitive Society*, London, 1926, pp. 14, 32, 43, 96, 206.

[2] *The Case of Benn* versus *Maxton, Being a Correspondence on Capitalism and Socialism to Which is Appended the Report of a Broadcast Debate*, London, 1929, p. 36; Labour Party *Conference Report*, 1928, p. 201.

any event, an entirely individualist matter for the Webbs, since, for all their 'socialism', they denied that 'the community as a whole' existed. There was no 'general will', they asserted, because even the individual had 'several different wills . . . which have no identity'; and the 'community' is an aggregate of individuals. For this reason, the *Socialist Commonwealth* denied that democracy can be 'simple, homogeneous and indivisible'; and, indeed, rather than 'democracy', spoke of 'democracies'—'of Consumers, of Producers, of Citizens'. At most, in other words, the Webbs still deviated from classical Victorian individualism only to countenance a corporatism, of which the centrepiece would be the array of trade unions, or 'vocational organizations' 'free, independent and voluntary'.[1]

Among the Labour Party's younger intellectuals after the First World War, few were as productive as Harold J. Laski, then professor at the London School of Economics. Laski was later an editor of the largely pro-Communist Left Book Club, and a leader of the left-wing Socialist League. But Laski, by British standards, was in fact an individualist of the most old-fashioned kind. He rejected the concept of a 'whole', which 'transcends the interests of the Many who compose that whole', as a 'mystic monism' which 'runs counter to some of the deepest convictions which we possess'. Laski himself favoured what he called 'the pluralistic theory of the State'. He regarded 'group competing against group' as 'a ceaseless striving of progressive expansion'. The state itself, he wrote, was 'only one of the associations' to which the individual 'happens to belong'; the 'good' that the state pursued would be 'that of a certain section', not that of 'the community as a whole'; and, in any event, in true utilitarian spirit, the state must 'prove itself by what it achieves'. In no sense is this collectivist doctrine and, since socialism is a collectivist doctrine, in no sense can it be socialist doctrine either.[2]

When Labour theorists reckoned with problems of the structure of what the Webbs called 'the Socialist Common-

[1] John Stuart Mill, *Utilitarianism, Liberty and Representative Government*, London, 1968, pp. 72–3; Sidney and Beatrice Webb, *A Constitution for the Socialist Commonwealth in Great Britain*, London, 1920, pp. 102–3, 167, 315.
[2] Harold J. Laski, *Studies in the Problem of Sovereignty*, New Haven and London, 1917, pp. 3, 15, 19, 21, 25.

wealth', the continuing conflict between a forlorn collectivism (as represented by Tawney or the young MacDonald) and a preponderant preference for individualism, or the closest practical approximation thereto (as represented by Laski and the Webbs), expressed itself in a tendency to define the details of Labour's ideal state and society in terms of the most elaborate compromise. Since very few of these theorists were out-and-out syndicalists, there was a certain emphasis on the state: even Independent Labour Party spokesmen like Brailsford, for example, urging that Parliament must retain 'final control' in 'broad outline'. On the other hand, the strong promptings of the *laissez-faire* tradition caused many Labour writers to emphasize also the variety and diversity of the socialist commonwealth. 'The British Labour and Socialist Movement' would actually 'maintain, strengthen and extend private property', declared the Webbs, explaining with due obeisance to redistributionism, that this would be done 'by preventing its monopoly in the hands of a small fraction of the population'. And so far as *public* ownership was concerned, there could be, given individualist principles, no single, correct, or 'scientific' form of organization. 'I do not assume', declared Laski, 'that any special formulae, whether of State socialism, guild socialism, or syndicalism, represent a universal truth applicable to all industry and under all conditions.'[1]

Moreover, all Labour thinking from the First World War onwards assumed not merely that there were to be many types of ownership and control in the socialist commonwealth, but that each type itself must allow for the free play of different, and indeed opposing, interests. W. H. Hutchinson, then Chairman of the Labour Party, told the Party conference of 1920 that nationalization would involve both 'workers' control' and 'full representation of the consumers as well'; and Tawney insisted that nationalized undertakings must represent 'at least those who supply the service and those who use it'. In other words, when members of the Labour Party, and those who generally thought with them, spoke of giving 'the workers' a 'large share of control' in industry, they in fact expected that 'share' to be no more, and perhaps much less, than half.[1]

---

[1] H. N. Brailsford, *Socialism for To-day*, London, 1925, p. 88; Webbs, p. 340; Harold J. Laski, *A Grammar of Politics*, London, 1941, p. 437.

And there were further complications. Even if the state was to have 'final control', it was to remain relatively weak. Claiming to seek 'protection against the evils of uncontrolled bureaucracy', the Webbs proposed 'to divide, and sharply to separate . . . strictly political government' from 'control of social and industrial administration'. The 'Political Parliament' would have to get its funds from a 'Social Parliament'; the latter would be advised on the running of the economy by a system of 'separate standing committees', each with 'continuous oversight' over one economic sector; but each committee would in turn rely on a 'national board' for the actual 'administration' of its sector, using the term 'administration' in 'its widest sense'. The Webbs' scheme was perhaps over-elaborate, and certainly, in part, controversial. Yet it specified the broad orthodoxy of the Labour Party; and this orthodoxy was summarized (in a discussion of coal nationalization) by a Labour Party Executive dictum of 1926, that government would be restricted to 'questions of general policy', while 'day-by-day conduct' of each industry notionally publicly controlled would be in the hands of a separate body.[1]

Such devolution of power must cast doubt upon the degree to which the state of the so-called socialist commonwealth would indeed be socialist; since the political and economic institutions envisaged for it seem opposed to any unitary, 'socialist' concept of the community and its activities. The socialist commonwealth might, then, be thought to approach the syndicalist ideal of untrammelled workers' control. Yet that ideal found little favour with the most influential Labour theorists after the First World War. Just as those theorists tended to water the principle of a collectivist state, so they tended to dilute the idea of syndicalist labour organization. For a start, trade unions must be transformed: in both Tawney's 'functional society' and the Webbs' socialist commonwealth, trade unions were to emphasize 'duty' not 'rights', 'service . . . to the community' not class 'warfare'—they must, as Brailsford put it, teach labour to regard ' "slacking" as treason'. In any event, the sphere of the workers' responsibility—and control—was to be strictly limited to the sphere of their own competence

---

[1] Webbs, p. xvi; Labour Party *Conference Report*, 1920, pp. 116, 181; Tawney, p. 148; Plebs League, *An Outline of Economics*, London, 1923, p. 134.

or 'technique'. Were manual employees, for instance, to be permitted to control non-manual elements of the productive process, this would be, in Laski's words, 'as absurd as to allow the patient to control the doctor'. Finally, the doctrine of the representation of a multiplicity of interests meant that the whole community (that is, the aggregate of those interests) should appoint and direct the management of industrial undertakings. How would the unions like it, the Webbs wondered, if the 'charwomen' at union headquarters should 'elect the General Secretary' of a union, 'instead of the right of election being vested in the whole membership of the trade union': a procedure which would, by definition, exclude in almost every case that union's own manual employees.[1]

These complex equivocations had, however, a fairly simple dénouement in the realm of practical proposals, even if that dénouement did not become apparent to labour for some years. The socialist commonwealth, the Webbs argued, would nationalize economic undertakings. Each undertaking would then be run ('day-by-day') by an independent 'National Board' acting through subsidiary committees and through individual managers. The 'National Board', and the subsidiary committees, would be appointed on 'the sole consideration' of ability; and the 'confusion of thought' responsible for the doctrine 'that the employees should elect their managers' would certainly be avoided. Yet the National Board would include representatives, both 'of the various vocations (manual-working and clerical) employed', and of 'the interests of the consumers and of the community as a whole'; and since such 'representatives' could not be elective, their representativeness must arise not from their manner of appointment but from their similarity with, and competence to speak for, the particular section of the population that they were said to represent. In other words, nationalized undertakings would be run—above all, at the national level—by a combination of technicians and bureaucrats ('ability'), ex-trade unionists (the 'vocations'), and ex-public servants and respectable managers of other nationalized, or even private, undertakings (the 'consumers', the 'community'): that is, by precisely the mixture favoured by the

---

[1] Tawney, p. 139; Webbs, pp. 149, 159; Brailsford, p. 93; Laski, p. 442.

Attlee administrations a quarter of a century after the publication of the Webbs' *Socialist Commonwealth*.[1]

The ratiocinations of Labour theorists would merit little consideration had not their conclusions received a more or less sympathetic hearing among the trade unions that supported the ever-expanding Labour Party. Quite regardless of what the theorists said, those unions were increasingly committed to the doctrine of 'workers' control'. Shortly after the First World War, the Transport and General Workers' Union added to its constitutional 'objects' the commitment 'to endeavour by all means' to 'control the industries' in which its 'members are engaged'; and the Amalgamated Engineering Union chose for its first 'object' 'the control of industry in the interests of the community'. Such phrases could of course cover both the boldest schemes of social reconstruction and the most old-fashioned techniques of workplace money-making: and that flexibility may have been intentional.[2]

What 'workers' control' meant most trade unionists would have been hard put to say; but they were quite clear on its purpose. In the first place, 'control' was to bring 'freedom'. Charlie Cramp of the National Union of Railwaymen did warn the 1923 Trades Union Congress that 'even in a Socialistic Government you cannot afford to allow everybody to do as he likes'; but that warning usually fell on deaf ears. In the second place, the 'freedom' obtained through 'control' was to be used to force up wages. A Trades Union Congress memorandum of 1925 remarked, of constitutional revisions such as those adopted by the Transport and General Workers and the Engineers, 'It is being recognized by thinking Trade Unionists that to secure maximum results for their members some means of control is desirable.' Both points were neatly summarized by John Cliff of the Transport and General Workers' Union, who observed in 1932 that, 'if we are going to get anything out of socialized industry it must mean that we are going to have greater freedom for the worker'.[3]

Workers' control might be sought through violent means but

---

[1] Webbs, pp. 160, 163, 173, 176–7.

[2] Transport and General Workers' Union *Rules*, 1922; Amalgamated Engineering Union *Rules*, 1920.

[3] Trades Union Congress *Report*, 1923, p. 306; 1925, p. 229; 1932, p. 390.

such means seemed neither attractive nor feasible about 1920; and those manual workers who hoped to gain from 'control of industry' adopted other expedients. One scheme especially popular among Engineers was the 'collective contract', a device for avoiding capital outlay, while controlling all matters relating to the terms and conditions of employment, by constituting a co-operative workshop in which the capitalists provided the workshop and labour provided the co-operative. Alfred Clifford, a leading exponent of collective contract, proposed 'a relentless crusade to expel the employers'; but what he meant by this was that workmen should band together to supply labour ('on wholesale terms') to a proprietor of manufacturing capital, who would merely take a percentage, and would allow the collective contractors to appoint 'foreman and charge-hands', arrange 'allocation of jobs' and be responsible for 'output and the productive process'.[1]

The collective contract was virtually ineffective; and little more success was enjoyed by post-war attempts to form co-operative workshops that owned both capital as well as labour. The Coventry Engineering Guild, the Midland Guild of General Engineers and the Guild of Engineers (London) Ltd. sought to exploit the labour shortage of 1919–20 by offering to undertake bicycle manufacture and repair, and maintenance work for local authorities. These schemes appealed to few metal machinists; but the Manchester Building Guild, and the Guild of Builders (London), which embarked on £2,000,000 worth of work and employed up to 6,000 workers, did arouse rather more support from an industry which had a strong tradition of sub-contracting and small-scale working. Like the engineering guilds, however, the building guilds relied heavily on the favour of local authorities. Assisted originally by loans from the Co-operative Wholesale Bank, the guilds had no reserves and relied on prompt payment, by instalments, to cover their costs. When this ceased, and when the post-war boom collapsed, the guilds failed too: partly, suggests Cole, because they lacked the managerial skills to cope with their financial difficulties. In any event, by 1923, all the guilds had been wound up.[2]

---

[1] Engineers' *Monthly Journal and Report*, June 1920, pp. 60–1; January 1921, p. 76.
[2] Tawney, pp. 120–2; G. D. H. Cole, *A Short History of the British Working-Class Movement, 1789–1947*, London, 1948, pp. 406–8.

LAW, POLITICS, AND THE GENERAL STRIKE

Despite these set-backs at least one group of workers continued, if only in an organized rather than an individual capacity, to pursue the ideal of 'workers' control'; and that group, the Miners, counted for a great deal in the British economy, in the Trades Union Congress and in the Labour Party. As early as 1894 the Miners' Federation of Great Britain resolved that 'the best interests of the nation will be served by the nationalization of the mines'. But the Miners then assumed, in Robert Smillie's words, that the nationalized mines would be 'held by the State and managed by the State'. In other words, nationalization would simply replace obstreperous private employers by what was hoped would be enlightened civil servants; while the managerial structure of mining would remain fundamentally unaltered. Most Miners expected that this programme would be realized by conventional legal and political means. But during the First World War the government itself undertook the general direction of coalmining through a system of public surveillance headed by a Coal Controller. The mine owners were not removed; but they were required to be more friendly to the Miners' Federation, which gained for the first time the convenience and bargaining opportunities of national wages settlements. By 1918 these developments encouraged some Miners to think that outright nationalization was much nearer than it had been in 1894.[1]

But by 1918, the Miners' concept of nationalization, and their ideas about how to get it, had also undergone change. *The Miners' Next Step* contained a policy statement, clause XIV of which read, 'That our objective be, to build up an organization, that will ultimately take over the mining industry, and carry it on in the interests of the workers.' '*Nationalization of the Mines* . . . simply makes a National Trust, with all the force of the government behind it', declared the authors of this statement: who proposed to achieve *their* syndicalist transformation of mining by 'a policy of open hostility' towards the employers, and 'all capitalist parties'. Of course these sentiments did not commend themselves to every Miner; but the Miners' leaders, at least, now favoured a shift away from the scheme of unitary

[1] R. Page Arnot, *The Miners, Years of Struggle*, London, 1953, p. 129.

state control of the mines. In 1918 the Miners' Federation resolved to seek 'State ownership' of the industry 'with joint control and administration by the workmen and the State'. 'We want the nation to own the mines and the miners to control them', Smillie told the Trades Union Congress of 1919.[1]

The Miners' new vision of a publicly-owned mining industry, managed by the Miners themselves, drew heavily on syndicalist notions about the ideal future society. Their idea of how to achieve such a system of workers' control also had a pronouncedly syndicalist character. Smillie boasted that the Miners 'could within a month, stop every mine in the country till the mines were nationalized'. The Lloyd George coalition government, formed after the 1918 general election, was based on 'fraud', he claimed; and he asked the Labour Party Conference of 1919, 'were the miners not to use the power of their organization in order to improve their conditions by means of nationalization if they thought it right to do so?' The question frightened many Party members. 'It is unwise and undemocratic because we fail to get a majority at the polls to turn round and demand that we should substitute industrial action', warned one of the Miners' critics within the Party. Another insisted that Labour was that party which above all 'ought to hold that the duly elected representatives of the people should make the laws'— not the leaders of a powerful sectional interest.[2]

These critics could point to a well-established tradition of British politics: namely, that positive action to require major political and social changes from the people was the prerogative of a duly appointed government supported by a majority of parliamentarians, able, in their turn, to claim the confidence of a majority, or at least a plurality of electors; and that external pressure designed to force such action from a government was in principle unconstitutional. The 'constitutional' and the 'unconstitutional' are always difficult to define in a state organized on individualist rather than collectivist principles, if only because the citizens of the former type of state have so hazy a notion of the state as a *whole*, whether characterized by

[1] *The Miners' Next Step Being a Suggested Scheme for the Reorganisation of the Federation Issued by the Unofficial Reform Committee*, Tonypandy, 1912, pp. 23, 25–6, 29; Arnot, p. 184; Trades Union Congress *Report*, 1919, p. 263.

[2] Labour Party *Conference Report*, 1919, pp. 113, 118; Trades Union Congress *Report*, 1919, pp. 262, 290.

a constitution, or by any other holistic attribute. In the United States of America, this deficiency is partly offset by the federal constitution; but in the United Kingdom, which has no written constitution, efforts to define the constitutional have to be expressed in a somewhat unsuitable and inadequate language derived from public custom, or from the details of statute or common law. In this language, the unconstitutional tends in general to be conflated with the unlawful, and in particular to be equated, if on a small scale, with 'sedition' and 'conspiracy', if on a large scale, with 'treason'.

The issues of 'sedition' and 'conspiracy' had been raised in 1843, when Thomas Cooper and other Chartists were charged with seditious conspiracy for urging men to strike till the Charter became law. At the Staffordshire Assizes, Mr. Justice Erskine observed that, if the Chartists had simply tried 'honestly and peaceably' to induce 'workmen to abstain voluntarily from work until the Charter should become the law of the land', and 'if the establishment of the Charter were a lawful object', then no charge would stand. But if the 'obvious peril of such experiment' convinced the jury that 'the defendants contemplated and intended, through the pressure of distress from a simultaneous cessation of all work, to produce discontent, tumult and outrage, and through the operation of such results to press on the Government the adoption of the Charter'; if 'their purpose was, by turning those hands out of employ, and keeping them out of employ, to raise tumults or such a force in the country as would intimidate the Government and compel them by terror, and not by sound reason and conviction, to adopt the Charter as the law of the land': then the charge of seditious conspiracy would stand. The jury found the defendants guilty; and the convictions were upheld when the case came to the Queen's Bench. There Mr. Justice Patteson emphasized that 'the Court does not say it is lawful for any man to continue not to do any work at all'; and added that, 'it is illegal for persons to compel other workmen throughout the whole country to abstain from work until the Charter becomes the law of the land.' Every man, Patteson declared, must disseminate his opinion on the alteration of laws 'in a proper manner, and relying on the change being made by those who by the constitution of the country are entrusted with the power of making it. All the people in the country have no right to make that change.'[1]

Five years after Cooper's case, the Treason Felony Act (a statute later deemed highly relevant to assessments of the Miners' and Trades Union Congress's policies) attempted to define a lower yet, so to speak, broader treasonable crime than treason itself, which, since medieval times, had been understood to signify 'levying war against the king in his realm'. The statute of 1848 declared that attempts 'by Force or Constraint to compel' the Sovereign 'to change' his 'Measures or Counsels', or 'by Force or Constraint' to 'intimidate or overawe' Parliament were treasonably felonious. Thus the Act generalized the judgement in *Rex* v. *Frost* (1839), another Chartist case, which had included under 'levying war against the king', 'insurrection' to 'inhance the common rate of wages', 'to reform some national grievance, to alter the established law' or 'for any other purpose which usurps the government in matters of a public and general nature', in which 'the insurgents have no peculiar interest', whether those insurgents sought to procure their ends with 'an armed force', or merely by strength of 'numbers'. Criminal lawyers therefore hold that the extension of the concept of treason by the concept of treasonable felony means the inclusion under 'levying war against the king in his realm' of something wider than 'warlike operations in the ordinary meaning of the term'.[2]

Jurists did disagree whether a strike in one, several or all industries might or might not constitute in certain circumstances a 'seditious conspiracy', a treasonable insurrection or other felony, and an attack upon the British political system. Syndicalists had no doubt that what they meant by a 'general strike' was just such an insurrection, the means whereby, in Marx's phrase, 'the expropriators are expropriated'. But by the time the syndicalists began to develop their doctrines, most men's perception of the legal and constitutional significance of strikes had been largely influenced by that classic document of *laissez-faire* ideology, the Trade Disputes Act of 1906. Under the

---

[1] W. C. Costin and J. S. Watson, *The Law and Working of the Constitution: Documents 1660–1914*, London, 1952, vol. 2, pp. 275–8.

[2] 11 and 12 Victoria c.12, sect. 3; J. W. Cecil Turner (ed.), *Russell on Crime*, London, 1958, vol. 1, p. 244.

vast immunities of that statute, any action legal or tortious, if committed by an individual, would be legal if done by employees 'in trade or industry', 'in pursuance of an agreement or combination', acting 'in contemplation or furtherance of a trade dispute': that is, in contemplation or furtherance of a dispute between employees, or between employees and employers, in trade or industry, regarding 'the employment or non-employment, or the terms of employment' or 'the conditions of labour of any person'. The labour-lawyer and Labour politician Henry Slesser doubted whether a 'political' strike, and in particular 'a strike to coerce the Government' would be a trade dispute so defined. Yet this interpretation, though very probably legally accurate, had little effect on the perhaps inevitable assessment of the statute's phraseology. For the statute appeared to give all possible protection in two sorts of concerted stoppage of work (whether in breach of contract or not, and on whatever issue), by most or even all citizens, even in circumstances which approximated to constraint, and perhaps insurrection or treason felony, and which did tend 'to coerce the Government'. In the first place, 'conditions of labour' was so vague a term that, even if the striking disputants demanded—say, government control of the rents of their dwellings (as occurred in 1915), or legislative transformation of industrial structure (as was demanded by Smillie in 1919)— the participants in a nationwide concerted stoppage, a general strike in the parlance of 1926, if not in the language of the syndicalists, could still claim to be disputing their 'conditions of labour', and hence to be engaging in a lawful 'trade dispute'. And in the second place, supposing that this could be contested at law, a nationwide concerted stoppage *simultaneously both* about less contentious 'terms of employment' or 'conditions of labour', such as wages or hours of work, *and* about matters such as government control of rents or structural changes in industry, would in practice remain legally inexpugnable, since the strikers could hardly be ordered to resume work on one count, and at once welcomed back on strike on the other.[1]

By the Armistice, the Miners had in any event a number of precedents for the argument, however specious, that strikes on

---

[1] Karl Marx, *Capital*, Moscow, 1961, vol. 1, p. 763; Henry Slesser, *Judgment Reserved*, London, 1941, p. 157; 6 Edward VII c.47, sects. 1, 3–5.

almost any issue did not amount to 'insurrection', or any other treasonable or treasonably felonious breach of the constitution; but were, on the contrary, lawful activities enjoying the approval of government and the blessing of the Trade Disputes Act. The Miners' Federation noted these precedents; and, in the spring of 1919, balloted its members to determine whether they favoured a strike to secure a wage increase; shorter hours; an industry-wide unemployment benefit scheme; and nationalization. This was a clever mixture of 'industrial' and 'political' ends, in simultaneous pursuit of which the Miners could perhaps strike with impunity. Complaints, both inside the Labour Party and out, about the 'unconstitutionality' of 'direct action', could be ignored; and the Miners, by seeking large social and political changes through the coercive power of a stoppage of work, might well take the industrialization of British politics a stage further.

When most Miners voted to strike, the government hastily appointed a Royal Commission, headed by Mr. Justice Sankey, and weighted rather heavily in the Miners' favour. All the Commission's members, except those that represented the mine owners' point of view, advocated nationalization. Sankey himself, and the government's other nominees, proposed 'either nationalization or a method of unification by national purchase and/or by joint control'. While this recommendation was much less explicit than the Miners liked to claim, Sankey clearly wanted a thorough reorganization of the mines; and 'reorganization', as a synonym or near-synonym of 'nationalization', became the watchword of the next few years. Meanwhile the government prevaricated. Though perhaps few ministers favoured nationalization, they kept the industry under the Coal Controller for the time being, and expressed general sympathy with the Sankey proposals. In August 1919, Lloyd George finally admitted the government's dislike of nationalization; in October 1920 the Miners' Federation wasted much of its strength in a national wages strike; and this stoppage was hardly ended before the post-war slump began. Nationalization of the mines no longer seemed—to the general public, at least—to be a serious issue, and in the spring of 1921 the government decontrolled the coal industry.[1]

[1] Arnot, pp. 200–1; Mowat, pp. 31–4, 42–3, 120.

But the Miners remained committed to their new version of nationalization, and to their new industrial tactics. While the government was withdrawing from the mines, the Miners' Federation, with the enthusiastic support of the now moribund Shop Stewards' and Workers' Committees Movement, was forming a new set of proposals, under which the mine owners should both concede a wage increase and agree to form, with the Miners, a *joint* National Wage Board; which, as a first step towards complete workers' control, would preserve the principle of a national wage, and prevent mine owners cutting pay or closing pits in districts where costs were high. This policy, supported by over 70 per cent of Miners in a ballot held in June 1921, sustained the Federation through an immense national stoppage that lasted from April to July of that year.

In the end, however, the Miners had to accept wage cuts and to surrender the substance, though not the name, of their National Wages Board. The Miners had hoped for sympathetic action from the Transport Workers and the National Union of Railwaymen, their partners in the so-called Triple Alliance. But on 'Black Friday', 15 April 1921, the Transport Workers and the National Union of Railwaymen refused to take such action, largely because the Miners insisted on their structural reforms. Had the 'Triple Alliance' not collapsed on Black Friday, the government might have been obliged to concede, or to force the mine owners to concede, many of the Miners' demands, on organization as well as remuneration. That the Alliance did collapse indicated, in the trade union movement as a whole, a flaw as serious, from the point of view of workers' control, as the contemporaneous failure of the guilds' self-management.[1]

For both realization and maintenance of any system of workers' control remotely approaching syndicalist ideals required labour to achieve not merely liberty and equality, but also fraternity, in the form of co-operation between as well as within the industrial organizations of labour; and such co-operation was, as 'Black Friday' showed, not readily to be found during the early 1920s. That this was so can be explained quite simply. Sooner or later, co-operation involves compromise; indeed, co-operation in any complex undertaking even involves

[1] Ibid., pp. 122–3.

the compromises inseparable from a surrender of personal or organizational autonomy to a directing individual or group. In this sense, fraternity is incompatible with equality: and, in the last resort, British trade unions have always preferred the latter. Thus Bevin, for example, deplored arguments in favour of Trades Union Congress intervention in the unofficial docks dispute of 1923, and declared that, 'the docker . . . does not want other people to interfere in his row.'[1]

Labour's sectionalist indifference to brotherhood alarmed some trade union leaders, who looked back on 'Black Friday' as a humiliation; and who were exceedingly anxious, should the Miners afford them an opportunity, to demonstrate their solidarity by rising to the occasion if not beyond it. The chance came in July 1925, when the Miners, opposing new proposals for wage cuts, and still pressing for the reconstruction of the coal industry, secured a guarantee of sympathetic action from Transport Workers, Railwaymen and Sailors, who agreed on this course under the aegis of the General Council of the Trades Union Congress. The government was unable to meet the unions' threat. Baldwin claimed to the House of Commons that 'no minority in a free country has ever yet coerced the whole country'; but he adopted the policy—as he later put it—of 'buying off the strike', both by a government subsidy to support Miners' wages, and by a promise of an 'investigation into the methods of improving the productive efficiency of the industry'.[2]

Though trade unions proudly dated this surrender 'Red Friday', 31 July 1925, the government did not intend to yield again to the Miners. During 1925–6 official and semi-official preparations to resist a widespread concerted stoppage of work continued in parallel with the hearings of the new Royal Commission, a body (headed by Sir Herbert Samuel) whose members were apparently chosen chiefly on the grounds of their probable hostility to the conclusions of the Sankey Commission. However, the Samuel Commission did not quite do all that the government expected of it. True, it condemned the notion of a special subsidy for the wages of one group of

---

[1] Trades Union Congress *Report*, 1923, p. 270.

[2] Keith Middlemas and John Barnes, *Baldwin, A Biography*, London, 1969, pp. 388, 390; Mowat, pp. 292–3.

employees as 'indefensible': which, on grounds of equity, it was. The Commission also warned of the 'grave economic dangers' of 'so vast and so hazardous' a project as 'nationalization of the mines', and it envisaged 'the continuance of the industry under private enterprise'. To this extent at least, the Commission rejected the Miners' 'main proposal' to it, namely, 'reorganization' on the principle that 'the industry' should be 'acquired by the State', and that 'the representatives of the miners should be given a large share in the general oversight' and 'detailed management of the mines'. Nevertheless, the Commission agreed that 'the demand for large changes', for 'an expansion of the miner's influence' over 'his working life' was a 'legitimate demand'; and it proposed nationalization of coal royalties; consultative 'joint pit-committees'; and statutory 'profit-sharing schemes'. The Commission's report was, in short, a foundation on which the Miners' negotiators could attempt to build the edifice of workers' control.[1]

The Trades Union Congress now had little choice but to grant the Miners power to call a very large-scale strike whenever they chose. Though the General Council was to abandon the Miners in May 1926, amid right-wing taunts of adventurism and left-wing taunts of capitulationism, in March 1926, when the Samuel Commission's report appeared, the Trades Union Congress had no doubt that it would aid the Miners at all costs. This certainty led to a nine-day stoppage by 1,580,000 workers, or about 11 per cent of the male labour force, in May 1926. Miners, railwaymen, dockers, and some electricity and gas workers, were among those who struck.[2]

Few if any strikes have aroused so much controversy. Some trade unionists and Labour Party members have freely described the stoppage as 'the General Strike': though, as late as 1941, Slesser preferred to speak of it as 'what has come to be called the General Strike'. The phrase may be used to signify a widespread stoppage, affecting more than one industry; but it may also be used to signify a widespread stoppage designed to expropriate private capital, and replace existing management

[1] *Report of the Royal Commission on the Coal Industry (1925) with Minutes of Evidence and Appendices*, vol. 1, *Pp.* 1926, vol. XIV, pp. 63, 73, 214, 233–5.
[2] A. H. Halsey (ed.), *Trends in British Society since 1900*, London, 1972, pp. 115, 118.

with workers' control: and this was its usage in the mouths of syndicalists, who popularized the phrase, and whose ideas influenced the utterances of Smillie and other Miners' leaders at least from 1918 onwards. It was precisely in order to avoid this significance, that some trade unionists and Labour Party members tried, in vain, to have the stoppage known as 'the National Strike'. Yet the chief definitional problem in 1926–7, a problem of permanent relevance to the analysis of industrial politics, was whether the 'General' or 'National' Strike was a trade dispute in the meaning of the Trade Disputes Act. For many people suspected that, were the stoppage in contemplation or furtherance of a trade dispute in the meaning of the statute, it would be legal and on the face of it constitutional, while, were it not such, it would be illegal and possibly unconstitutional. And, given the wording of the Act, the precise nature of the *parties to* and the *substance of* the dispute therefore assumes considerable significance.[1]

In an action for an interim injunction brought during the strike, Mr. Justice Astbury denied that the stoppage arose from a trade dispute in the 1906 sense, because the 1906 Act defined a trade dispute as a 'dispute between employers and workmen, or between workmen and workmen': while the dispute then in progress appeared to involve 'the Trade Union Congress on the one hand and the Government and the nation on the other'. This point, which had in practice been ignored during the previous twenty years, was taken up by Sir John Simon, who told the House of Commons that 'a strike is a strike against employers to compel employers to do something, but a General Strike is a strike against the public to make the public, Parliament and the Government do something.' Against Astbury and Simon, A. L. Goodhart argued that the stoppage was 'perfectly legal', among other reasons because legal dicta had established the doctrine that a trade dispute in the 1906 sense could involve not only parties directly concerned in the dispute (such as the Miners), but also other 'interested' parties (such as the Railwaymen, or the Trades Union Congress); and Slesser took the same line when he claimed that the stoppage 'was a lawful sympathetic strike'. Whether any or every 'sympathetic strike' is lawful, however, the judgement

1 Slesser, p. 154.

cited by Goodhart, namely, that of Lord Loreburn in *Conway* v. *Wade*, did not sustain Goodhart's point. For Lord Loreburn used the example, not of Railwaymen or the Trades Union Congress organizing a strike in furtherance of a dispute in mining, but of the whole mining industry organizing a strike in furtherance of a dispute 'in a single colliery'. Moreover, whatever trade unionists' inferences from practice, the parties to a trade dispute in the 1906 sense were to be persons employed or employing in 'trade and industry': which the trade union negotiators (including Arthur Henderson and the General Secretary of the Trades Union Congress), and the Cabinet, at the very least, were not. In this respect, then, the 1926 stoppage did not strictly conform to the 1906 model of a 'trade dispute'.[1]

But the 1906 Act also states that a trade dispute is a dispute whose substance concerns 'employment or non-employment', 'terms of employment' or 'conditions of labour'; and if the substantive issues with which the 1926 stoppage dealt were not such issues as these, then the stoppage was not in furtherance of a trade dispute in the 1906 sense. Here the Miners revealed their tactical skills. Their case involved three substantive issues: maintenance of wage levels, continuance of a government subsidy to that end, and 'reorganization' of the mining industry. The first of these demands is just the kind of issue that causes trade disputes: and this point was strongly emphasized by Labour spokesmen. J. H. Thomas, for example, told the Commons that the stoppage was caused by 'merely a plain, economic, industrial dispute, where the workers say: "We want justice".' But the second is by no means so simple a question. When citizens strike to obtain a government subvention to the wages of a single group of workers, the strikers may be thought by some to have strayed from economics into politics: and this point was emphasized by Labour's opponents. Churchill, for instance, declared that the stoppage did not arise from a trade dispute properly speaking, but was 'a general strike to force Parliament to pay a subsidy'.[2]

The Miners' third demand is still more difficult. Some commentators on the 1926 stoppage simply ignore it. Thus Slesser

---

[1] 1926, Ch. 536; *House of Commons Debates*, vol. 195, cols. 861–2; A. L. Goodhart, *The Legality of the General Strike in England*, Cambridge, 1927, n.p.; Slesser, p. 158.
[2] *House of Commons Debates*, vol. 195, cols. 81, 121, 314.

hints that the strike should be seen as 'a sympathetic strike on a wide scale to compel the mine owners, if they wished for the labour of the miners, to remunerate them on what the trade union of Miners conceived to be an adequate basis'; and he says nothing about the 'reorganization' of the mines, and their owners. Yet such 'reorganization' was given considerable emphasis by the disputants in this stoppage, a stoppage which, as the President of the 1926 Trades Union Congress put it, expressed 'the growing discontent of the workers with the whole structure and policy of the industrial system'. Certainly, as Mowat observes, the Miners 'harped upon "reorganization".' They accepted the more or less limited suggestions of the Samuel Commission only as part of their goal. For they committed themselves to a Trades Union Congress formula that required 'drastic', 'speedy and effective reorganization'; and they stated (with rather uncertain logic) that, 'until . . . reorganization brings greater prosperity to the industry, the miners should not be called upon to surrender any of their present inadequate wages and conditions'. Finally, the Miners insisted that they would accept wage reductions only when the scheme for reorganization 'will have been initiated by the Government': and the stoppage immediately followed disagreement on this point.[1]

Up to and throughout this period the Miners' Federation advocated nationalization of the mines under a system of joint control, 'in order to improve their conditions', as Smillie told the 1919 Labour Party conference. As the Miners and the Trades Union Congress demanded in 1926 that the government forthwith 'initiate' 'drastic' reorganization, such as would bring 'greater prosperity to the industry', they are not likely to have had any very different policy in mind. A stoppage to secure the policy of nationalization and joint control of an industry might be described as a stoppage in furtherance of a dispute over 'terms of employment' or 'conditions of labour'. On the other hand it might not. No such stoppage had occurred before the 1906 statute was enacted: and it is not easy to show that the Parliament which passed the Act would have so described such a stoppage had one occurred up to that date. That is the force

---

[1] Slesser, p. 157; Mowat, pp. 298–9; Arnot, pp. 412, 415; Middlemas and Barnes, p. 404.

of Slesser's belief that the Act did not cover strikes for political purposes. The meaning of the Trade Disputes Act is, then, not such as to guarantee the legality of the 1926 stoppage, in so far as the substance of the dispute that led to that stoppage arose from a demand for 'reorganization' of the mines. It cannot be argued, by reference to the Trade Disputes Act, that the 1926 stoppage was manifestly legal, and hence prima facie constitutional. Indeed, many observers thought the strike manifestly unconstitutional, and hence prima facie illegal. Lord Hugh Cecil, for instance, described the stoppage as 'an attack upon the State'; while Harry Pollitt called it 'a fight against the Constitution of the country'.[1]

Yet Slesser, at least, thought the question of the relationship between the 1926 stoppage and the Trade Disputes Act merely irrelevant. 'It seems to have been assumed', he wrote in 1927, 'that if a particular dispute does not fall within the ambit of the' Trade Disputes Act 'it is *ipso facto* illegal'. All the Act did, Slesser claimed, was 'to defeat' attempts to secure a common law action against a trade union for 'procurement of breach of contract'. The statute 'can be of no assistance whatsoever in deciding' the 'constitutional question whether General Strikes *per se* are lawful or unlawful', he claimed. Quoting Erskine's judgement in *Cooper*'s Case, Slesser concluded that 'the mere honest and peaceable advice to the working classes to agree to a simultaneous cessation of work for a purely political purpose is not, in itself, unlawful'; though he conceded that promotion of 'discontent, tumult and outrage' in order to 'press upon the Goverment' a 'purely political' object was 'indictable conspiracy'; and that, if the 1926 stoppage contained 'elements of sedition or treason', it would be unlawful.[2]

Such arguments lay weight not on the legal (or constitutional) significance of the substance of, or parties to a dispute, but on the method by which the disputed objectives are pursued; and Slesser may have misinterpreted the methods adopted in 1926. Thus it was perhaps not correct, as he later claimed, that the 1926 stoppage was not in any sense 'a strike directed against the State'. The stoppage was, in Brailsford's words, designed

---

[1] *House of Commons Debates*, vol. 195, col. 338; Labour Party *Conference Report*, 1926, p. 249.
[2] Slesser, pp. 157, 163, 165.

'after all, to compel the Government to do something . . . neither it nor the majority behind it in the House wished to do'; and, both before and after the stoppage, more electors voted for the party that formed the government in 1926 than for the Labour Party. Moreover, Slesser's appeal to Erskine is somewhat obscure. Erskine did not state that the Charter was a lawful object; he noted the 'obvious peril' of procuring a widespread concerted stoppage to secure that object; and he condemned any attempt to 'intimidate the Government and compel them by terror, and not by sound reason and conviction, to adopt the Charter.' Were the defendants engaged in any such attempt, he concluded, the indictment for seditious conspiracy would stand: and the jury may have agreed with this proposition since it found the defendants guilty. Finally, when the case went to a higher court, that court upheld the defendants' conviction; and affirmed that men must seek to alter laws 'in a proper manner, and relying on the change being made by those who by the constitution of the country are entrusted with the power of making it'. In short, to prove the 1926 stoppage legal and constitutional one would have to prove that it was not like but unlike the actions of Cooper and his fellow Chartists.[1]

In effect Slesser himself tried to do this by denying that those who organized the 1926 stoppage intended or effected what Erskine called such 'pressure of distress' as 'to produce discontent, tumult and outrage' sufficient to cause the government to change its policy through 'terror' and not from 'sound reason and conviction'. A. L. Goodhart made a very similar point by appealing to the Treason Felony Act as the statute most relevant to the question of any 'elements of sedition or treason' there might have been in the 1926 stoppage. That Act, Goodhart noted, stated that treasonable felony consisted in levying war against the government 'in order by Force or Constraint' to 'compel' the government to change its 'Measures or Counsels', or 'to intimidate or overawe' Parliament. Goodhart concluded that levying war meant 'Force', and that 'Force' meant violence: though he made no reference to 'Constraint', a term quite probably applicable to strikes general or not. 'It is difficult to see how a deliberate refusal to work can

[1] Ibid., p. 158; *House of Commons Debates*, vol. 202, col. 610.

constitute violence', he remarked, although he freely conceded that the stoppage was designed to 'force the government to intervene in a trade dispute' (one object of which was drastic 'reorganization' of an industry).[1]

The methods used in the 1926 stoppage plainly did not amount to 'levying war', in the sense of a resort to armed violence. The Trades Union Congress condemned such practices; and those who followed the Congress's strike call did not engage in them. However, the Congress did call one-and-a-half million men out of work; closed the pits; stopped almost all public freight and passenger traffic; halted movements of food; and stopped all supplies of electricity and gas except those continued by the army and navy and by trade unionists who disobeyed Congress. In 1919 some Labour Party members thought a stoppage in the coalmines to secure nationalization of the mines 'unwise and undemocratic'. The 1926 stoppage went far beyond the pits. It might well be thought to have intimidated, or to have been designed to intimidate, both government and citizens. In *Cooper*'s Case Erskine held that *either* 'tumults' *or* a 'force' of many unemployed persons might intimidate; and the judgement in *R.* v. *Frost* held that 'insurrection' might be procured *either* by 'an armed force' *or* by mere 'numbers'. The numbers who left work in 1926, and the manner and consequences of their so doing, were such as to lay the Trades Union Congress open to accusations of intimidation if not insurrection. Slesser claimed that these accusations did not influence the General Council's decision to call off the strike on 12 May: but his information may not have been entirely precise.[2]

Thus the stoppage of 1926 in support of the Miners very probably was not a stoppage in contemplation or furtherance of a trade dispute in the sense of the Trade Disputes Act; and the methods of the stoppage—the intent to put pressure on the government, for the objects envisaged; the numbers involved; the duration of the strike; and the effects of the stoppage on transport and food and fuel supplies—were not methods of undisputed legality. Finally, the stoppage did offend against the British traditions of political change succinctly summarized by

[1] Goodhart, loc. cit.
[2] Slesser, p. 155.

Mr. Justice Patteson in *Cooper*'s Case. In this sense, even if, in intention and execution, the 'General Strike' fell far short of the syndicalists' ambitions, the stoppage embodied the principles of industrial politics. For, had it succeeded, it would have given the unions power sufficient to make the Labour Party redundant, and to replace the project of labour parliamentary representation by a system of direct action bordering upon syndicalism. If, indeed, the strike had produced drastic reorganization in the sense of workers' control in nationalized collieries, such 'reorganization' might have spread to other sectors, including the railways and certain branches of engineering. The failure of the strike revitalized labour politics and caused trade union leaders to rethink many of their social and economic ideas.

THE CORPORATISM OF MOND-TURNER

The initial impetus towards workers' control arose from left-wing responses to pressures for a more collectivist, or at least a more corporatist, social system. In some respects, the specifically syndicalist response to those pressures was shaped by an optimistic expectation that a new social order would afford special opportunities to exploit the economy in the interests of manual workers. But organized labour and its advisers usually regarded any shift towards more corporatist social or economic structure as a mere defensive measure forced upon them by the decay of a *laissez-faire* system which, in an ideal world, they would have been very happy to preserve. The vision of a worker-controlled coal industry expressed an optimistic form of syndicalism; and after the General Strike had collapsed and while unemployment persisted at about 10 per cent, labour's thinking took on a more pessimistic colour.

The low prices of the late 1920s encouraged manufacturers to cut costs by 'rationalization', that is, by a capital investment (or by simple rearrangement of production) which would enable them to reduce their labour force. Rationalization of this sort frightened trade unions, who were in any event anxious, after their defeat at the hands of the Baldwin government, for a new understanding with the employers. The more skilful trade union officials now tried to evade all accusations that they engaged in advanced or extremist social thought, and sought to emphasize their own realism and pragmatism. 'Our political party is working for change' Bevin conceded, but 'the industrial leader has every day of his life to deal with the facts as they are.' George Hicks made a rather strange presidential speech in this vein at the 1927 Trades Union Congress. He defied 'the powers of the capitalist State'; and he warned that 'more and more workers are aiming at obtaining a share in the control and administration of industry through the Trade Unions.' But he also urged a 'joint conference' in each industry between 'representatives of the great organized bodies who have responsibility for the condition of industry'—that is, the employers and the trade unions—to start 'a common endeavour to improve the efficiency of industry and to raise the workers' standard of life'.[1]

Hicks' speech amounted to an espousal of the bipartite corporatism first propounded in the late nineteenth century by employers' spokesmen such as H. C. S. Dyer. The speech brought a speedy response from a self-appointed group of capitalists headed by Sir Alfred Mond. The so-called Mond-Turner conferences between this group and the General Council persisted for some years, despite many employers' reluctance and certain labour leaders' open hostility. 'Mond-Turnerism' rested on a very simple principle, namely, that, as Clynes puts it, 'there are many points' on which 'employers and employed can find common ground in joint promotion of what is called the interests of industry.'[2]

Among those points, two were particularly significant. First, as was agreed early in the conferences, the 'organizations on both sides' should accept 'the responsibility of industry as a whole for the avoidance of stoppages': in other words, there should be a new system of co-operation to reconcile conflicts of interest in industry. Secondly, despite the old-fashioned Gladstonian economics of men like Philip Snowden and Winston Churchill, employers and trade unionists in manufacturing industry favoured an inflationary stimulus to production rather than a deflationary restoration of confidence as

---

[1] Trades Union Congress *Report*, 1927, pp. 62, 66–7; 1928, p. 448; 1931, pp. 362–3.

[2] Ibid., 1928, p. 432.

the means to economic expansion. In particular, they desired both devaluation of the pound from the pre-war parity with the dollar, to which the pound had been revalued by the return to the gold standard in 1925; and a reduction of the bank rate from the high levels of the late 1920s to the lower levels characteristic of the pre-war world. Such changes, it was believed, would aid exports and home consumption. Thus in 1928 the two sides condemned the gold standard, and called for 'a full enquiry' into 'credit policy'; and as late as 1932, the General Council could utter the sentiment—altogether pleasing to manufacturing capitalists—that industry 'has been badly treated by the banking world'.[1]

When the Mond-Turner conferences ceased in the early 1930s, they could show few concrete results, but the policies they had at least publicized, if not in every respect furthered, did indicate new tendencies in both industry and society. Organized labour had in effect abandoned the pre-war syndicalist programme, in favour of closer co-operation with employers. But the employers, who had been advocating different versions of such co-operation ever since the 1890s, now envisaged more ambitious goals for bilateral action. No longer content with achieving industrial harmony, the employers wished also to obtain labour's aid in securing public assistance for industrial expansion: an object with which unions felt some sympathy. The later results of such a policy—that is, redistributive fiscal and welfare measures to raise purchasing power, and deficit budgeting and public investment in manufacturing and construction to stimulate economic activity— were but dimly glimpsed in the 1920s: indeed, such measures would then have alarmed most industrialists, and some trade unionists. But the Mond-Turner conferences' obsession with credit and banking indicated the lines of economic change over the next few decades; while the very logic of the conferences, their inarticulate striving towards the creation of a unified bilateral manufacturing pressure group able to dominate public policy, presaged many of the innovations of the years after 1940.

Mond-Turnerism sought to transform manufacturing industry into an autonomous corporate system able to settle its

[1] Ibid., 1928, pp. 227, 230; 1932, pp. 215–16.

own internal problems (problems of production and industrial relations) with relatively little interference from without; and able, too, to solve its external problems (the problems of selling its product) by summoning to its aid, almost regardless of all other interests, the largest available resources of public and private credit. The success of Mond-Turnerism would not have meant workers' control, in the sense of a surrender of supreme power to the organized manual workers. But like the unions' earlier bid for workers' control, culminating in the general strike, it would, if successful, have rendered the Labour Party (perhaps all parties) superfluous. For parties are concerned with government; but Mond-Turnerism proposed to transform government into a merely administrative system to be controlled and directed for—and, to a large extent, by—one great overweening interest, namely, 'industry'. Mond-Turnerism, in short, like workers' control, sought to industrialize politics.

MACDONALD AND THE NATIONAL INTEREST

In the late 1920s, however, Mond-Turnerism was too *avant garde* for many trade union leaders who, though they would no doubt have dispensed with politics, could they have seen their way to doing so, still thought themselves devoted followers of a Labour Party whose 8,000,000 votes gave them, after all, prestige, patronage, and claims on government that their own 5,000,000 members (only 2,000,000 of whom paid the political levy) did not. And in so far as they thought of themselves in this fashion, trade union officials linked themselves to an institution whose leader's political collectivism remained, by British standards, daringly advanced: even if his economic liberalism, like that of almost all other Party members, was by now somewhat out-dated. Especially since Labour's spell in office in 1924, MacDonald had zealously tried to shake off the Party's original sectionalism; and this revival of the strongly Rousseauesque doctrines of his youth did not bode well for the trade unions. In fact Labour's relatively bad showing in the 1929 election, when it polled slightly less than the Conservative Party, and secured the support of under 29 per cent of the total electorate, gave it a rather poor claim to represent the whole. At that date, it was still true, as a Labour historian recently put it, that the Party 'had no life apart from the unions', with which it was 'inextricably linked'. But Labour politicians thought, in Herbert Morrison's words, that in the 1929 election, MacDonald 'convinced the country that the Labour Party were a Party of the nation, and not the instrument of a section.' In any event, once returned to office, MacDonald, it has been noted, 'considered his first duty was to the "national interest" as it was almost universally conceived'.[1]

During MacDonald's second government fulfilment of that duty, as universally conceived, meant, first and foremost, economic recovery. According to various indices, between 1929 and 1931 United Kingdom exports fell 38 per cent; industrial production including building fell 10 per cent; and domestic wholesale prices fell 23 per cent. Unemployment, which had remained at about 10 per cent during 1924–9, rose to over 20 per cent by mid-1931. British dependence on exports made efforts to increase economic activity the more difficult, since government economic advisers and other economists feared (probably wrongly) that any such efforts would soon raise prices and make British products less attractive in the world market. Nevertheless some stimulus to the domestic economy seemed highly desirable, not least among Labour supporters who made up the bulk of the unemployed.[2]

Yet almost any sort of government activity was apparently unacceptable to Labour ministers who, even if they shared MacDonald's political collectivism, had a near-superstitious reverence for traditional British economic arguments. Even after the downfall of the Labour government, Arthur Henderson could repudiate the reflationary policy of deficit financing by insisting that every government ought to do its best 'to balance . . . its Budgets'; while the chairman of the Labour Party Conference of 1931 solemnly assured that body that 'no Party in the state stands for an unbalanced budget'. J. H. Thomas, when minister with special responsibility for unemployment, rejected proposals for direct government intervention in industry on the grounds that it was 'practically . . . impossible'

---

[1] Labour Party *Conference Report*, 1929, p. 150; Ross McKibbin, *The Evolution of the Labour Party, 1910–1924*, London, 1974, pp. 241, 246; Robert Skidelsky, *Politicians and the Slump, the Labour Government of 1929–1931*, London, 1967, p. 387.

[2] B. R. Mitchell and Phyllis Deane, *Abstract of British Historical Statistics*, Cambridge, 1971, pp. 272, 329, 477–8; Halsey, p. 119.

to find 'a fair, equitable and business-like basis' for such intervention; and almost everybody in the Labour Party agreed
that anything in the way of tariff barriers to protect British
industry would be 'unthinkable'. Sir Oswald Mosley, who was
for a while Thomas's deputy, did call for 'a great national
effort', in which 'the Government and Parliament must give a
lead'. He favoured what has been described as 'a vigorous
policy of public works and home development', exploiting the
large closed market that could be provided by the colonial
Empire. Lansbury, who was shortly to succeed MacDonald as
leader, condemned Mosley's programme as 'crying for the
moon'. After fourteen months in government, the public
works introduced by MacDonald's administration employed
67,000 of the 2¼ million men out of work, and amounted to an
expenditure of £43,000,000, a sum equivalent to 0·9 per cent
of the gross national product in 1931.[1]

Meanwhile, according to some calculations, state unemployment benefits were costing the Treasury over £50,000,000 a
year; and the government was borrowing over £40,000,000 a
year to meet further calls on the unemployment fund which
was in debt to the sum of more than £70,000,000 by 1931.
Indeed, the government increased pressures on the unemployment fund during the years 1929–31 by statutory and administrative changes which so liberalized the unemployment
insurance scheme that, in the Government Actuary's opinion,
persons obtained 'legal title to benefit in circumstances which
the Trade Unions would not have recognized as unemployment'. From the autumn of 1930 onwards, Snowden argued,
as Chancellor of the Exchequer, that the foreign and domestic
confidence necessary to avoid complete economic collapse
would be badly damaged by the 'psychological effect' of the
increased taxation or increased borrowing needed—as the
number of unemployed rose—to maintain existing rates of unemployment benefit; and that those rates must therefore be
reduced. Thus while the deflationary ideal of balanced budgets
hindered the Labour government from translating MacDonald's
revitalized collectivism into practical policies, pursuit of the

---

[1] Ibid., p. 81; Labour Party *Conference Report*, 1930, p. 203; 1931, pp. 156–7;
Trades Union Congress *Report*, 1931, p. 399; *House of Commons Debates*, vol. 239, cols.
1372, 1433; Skidelsky, pp. 167–8, 179.

same ideal hastened the moment at which the government must clash with its own sectional supporters over the insurance benefits of unemployed manual workers.[1]

Early in 1931 MacDonald appointed a committee, headed by Sir George May, the Secretary of the Prudential Assurance Company, to propose economies in government expenditure. The May Report was published on 31 July 1931, at the end of a fortnight in which, amid severe financial crises in central Europe, gold was being withdrawn from London at a rate of £2½ million a day. The Report proposed increased taxation, cuts in civil servants' and teachers' salaries, and a 20 per cent cut in unemployment benefits. Faced with the urgent need to raise loans in Paris and New York, MacDonald saw no alternative but to accept the May Committee's recommendations, though whereas May wished to take 80 per cent of his economies from pay and benefits, and only 20 per cent from taxation, MacDonald proposed to take 44 per cent from pay and benefits and 56 per cent from taxation. The Labour left declared that the May Report reversed the 'principles of the Labour movement': that is, of course, economic redistribution. The Trades Union Congress stated that, 'it is inequitable and indefensible to levy upon the workers the heaviest sacrifices called for in a financial emergency'. On 20 August the General Council rejected all the government's economy proposals. Three days later, the Cabinet split 11–9 for and against various measures, including a 10 per cent cut in unemployment benefit (equivalent to a real reduction of about 3 per cent). When MacDonald found himself in this very small majority, he resigned as Labour Prime Minister and formed the National Government, which lasted, in various guises and under different prime ministers, till the German defeat of the British forces in Norway in 1940.[2]

The collapse of MacDonald's Labour administration, and the formation of the National Government, did much damage to the Labour Party and some of its longest-serving leaders; and the bitterness caused by the events of 1931 produced a decade of disunity at a time when Britain's national survival almost depended upon the country's ability to display unity of purpose

---

[1] Ibid., pp. 113, 123 ff., 298, 309–11, 326.

[2] Ibid., pp. 351, 378–80; R. Bassett, *Nineteen Thirty-One, Political Crisis*, London, 1958, pp. 59, 101, 120, 137 ff.; Trades Union Congress *Report*, 1931, p. 66.

to the outside world. The fundamental charge against Mac-Donald, and that majority of the Cabinet which voted with him, was that the economy proposals of 23 August 1931 were both inequitable—in that they laid too heavy a burden upon the poorest citizens—and inexpedient—in that, by reducing domestic demand, they merely deepened the depression.

The defence of MacDonald and his supporters must derive first from the character of the advice available to them, and secondly from the duties which they felt that advice laid upon them. In the first place, the advice that the MacDonald government received as it attempted to deal with the great financial crisis of August 1931—whether that advice came from civil servants, government appointed advisers or independent experts such as J. M. Keynes—indicated, without dissent, that financial confidence had to be restored: and, given the May Committee's recommendations, the measures that were to be adopted were generally expected to include tax increases and pay and unemployment benefit cuts. The General Council of the Trades Union Congress, however, urged the government not to overrate the crisis, and, if it insisted on doing something, to confine itself to tax increases, and to suspension of interest payments on government debts (a measure not likely to restore financial confidence, however).

The government could scarcely escape some kind of economy measures therefore; and could barely avoid regarding the General Council as frivolous—unless the government were to assign some kind of monopoly of the truth to the sectional interest that dominated the Labour Party. The government did rewrite the recommendations received from outside the General Council, by shifting much of the proposed economies on to the tax payer, and by reducing the change in unemployment benefit to a real drop of 3 per cent. But this produced no concessions from the General Council, whose immovability immediately led to the break up of the Labour government. 'The General Council are pigs,' complained Sidney Webb, who supported MacDonald on 23 August but did not join the National Government, 'they won't agree to any cuts'.[1]

This confrontation raised the second point that may be cited in MacDonald's defence. Throughout the crisis, and especially

---

[1] Bassett, pp. 97–8, 101; Skidelsky, pp. 374, 379, 387.

after the General Council had revealed its *non possumus* attitude, MacDonald, his supporters, and very probably some of his opponents, perceived the government's position as one that required it to protect real 'national' against apparent sectional interest. Snowden, for example, argued that Britain faced 'national bankruptcy' and that, in this 'national crisis', 'national retrenchment' was vital to restore 'national solvency'. He deplored what he called 'dictation' by the General Council, which he also accused of misinterpreting its constituents' true needs: for he claimed that, even if retrenchment might not be consistent with labour's apparent interests, the economy measures were 'serving the best interests of the working-classes'. The issue thus resolved or perhaps complicated itself into one of obligations. Given the conflict between the best available advice and the attitudes of the leaders of organized labour, was the administration to respond to what it regarded as the responsibilities laid upon it by the suffrages of eight million voters, and the duties to the whole people imposed by government; or was it to yield to the trade unions' demands, either by abandoning its policy or resigning from office?[1]

MacDonald did not doubt that, once he had discovered, to the best of his ability what the national interest was, he must pursue it above all other ends: and, in this respect, collectivists (socialists included) may well cite his course of action in 1931 as a bad case for a good principle. Trade unionists could not agree. They opposed unemployment benefit cuts chiefly on the grounds that the incomes of the unemployed were already far too small; and they opposed public sector pay cuts especially because they feared these would set off a general round of reductions in wages. Their aggregative concept of the community encouraged them to deny the existence of a national interest, or a common good; and they required the Labour Party to return forthwith to its original role, namely, that of a trade unionists' parliamentary pressure group. The point was well put by the president of the Amalgamated Engineering Union, which abolished some of its unemployment benefits, and raised higher-paid members' contributions by a third, and lower-paid members' by a half, on the day the General Council rejected the government's economy proposals. 'Labour . . . should

[1] Bassett, pp. 444–9; Skidelsky, p. 387.

recognize our importance as the creators, the financiers and the backbone of the political movement', the Engineers' president declared in 1932. 'Who must control the Labour Party? . . . The Trade Unions must be in control.'[1]

THE COMMUNISTS' SECOND LOST OPPORTUNITY

But the situation that confronted both the Labour Party and the trade unions was much more complex than this clear-cut pronouncement might suggest. In Parliament, though not among the electorate, the Party was reduced to its pre-war strength; while the failure of the General Strike, and the devastations of the slump, virtually precluded any major resort to 'industrial action' as a means whereby labour might achieve its ends. Moreover, those ends were themselves obscure. As early as the 1930 Labour Party conference, Maxton, sensing the disasters that lay ahead, told delegates that 'they had got to start again as a mere propagandist organization, to tell people that Socialism was the only hope of the workers.' Yet few could agree what 'socialism' was, and few could expect much guidance on this matter either from the denuded leadership of the Labour Party, or from trade union leaders who had got little farther than vague if persistent commitment to 'workers' control', whatever that might be.[2]

In these circumstances the Community Party was presented with a new opportunity to achieve an ideological reformation of the organized British manual workers; a task in which it was greatly helped by the public's increasing fear of Nazism and Fascism. From 1934 onwards, trade union (and middle class) left-wing orthodoxy held that 'capitalism', struggling with an economic world crisis, would resort to either 'War or Fascism' —or both. Communists claimed to provide a bulwark against these menaces. They pointed to Russia—'the land of the Soviet', where 'the workers have freedom' and 'where the exploitation of the capitalist class has ended', as a delegate to the 1934 Trades Union Congress put it—and they drew attention also to the alleged struggles of the Communist Parties of every

---

[1] Amalgamated Engineering Union *Monthly Journal*, September 1931, pp. 5–6; *National Committee Minutes*, 1932, p. 69.
[2] Labour Party *Conference Report*, 1930, p. 188.

country against fascist encroachments on the workers' rights and powers. The Spanish Civil War gave the British Communist Party the chance to assert itself forcefully as the workers' champion against fascism, in contrast to the Labour Party which chose to play a more cautious role during this difficult period. Thus from 1936 till the signing of the Nazi-Soviet Pact in August 1939, the Communists enjoyed a special ascendancy in labour circles.[1]

Yet this ascendancy was limited by circumstances beyond the Communists' control, as can be seen from the character of their attempts to establish a 'front' against fascism. The Franco-Soviet *rapprochement* of 1934, and the Union of Soviet Socialist Republics' entry into the League of Nations, indicated that Russian policy during the mid-1930s was to seek a diplomatic and military counterpoise against Nazi Germany. If Britain was to contribute to the realization of this policy, the United Kingdom had to obtain a type of military capacity that could not be reached unless conscription were to be introduced; and considerable advantages would probably accrue to the Soviet Union were Britain to rearm in this and other ways, not least by reinforcing the French against Germany. But for several reasons the British Communist Party could go little farther than the vague advocacy of an anti-fascist 'front' of all left-wing groups, a scheme that did little more than update the Party's long-standing demand for affiliation to the Labour Party.

One major difficulty in the way of a pro-conscription policy was the argument, widespread in labour circles by 1935, that the National Government was itself fascist, and that rearmament would therefore strengthen rather than weaken fascism. But this argument (in so far as it did not arise somewhat uncritically from an understandable desire for revenge among the vanquished of 1931) merely concealed a further and larger difficulty. Organized labour looked back with dismay to the First World War when military conscription, and coincidental government control and regulation of manufacturing (usually dubbed 'industrial conscription') either put trade unionists' lives at risk, or reduced their freedom to maximize their earnings, or both: and in either case deeply offended against the *laissez-faire* principles dear not only to Asquithite Liberals but

[1] Trades Union Congress *Report*, 1934, pp. 265, 321–2.

to leaders of trade unions and Labour Party alike. Already by 1922, the Labour Party conference was demonstrating its pacifism by resolving, with virtual unanimity, not only to 'oppose any War entered into by any Government, whatever the ostensible object of the war', but also to make no exception in favour of the 'support of any nation' forced 'by armed aggression to defend its independence or its democratic institutions'. This policy persisted for more than ten years. Thus George Lansbury, then leader of the Party, told the electors of East Fulham in 1933: 'I would close every recruiting station, disband the Army and disarm the Air Force. I would abolish the whole dreadful equipment of war and say to the world "do your worst".'[1]

In this context any case for conscription could receive scant welcome from trade unions. The 1936 Trades Union Congress, held after Hitler had finally destroyed the Treaty of Versailles by introducing conscription and by remilitarizing the Rhineland, voted to 'actively resist' all attempts to introduce 'industrial' or 'military conscription' in Britain. A. G. Tomkins of the Furnishing Trades Association, moving the resolution, emphasized the threat conscription posed to the 'absolute independence' of the 'Trade Union movement', especially from 'the industrial point of view'; and P. Allott of the Shop Assistants quoted John Bright, that great symbol of *laissez-faire* liberalism, in support of Tomkins. Thereafter nothing changed, at least for labour. In May 1939, when Hitler had intervened in Spain, annexed Austria, and destroyed Czechoslovakia, a conference of Trade Councils rejected conscription, which, it resolved, was merely a means 'to undermine British democracy' above all by opening the way for 'industrial conscription and the attack on the Trade Unions'. When Hitler invaded Russia, therefore, the Soviet Union faced an enemy whose armed forces had been based on conscription for six years, and had from Britain, its sole ally, the assistance of a power which had introduced conscription only two years before and which, not least because of its lack of large-scale land forces, had already been defeated on, and excluded from, the European mainland.

[1] J. T. Murphy, *Modern Trade Unionism, A Study of the Present Tendencies and the Future of Trade Unions in Britain*, London, 1935, pp. 75–6, 85; Labour Party *Conference Report*, 1922, pp. 200, 203; Middlemas and Barnes, p. 745.

Nevertheless, paralysed by labour attitudes to conscription, the British Communist Party could go no further, during the 1930s, than vague slogans for a 'United Front', and for 'collective security'.[1]

The same failure to overcome well-established indigenous attitudes attended the Communists' efforts to transform labour's approach to issues larger if less urgent than conscription. The Communist bid to re-educate the British in social and political theory culminated in the work of John Strachey, later minister for food, and finally for war, under Attlee, but at this period of his life if not a member of the Communist Party, at least its most brilliant advocate. Strachey's publications gained considerable respect from left-wing intellectuals; but their particular influence would be very hard to trace outside specifically Communist circles; while their contents are such as to suggest that even this avowed apologist for collectivism possessed a characteristic British tendency to introduce anti-collectivist elements into his thought. Strachey did claim that 'Communist theory and practice' was 'the only possible policy for the workers of Britain'. He extolled Russia as the country of true liberty, true democracy, and true working-class power; he urged support for the British Communist Party, 'the essential political organization of the workers as a class'; and he argued the necessity for 'a revolution' followed by 'a working-class dictatorship' with its own 'apparatus of coercion'. These fairly commonplace Communist positions were associated, in Strachey's writings, with quite explicitly collectivist if not totalitarian ideas. Strachey held that 'scientific socialism' was a doctrine which provided 'the true view' of 'basic questions of social theory'; and he proposed that this 'one unified ideology' should be 'binding' on all members of the revolutionary 'new model party' which, he intimated, the Communist Party of Great Britain either was or would become. 'In Britain and America', he noted, 'most of us shallowly conceive of political activity as something cut off from everyday life', or 'as a sort of hobby'. But the kind of politics he favoured would be 'a way of life', in which members of the new model party would live 'the whole of their time' as 'members of the party'. In this way, men could eventually achieve socialism, which was,

[1] Trades Union Congress *Report*, 1936, pp. 389–90; 1939, p. 136.

wrote Strachey, a society marked by 'a genuine identity of interest between all citizens'.[1]

These ideas contradicted the leading principles of normal British political discourse, and Strachey himself felt an evident unease about some of his arguments. Thus, while he frequently accused the Labour Party of 'accommodation' to capitalism, he himself practised a distinct 'accommodation' to British politics, especially as espoused by labour. He scorned 'the majestic bemusements' of theories of the State derived from Hegel ('that mighty thinker', as Marx called him), and paradoxically asserted that the Anglo-American tradition of 'self-government, self-reliance, and independence' would prove essential in 'building up a socialist society'. Strachey expressed his horror of government by a 'horde of officials'; reaffirmed the Labour Party's hostility to direct government control of industry; freely admitted that, even in a socialist society, there would be conflicts between 'the interests of the workers' and those of 'over-enthusiastic "planners" '; and insisted that, though trade unions were 'inevitably to some extent sectional organizations', they must always 'play an important part in organizing' the 'economic system'.[2]

Above all, he persistently attempted to reduce collectivist notions to the individualistic or sectionalist economism that, as Lenin frequently observed, characterized labour industrial organizations. 'Democratic centralism' was no more than the principle on which trade unions were 'in effect usually organized', claimed Strachey; he believed that 'socialist theory' was 'deduced from the wage-workers' efforts to improve their lot'; and 'communism', he claimed, was simply a 'summing up of the workers' reactions' to the capitalist crisis. For these reasons, he concluded, socialism must and should be presented, not as an 'abstraction', but as the 'indispensable means of getting simple concrete benefits' for wage earners, such as 'a living wage' and 'tolerable hours of work'.[3]

[1] John Strachey, *The Coming Struggle for Power*, London, 1932, pp. 326, 349, 356–8, 383; *The Theory and Practice of Socialism*, London, 1936, pp. 158–9, 176, 199, 204, 206; *What Are We to Do?*, London, 1938, pp. 166, 258, 261, 382.

[2] Strachey, *Theory and Practice of Socialism*, pp. 141–2, 209; *What Are We to Do?*, pp. 67, 177, 222–3; *Why You Should Be a Socialist*, London, 1938, pp. 64–5; Karl Marx, *Capital*, vol. 1, Moscow, 1961, p. 20.

[3] Strachey, *What Are We to Do?*, pp. 60, 173, 331, 335.

PLANS FOR A NATIONALIZED ECONOMY

On this feeble note ended the Communists' interwar efforts to introduce some genuine collectivism into labour's demands for workers' control. Nevertheless, both the Labour Party and the trade unions continued to elaborate demands for social and economic innovations; and they generally related the various proposals and projects that they produced during the 1930s to the traditional stock-in-trade of British political thought. In short, they still assumed that society was an aggregation of competitive individuals, each of whom would seek to maximize his own material gains; and that, wherever organizations appeared, they would act only as collections of individuals. Government should provide whatever services could not possibly be supplied by any other agency but should otherwise be restrained within the role of making such 'fair' rules as would render this competition perfect. After 1931 organized labour advocated only two seeming exceptions to this schema, namely, planning and nationalization; but both these were seen as measures for perfecting the 'opportunity' of individuals to compete (by redistributing resources from the over- to the under-advantaged), rather than as meaningful attempts to replace competition by 'co-operation'.

The notion of planning, as conceived by organized labour, had received some currency during the 1920s. The government spent public money to maintain wages in one section (namely, coalmining) during 1925–6; and from 1929 did spend more money providing jobs for the out-of-work. The Mond-Turner conferences' demand for special credit facilities for manufacturing industry had touched on the principle of economic manipulation in favour of production. During the 1930s the National Government introduced both tariff barriers on manufactures and production quotas in agriculture; and took certain very modest measures to assist the 'special' or 'distressed' areas where unemployment was particularly high. Meanwhile Keynes and his followers adumbrated the abstract theories of economic expansion *via* inflationary demand-management policies; and, farther off still from the lives of British wage earners, but no less potent for that, from 1934 onwards 'the land of the Soviet', the proletarian paradise, was rapidly gain-ing prestige as the country which had solved the workers' problems by 'economic planning'.

As early as 1931, Arthur Pugh, on behalf of the General Council of the Trades Union Congress, called for 'a planned and regulated economy' to meet 'the needs of the present day', since 'individualistic *laissez-faire* institutions' could not secure 'the economic and social progress of the people', i.e. could not prevent unemployment. By the outbreak of war, this argument had become commonplace. Thus Stafford Cripps wrote in 1939 that, while he rejected any society in which men were mere 'mechanical units in a vast machine', the 'days of *laissez-faire*' were 'now definitely past' and 'the State must attempt to plan in some degree' its own 'economic life and that of its citizens'. The theory of this reform was quite clear to Cripps. He held that 'liberty' did consist in 'permission to do what the individual wishes'; but that, given the inequality of individuals, the state must interfere with 'the free action' of individual members of society not simply (in Mill's phrase) 'to prevent harm to others', but to create in certain individuals, who would otherwise lack it, the ability 'to take advantage of that permission'. As ever in labour's political thought, therefore, the goal of social change was modification (in labour's favour), and not supersession, of *laissez-faire*.[1]

However, the precise advantages of 'planning' still seemed somewhat uncertain to organized labour, whose leaders showed relatively little interest in the possible machinery of such an undertaking. The one aspect of such machinery frequently mentioned by Labour Party and trade union spokesmen (who did not, however, greatly elaborate on it) was the notion of a governmental 'Planning Department' or 'Economic General Staff', first propounded in 1929 by a civil servant attached to the Ministry of Labour. What did hold manual wage earners' attention at this time was, in fact, not 'planning' but 'socialization' or 'nationalization' of private industry. In 1931 the Transport and General Workers carried through the Trades Union Congress a resolution on the control of nationalized industries that stimulated the General Council to present to the next Congress a report on 'The Public Control and Regula-

[1] Trades Union Congress *Report*, 1931, pp. 406, 408; Stafford Cripps, *Democracy Up-to-Date*, London, 1939, pp. 18, 20, 32–3.

tion of Industry and Trade'. After criticism, this report was somewhat redrafted and presented to the 1933 Congress under the title 'Public Control and Regulation of Industry'. The document was approved, on a card vote, by 58 per cent; and became, to a large extent, the basis for detailed (and very similar) constitutions for nationalized iron and steel, coal, cotton and electricity distribution corporations, which the Trades Union Congress published from 1934 onwards.[1]

The debate on nationalization during the 1930s reaffirmed two principles that had become well established by 1920: that nationalized industries should somehow be 'independent' of government; and that the 'workers' should somehow control them. The contrast between 'general policy' as the proper sphere of government, and 'day-to-day' affairs as that of the management of an independent if socialized undertaking, stood labour leaders in good stead as they endeavoured to reaffirm the first of these principles. Morrison summarized the point in his speech on the London Passenger Transport Bill in 1931. 'The old idea of Departmental nationalization' was 'not the appropriate way', Morrison declared, 'for a great business undertaking of this kind.' After 1931 this doctrine was widely accepted. 'Direct administration by a Minister through a Government Department is apt to be regarded nowadays as an old-fashioned form of Socialism', wrote Hugh Dalton in 1935. True, the government should have 'ultimate control' over 'general policy'; but there must be no 'day-to-day intervention by politicians in the details of administration' of the nationalized public corporations, which should indeed 'stand a little detached' from 'a Minister in Parliament'. The General Council agreed. 'According to modern Socialist ideas', no advantage was gained from 'direct State operation' of nationalized undertakings, it declared in 1932: and then proceeded to write 'independence' into the constitutions it drafted during the next few years.[2]

---

[1] Skidelsky, pp. 134–6, 172–4; Hugh Dalton, *Practical Socialism for Britain*, London, 1935, p. 315; G. D. H. Cole, *The Machinery of Socialist Planning*, London, 1938, pp. 9, 66; Trades Union Congress *Report*, 1931, pp. 433, 439; 1932, pp. 206 ff., 397, 400; 1933, pp. 210 ff., 379; 1934, pp. 200 ff.; 1935, pp. 204 ff.; 1936, pp. 210 ff., 220 ff.

[2] *House of Commons Debates*, vol. 250, col. 55; Dalton, pp. 94–5, 100, 315; Trades Union Congress *Report*, 1932, p. 210.

But no such certainties, however spurious, allowed the General Council to end the debate on workers' control. 'For many years the demand for "workers' control" ' had been 'something of a slogan in the Labour Movement', the Council conceded; but it was a slogan on which labour's ideas were 'very vague'. Charles Dukes, of the National Union of General and Municipal Workers, who did more than anyone else to dispel this vagueness, carried through the Labour Party conference of 1933 a resolution requiring that the 'right', of 'wage-earners of all grades and occupation', to 'an effective share in the control and direction of socialized industries which their labour sustains', be 'acknowledged by law'. Dukes, like other labour leaders, chiefly envisaged the means of such control as participation in the highest managerial board of a nationalized undertaking, and he required that the relevant trade union in each case be 'the recognized nucleus of representation' for such participation.[1]

The General Council disliked parts of Dukes's arguments. Even the Council's more radical report of 1933, reserved 'day-to-day administration' of nationalized undertakings to 'trained business administrators'; and the report of 1932 treated 'questions of technical and commercial policy' as matters related to 'the manager's "craft",' but 'outside the competence' of 'a worker as such'. Action in accordance with these principles could not produce 'workers' control' as most trade unionists understood it: for trade unionists regarded management as 'bosses' men', and even 'the capitalists'; and excluded any 'special class in the field of management' from what they called 'labour'. Realization of their form of 'workers' control' required some kind of displacement of 'the capitalists' (that is, members of the managerial class, regardless of their property) by 'labour' (that is, by members of the manual wage-earning class, regardless of their property).[2]

That displacement could be achieved in either or both of two ways. In the first place, as a delegate from the Distributive and Allied Workers put it to the 1933 Trades Union Congress,

[1] Trades Union Congress *Report*, 1932, p. 215; 1933, p. 371; Labour Party *Conference Report*, 1933, pp. 205–6, 210.

[2] Ibid., p. 208; Trades Union Congress *Report*, 1931, p. 362; 1932, p. 217; 1933, pp. 210, 372.

the 'administrator' and 'the technical expert' could be put 'under the instructions of the workers who should have the control and direct the policy'. And in the second place, at least some of 'the workers' might turn themselves into administrators: perhaps by 'training in management and administration', perhaps by that training 'in the actual field of operations' which, Dukes assured the Congress, was as good as the 'theoretical or technical training' boasted by 'these so-called specialists' in management. In the first of these cases, managerial 'experts' would take orders from manual wage earners; in the second, manual wage earners would either become experts themselves, or at least learn the experts' techniques as a means to expedite the issue of orders to the experts; and such transformation of manual wage earners into managerial experts might be achieved by the two quite different processes of 'on the job' learning (the 'job' in this instance being, in fact, the manual worker's job, not the expert's), or of full- or part-time formal business education.[1]

No one explained how manual wage earners could control the managers without becoming managers themselves, or how, given trade unionists' intense sectionalism, such metamorphosed manual wage earners could remain as representatives acceptable to the other, untransfigured manual wage earners. Nor was any evidence offered to establish the efficacy of experience 'in the actual field of operations' as an alternative preparation for managerial work. Nevertheless the General Council stated, in all its nationalization projects of the 1930s that appointments to boards of nationalized undertakings should be justifiable 'on . . . grounds of . . . competence', a requirement which did presuppose that any wage earners' representative on the boards would indeed be managerially proficient, whatever his other qualifications.[2]

During the 1930s labour leaders hinted at two methods whereby their influence might be brought to bear on the boards of nationalized undertakings. On the one hand, it was felt that, supposing all appointments to such boards were within the sole power of a responsible Minister, the Minister should make

[1] Ibid., 1927, p. 66; 1933, pp. 371, 375; Labour Party *Conference Report*, 1933, p. 206.
[2] Trades Union Congress *Report*, 1934, p. 203; 1935, p. 207; 1936, pp. 210, 220.

'some of the appointments' to the Board 'only after consultation with the Trade Unionists in the industry', to use Dalton's words. The General Council accepted the idea that one or more places on a board should thus be allotted to the trade unions' patronage (though at first they were disposed to restrict exercise of such patronage to appointments to 'Advisory or Consultative', rather than executive, boards); and they wrote into their nationalization schemes provision for unions 'to nominate from among their number persons with the necessary capacity' to serve on the Boards. On the other hand, some trade unionists, notably Dukes, required a formal process of worker representation, rather than an informal system of 'consultation' with trade union leaders. Indeed, Dukes carried through the 1934 Trades Union Congress a resolution demanding statutory allotment of '50 per cent of the representation of Managerial Committees' of nationalized undertakings to 'workers' representatives' able to express 'the mind of the men in the workshop regarding matters of managerial control'. The scheme for nationalization of coal, first published in 1936, adopted this principle by including a clause for 'statutory provision' for 'the representation of the workers in the industry' on its various boards.[1]

But almost any scheme for worker participation in nationalized management raised the problem of interests which had always been emphasized by critics of workers' control. In 1931 Morrison propounded the principle of 'public ownership for public service and for the public good'; and the General Council later required that each nationalized enterprise should be 'a public body working solely in the public interest'. Yet this programme could only be realized if the manual wage earners' interests were always identical with those of the public; because trade unionists insisted that the overriding purpose of nationalization be to benefit the workers in the industry nationalized. The General Council's coal scheme of 1936 made this perfectly plain. Coal prices, the Council stated, could be determined by 'only one approach': namely, by fixing those prices which would sustain 'a proper level of wages'. That level was to be found by negotiation between 'the miners' organization and the

[1] Dalton, p. 164; Trades Union Congress *Report*, 1934, pp. 304, 371–2; 1936, pp. 210 ff.

Corporation' established to run the industry; and if, when those parties had taken due note of 'the existing low earnings' and 'the unpleasant and dangerous nature of the miners' work', etc., they were to fix wages at a level altogether too high for the world market, 'it might be found expedient, from time to time, to charge higher home prices in order to subsidize foreign sales'. In other words, all domestic coal consumers, both private and public, should pay a price for coal high enough not merely to raise wages to the point that satisfied the miners, but also to subsidize coal consumed by foreign nationals, so that miners in the export trade could keep their jobs and, despite their high wages, not price themselves out of the world market. Such a promotion of the miners' interests, here so clearly stated, cannot automatically be equated with promotion of the interest of the whole community.[1]

For all the General Council's talk of nationalization 'solely in the public interest', public and sectional interest could, then, conflict both in coal mining and in other nationalized industries. Hence, were there workers' control (in the sense of control of each 'industry' by the 'workers' of each 'industry') the workers' representatives must either flout the public interest, or compromise their constituents' interests; and while, in the first case, they would make a mockery of socialism, in the second they would make a mockery of what labour leaders understood by 'workers' control'. Herbert Morrison stated these alternatives in a debate on nationalization at the Labour Party conference of 1932. 'Once you concede . . . the right of representation', he warned, 'your Board will be run by interests, thinking of their interests with sectional minds', and 'your Socialist undertaking will be in danger of failure.' On the other hand, he argued, if the workers' representatives did not adopt sectional policies, 'within a year the Trade Union delegate will be regarded by the rank and file as a man who has gone over to the boss-class and cannot be trusted any more.'[2]

Morrison believed that, for all labour's grand talk of socialism and workers' control, the trade unions should settle for a system of nationalization that signified no more than

[1] *House of Commons Debates*, vol. 250, col. 53; Trades Union Congress *Report*, 1934, p. 202; 1936, p. 213.
[2] Labour Party *Conference Report*, 1932, p. 214.

a transfer of property to the state and changes in higher management; and that preserved existing trade union practices in their entirety, free from all these newfangled complications. 'It would be better', he concluded, 'if you want a trade union fighting policy, that your officials should not see too much of the other side', but 'have a free hand to bargain'. With this conclusion the General Council could not but agree; and thus they solemnly included in all their schemes for the socialist commonwealth to come—with its unity, harmony and fraternity—a proviso that guaranteed what can only be called 'the two sides' of industry, respectively, 'the right to strike and equally . . . the right to lock-out'.[1]

COLLECTIVISM AND WORLD WAR

The higher sectionalism implicit in this curious version of socialism still remained unchallenged when renewed conflict with Germany generated (in the words of one industrial reformer) the recognition of 'a transcendent common interest— the winning of the war—which overrides sectional interests of every kind'. During the first four or five years of war, however, the Labour Party made little effort to move beyond the thinking of the 1930s: and indeed the impasse then reached by the proponents of nationalization made any such advance scarcely likely. Yet the period of hostilities saw new developments that were both instructive and, in one instance at least, highly influential.[2]

Outside the ranks of the Communist Party, probably the most striking wartime innovation in left-wing political thought was the Commonwealth Party, led by Sir Richard Acland, which appealed to certain elements (and especially Christian Socialist intellectuals) among the membership of the Labour Party. Acland himself sat as Commonwealth Member of Parliament for some years; and in the 1945 general election the Commonwealth Party polled 111,000 votes, or 8,000 more than the Communist Party. Acland condemned the doctrine that

---

[1] Trades Union Congress *Report*, 1934, p. 205; 1935, p. 208; 1936, p. 212.
[2] G. S. Walpole, *Management and Men, A Study of the Theory and Practice of Joint Consultation at All Levels*, London, 1944, p. 28.

'the very best way of promoting a prosperous and harmonious society' was to encourage 'each man to promote his own self interest'. This 'self-regardant' individualism produced in Acland's opinion (as in Tawney's before him) a 'sordid struggle' among men and 'an immoral society'. Acland favoured a new society, based upon the principles of ' "Vital Democracy" and "Common ownership" ', in which the individual would see at least his work—and perhaps his life—'first and foremost in terms of service' to 'the community as a whole'. That society would be organized on a 'plan', the priorities of which would be determined by 'Parliament and Cabinet', working through an 'Economic General Staff'. The 'plan' would co-ordinate 'industries', each run by a council, the 'great majority' of whose members would represent managers, technicians, and 'workers in the industry'. Meanwhile, every factory in the industries thus co-ordinated would be controlled by 'an executive team' of 'managers and technicians' together with 'perhaps an approximately equal number of representatives of the . . . workers employed'.[1]

The details of Acland's future society obviously owed much to the main elements of Labour Party and trade union thought. But there were two ways in which Acland diverged from his predecessors. First, he laid great stress on a moral (or perhaps cultural) change that he thought inseparable from the social and economic changes which he advocated. Thus he spoke of 'the rediscovery by a whole nation of its very soul'; he called men to 'work together in a wholly new spirit for the rebuilding of a nobler country'; and he claimed that there must be a 'fundamentally religious' transformation of men. In other words, Acland did not accept the Labour Party's and the trade unions' assumption that the individuals of existing society, complete with their own ideas, attitudes and expectations, could achieve Socialism—or workers' control. Secondly, though Acland hoped for Labour support, he repudiated 'the present Labour Party machine', and ignored the trade unions. He saw no way whereby either Party or unions could go beyond existing society, of which they formed apparently inseparable

[1] Richard Acland, *Question and Answer from Commonwealth Meetings*, London, n.d., pp. 13, 19, 21, 86–7; *What It Will Be Like in the New Britain*, London, 1942, pp. 50, 76, 80, 153–4.

organs. Any attempt to construct a new society on the basis of these institutions must, he intimated, fail.[1]

Acland's intellectual case against the possibility of a labour road to socialism was simultaneously vindicated, in practical terms, by the Communist Party which, between 1941 and 1945 embarked on the first serious test, in existing social and economic conditions, of the shibboleths of workers' control. Once the Nazi-Soviet Pact was signed, Communists denounced all resistance to Germany as 'imperialist war'. They urged 'the people' to 'take their destiny into their own hands'; and in January 1941 they organized a 'People's Convention' or 'People's Parliament' to call for 'A People's Peace that gets rid of the causes of war'. They also encouraged the trade unions' fairly extensive resistance to the efforts of both Chamberlain's Conservative administration and Churchill's Conservative-Labour coalition to hasten rearmament by those measures of production control that labour traditionally condemned as 'industrial conscription'. The *Daily Worker* explained, in the last issue before it was suppressed by the government, that 'The Communists are the defenders of trade unionism, of the rights of the workers, of established practices and customs'; and, when Bevin advocated joint representative 'factory councils' to raise productivity, the paper dismissed the councils as replicas of 'the Nazi system of factory organization', designed 'to whip up production to unheard of peaks'.[2]

These pronouncements presumably bore some relation to the Soviet Union's desire not to antagonize Germany. But on 22 June 1941 Hitler's forces invaded Russia; and, in the course of that day, the Communists turned from appeasement to super-patriotism in their determination to assist the Soviet Union both by the supply of arms, and by the acceleration of Britain's preparedness to send armies to continental Europe.

> MOBILISE every able-bodied man and woman for war-service in the armed forces, civil defence and industry. No evasions to be tolerated. SPEED the training and placing of women in all industries to release large numbers of men for the armed forces. . . .

[1] Loc. cit., pp. 9, 13, 159–60.
[2] *The Daily Worker*, 17 August 1940, p. 4; 19 September 1940, p. 4; 28 December 1940, p. 1; 11 January 1941, pp. 1, 8; 21 January 1941, p. 4.

declared the *Daily Worker* on the day on which it restarted publication. Communists had discovered that one 'transcendent common interest' did now override all others; and, in the pursuit of that interest, they were willing to press manual wage earners as far as they could towards attitudes and actions consistent, in many respects, only with larger social arrangements founded on principles of the most far-reaching collectivism: even though such arrangements virtually did not exist. In short, the Communists sought to make labour truly socialist in a still liberal-individualist country.[1]

The chosen instruments of this transformation were to be elective representative 'joint production committees' exceedingly similar to Bevin's 'factory councils'. Up to July 1941, there were ten joint production committees in Britain; by December 1943, nearly 4,500 committees or similar procedures, all involving co-operation between management and worker representatives on many matters of production, had been established throughout industry. As one large armaments works reported in the spring of 1943, 'the men have welcomed' the production committees 'as a step in the direction of enabling them to deal with problems hitherto recognized as the Management's responsibility'. But the managerial powers already essential even to this degree of workers' control also brought managerial duties; and these—above all, the discipline of the work force—proved entirely unacceptable to most trade unionists, who really wanted, in wartime as in peace, what Morrison called 'a trade union fighting policy', and who accepted the joint production committees only under pressure from every quarter, above all from Communist erstwhile 'militants'. An agreement signed by the trade unions and the government in February 1942 placed a wide range of complex technical questions within the legitimate purview of joint production committees. In practice, however, the worker representatives' chief contribution to production was their power to get their members to produce. Hence a draughtsmen's delegate complained to the 1942 Trades Union Congress that 'absenteeism' was already 'the preoccupation of the majority of the Committees'.[2]

---

[1] Ibid., 7 September 1942, p. 1.

[2] P. Inman, *Labour in the Munitions Industries*, London, 1957, p. 381; Engineering

The significance of the episode of the joint production committees was this. The ideal of workers' control inescapably requires workers' control not merely of capital (or 'capitalists'), but of workers. Unless workers' control means only the industrial elysium of high wages, fixed prices, and subsidized production, envisaged, for instance, in the Trades Union Congress's 1936 scheme for coal nationalization, workers' control of workers must eventually involve the workers' representatives in decisions apparently inimical to those they represent: decisions, for example, to lower costs through wage cuts, or through pressure for extra productive effort, or curbs on absenteeism and unpunctuality. Decisions of this type may be accepted from governments, even by the citizens of *laissez-faire* states; but they are highly unlikely to be tolerated by British trade unionists, either from their officials or from worker representatives. For British trade unionists will regard those who make such decisions, even in nationalized industries, and very probably even under full-blown socialism, as 'the boss-class' (to use Morrison's term): and they will treat both the decisions and the decision-makers accordingly. True, under the momentary extremity of threatened defeat in war, and under incessant pressure from the former self-styled 'defenders of trade unionism', organized labour temporarily tolerated the unitary corporatism of the joint production committees, those partial prototypes of workers' control: but only by suppressing, for a while and quite unsuccessfully, its passionate desire to return to the bipartite corporatism of collective bargaining, as the best practical approximation, in modern conditions, to the free-for-all of pure Victorian *laissez-faire*. 'Some of the more conservative brothers', the Engineers' President drily observed in 1945, thought the joint production committees 'a piece of class collaboration'.[1]

THE ATTLEE VERSION OF NATIONALIZATION

The trade unions' dislike of joint production committees foreshadowed the policies and attitudes of the Labour government

---

Employers' Federation, 'Joint Production Consultative and Advisory Committees. Summary of Replies to Enquiry', April 1943; Trades Union Congress *Report*, 1942, p. 172.

[1] Amalgamated Engineering Union, *Minutes of National Committee*, 1945, p. 215.

which was formed by Clement Attlee after the Labour Party polled twelve million votes, or 48 per cent of the total, in July 1945. For all the new government's professed socialism, its attitudes were very largely individualist. Attlee's ministers shared the opinions of Walter Citrine, ex-general secretary of the Trades Union Congress, and chairman of the Central Electricity Authority from 1947 onwards, who claimed that 'British history has shown the desire to organize the community with a minimum of interference with the individual.' 'British people prefer to have direct control over the things that affect them irrespective of whether these things may be done less efficiently than at some higher level', declared Citrine, who praised this 'healthy and natural assertion of individuality'.[1]

When, in 1945 Hartley Shawcross, then a new Labour member of Parliament, uttered the famous pronouncement 'We are the masters now', he meant not that Labour's victory indicated (as a socialist might hope) that henceforward there would be no masters, but that, while the liberal-individualist *system*, with its masters and men, remain unchanged, the identity of those who played out each role was to be reversed. Shawcross himself was later to quit the Labour Party, but it is open to question how far the Party quitted Shawcross's position in 1945. As the Attlee years progressed, the philosophy of 'government by persuasion', in J. C. R. Dow's phrase, became more predominant. Labour's repudiation of any truly collectivist economic system during these years was symbolized by the transformation of planning 'targets' into 'estimates', in successive government economic forecasts, and by Harold Wilson's 'bonfire' of wartime controls in November 1948. Decontrol, refusal to set production targets, the resort to 'persuasion', were none of them socialist measures.[2]

Nor necessarily was nationalization, though this was to become the chief test of the Attlee government's socialist *bona fides*. The Trades Union Congress's 1944 'Interim Report on Post-War Reconstruction' put the need for the 'workpeople' to have 'a share in the control of industry' third in its list of

---

[1] W. M. Citrine, 'Problems of Nationalised Industries' (Sidney Ball Lecture, 1951), n.p., n.d., p. 6 (typescript in Bodleian Library).

[2] Earl of Kilmuir, *Political Adventure*, London, 1962, p. 137; J. C. R. Dow, *The Management of the British Economy, 1945–1960*, Cambridge, 1970, pp. 33–4; Sidney Pollard, *The Development of the British Economy 1914–1950*, London, 1962, p. 374.

priorities (in which 'maintaining and improving wages, hours and conditions of labour' and ' "Full Employment" ' came, respectively, first and second). Organized labour's doctrine of industrial reorganization must, as ever, be understood in this frankly redistributive sense. In 1944 the wartime coalition administration had agreed that one of the 'primary aims and responsibilities' of post-war government would be 'the maintenance of a high and stable level of employment'. That policy had to be redistributive, both because it was to be achieved partly through inflationary government expenditure financed by taxes on capital and on higher incomes; and because, however achieved, full employment would create those permanent labour shortages which constitute the ideal conditions for the exercise of trade union power. During 1944–5, however, these possibilities were at most only partly comprehended by organized labour, which believed that nationalization, not demand management, would prove to be the manual wage earner's salvation. Nationalized management, labour leaders expected, would neither sack employees nor resist wage claims. Many sectors would remain unnationalized; but what the Trades Union Congress euphemistically called 'planning, regulation and control' would, it hoped, nevertheless, bring nationalization's benefits wherever a paper transfer of ownership had not yet occurred.[1]

Since nationalizaiton was designed not to transform the traditional *laissez-faire* structure of the British economy, but simply to convenience manual wage earners, the Attlee government did little to establish nationalized undertakings on a collectivist footing. The Trades Union Congress's 'Reconstruction' Report merely reaffirmed the principles of nationalization already prevalent in labour circles, namely, a property transfer to the state, and the organization of the enterprise nationalized as an 'independent public corporation' whose 'day-to-day management' was vested in a board 'ultimately responsible' to government, which would determine only 'general policy'. Writing seven years later, Citrine restated these ideas. Since 'nationalized industries should be able to operate free from undesirable political restrictions', he declared, 'the public corporation type of organization', with 'ultimate

[1] Trades Union Congress *Report*, 1944, p. 397; Dow, p. 1.

responsibility' for 'general policy' vested in Parliament, was the ideal method of nationalization.[1]

Whatever method was to be adopted, the Trades Union Congress remained sceptical of the possibility of realizing 'workers' control' through structural changes within undertakings nationalized. Such changes, the General Council feared, would compromise or distract trade unions and confuse the merely managerial policies of the enterprise. Nationalized industries, Congress declared in 1944, must act 'solely in the public interest'; and, if this principle were to be observed, 'members of the governing body' of the industry could not 'at the same time answer to the workers . . . as their representatives, and bear responsibility to the Minister' in Parliament. In any event, Congress concluded, in 'the best interest of the workpeople of a nationalized industry', the trade unions in that industry must 'maintain their complete independence' and 'power of independent criticism'. The Union of Post Office Workers pressed the General Council to support the Dukes scheme of 'joint administration' by an equal number of representatives of 'the management' and 'trade union representatives elected by and responsible to their membership'. The Council claimed that such a scheme 'would be destructive of the independence of the trade Unions'. The Post Office Workers then accused the General Council of assuming 'a divergence of interests between the workers in industry and the community at large': but on this point the General Council preserved a diplomatic silence.[2]

Had either the unions or the Labour Party been clearer or firmer about their policy for workers' control, the demand for workers' representation, on the Dukes pattern, might have persisted. Yet it did not; and the Attlee government, in concert with the General Council, proceeded to its own satisfaction, if to no one else's, to solve the difficulties of workers' control by a device envisaged by labour theorists for nearly three decades. 'Statutory provision should be made', the General Council urged, not for workpeople, but for 'the interests of' workpeople, to be 'represented on the governing Board' of each industry nationalized. In other words, the government should give trade

[1] Trades Union Congress *Report*, 1944, p. 400; Citrine, pp. 1, 5.
[2] Trades Union Congress *Report*, 1944, pp. 411–12; 1948, p. 238.

unions legal powers to 'nominate' to such boards appointees who (though 'in no way accountable to any other interest than the public') would nevertheless 'ensure that the views of the . . . workers . . . receive full consideration' by nationalized management. The General Council did not say whom the unions should choose: but it did seem to favour nomination of established trade union leaders, not least since it emphasized that 'experience in the day-to-day work in the Trade Union organization of industry' was a preparation for 'undertaking administrative responsibility' in no way inferior to that afforded to those whose 'social advantages' conferred on them the privileges of further education.[1]

Many trade unionists doubted whether long-tenure national union leaders responded adequately to the 'views of the workers' even while they remained union officials; and were not likely to find those views well represented by the same leaders once translated to the boards of nationalized industries. Certainly this system of non-elective expression of 'the views of the workers' was unlikely to correspond to workers' control. Nevertheless, the Trades Union Congress pressed the government to draft nationalization statutes that gave the unions some such right of nomination; and, though the government resisted this pressure, it agreed that informal consultation with unions should be used to settle at least some managerial appointments in nationalized industries. In the coal industry, for example, the government indicated that 'in practice' it would 'seek the views' of the Trades Union Congress on one, and the National Union of Mineworkers on another, appointment to the National Coal Board.[2]

In this somewhat haphazard fashion, the Attlee government began to approximate to the unitary corporatism planned from the late nineteenth century onwards. For the government's nationalization schemes maintained a unitary managerial structure that claimed to know 'the views of the workers' for itself, and to be able to take due account of those views without any necessary intervention in management by organized labour. True, the bipartite corporatism implicit in collective bargaining was still to obtain in nationalized industries—along

[1] Ibid., 1944, pp. 400, 410, 412.
[2] Ibid., 1946, p. 209.

with the 'right to strike and equally the right to lock-out'—but the special claims of nationalized management, which disposed of a capital that was not private but state property, and which included among its numbers experienced ex-trade unionists in good standing with organized labour, gave collective bargaining in nationalized industries a position in theory at least distinctly more precarious than that which it had enjoyed in privately owned and managed industry during the first half of the twentieth century. Under private industrial management, collective bargaining (with its concomitant industrial action) had been accepted by all parties as one conformable element in a *laissez-faire* whole; but under nationalization, it appeared to go somewhat against the grain.

Meanwhile, workers' control—a unitary corporatism in which the manual wage earner obtained supreme power—seemed to have been displaced by managerial control. Sir Stafford Cripps, then President of the Board of Trade, remarked in 1946 that 'the workers' were not 'capable of taking over large enterprises'; and he added, 'I think it would be almost impossible to have worker controlled industry in Britain, even if it were on the whole desirable.' Cripps apparently expressed the opinion of the entire Attlee administration, given the scant attention that workers' control received from the authors of the nationalization statutes. For all the nationalization his government had introduced, Attlee had granted the worker no 'opportunity of running . . . industry' complained a Chemical Workers' delegate to the 1950 Trades Union Congress. What had occurred was not 'the Social democratic revolution' but 'the managerial revolution', the 'revolution of the technicians and managers who today have more power than Hitler ever dreamed of'.[1]

This complaint would have had more force if labour had shown itself less satisfied with a species of nationalization that merely gave property to the state, and power to a managerial class. As it was, however, unions made little effort to exploit what opportunities they had for participation in nationalized management. 'There was some reason to believe', Morrison told the General Council in July 1949, 'that the Unions concerned had not been as anxious to take advantage of the

---

[1] *The Times*, 28 October 1946; Trades Union Congress *Report*, 1950, p. 513.

willingness of the Boards to discuss matters concerning the industries (other than wages and working conditions) as they might have been.' To this point Council made little reply, since unions affiliated to Congress now showed exceedingly little interest in any form of workers' control.[1]

The National Union of Railwaymen, for example, called for 'a 50 per cent share in administration and management' at the 1949 Trades Union Congress. But the Union's enthusiasm for this policy was perhaps best expressed by a railwayman who wrote to the *Railway Review* in that year that 'one reads nearly every week, that what the railway workers want is a share in management.' That, the writer agreed, was the policy of the National Union of Railwaymen. But, he added, 'I venture to suggest that, the rank and file railwaymen do not desire that so much as they desire an increase in their wage packet.' In the end, the railwaymen's stake in the new nationalized management extended little further than the transfer of the general secretary of the National Union of Railwaymen to the board of the British Transport Commission. Such an arrangement, which the Union accepted with relatively few quibbles, consisted of little more than 'the same old racket under a different name', in the words of a St. Pancras porter quoted by one delegate to Congress.[2]

The National Union of Mineworkers underwent similar experiences. When the mines were nationalized on 1 January 1947, the Mineworkers placarded the pits with notices stating that, 'this colliery is now managed by the National Coal Board on behalf of the people'. That state of affairs seemed soon to produce the redistributions always promised by labour advocates of nationalization: for at the 1947 Trades Union Congress, Will Lawther, the Union's president, declared 'We as miners have had more concessions . . . in six months from the Coal Board than in a hundred years under private ownership.' Yet within two years the Union reported the onset of 'cynicism' about coal nationalization. Even public ownership did not mean the wage increases the Mineworkers desired; while the structural innovations promised by nationalization had little appeal for miners. The National Coal Board 'must function like employers',

---

[1] Loc. cit., p. 230.
[2] Ibid., 1949, pp. 50, 416.

little different from the agents of private capital, Arthur Horner, the Mineworkers' leading Communist official, told the Trades Union Congress, because 'the fundamental relationship between the buyer and seller' of labour 'remains after an industry has been nationalized'. The South Wales Miners, meanwhile, kept faith with their syndicalist past by urging the Mineworkers' annual conference to secure 'a greater measure of workers' control in the organization and general direction of the coalmining industry'. But Lawther was able to counter these demands for workers' control with the observation that 'when the truth comes to be told about the steps the Board took'—all in vain—'to get people from our own ranks to go into the various jobs, then there will be some revelations.' And in 1953 Arthur Deakin reminded the Labour Party conference that, 'The miners know how much difficulty they had to face in securing that representation that was accorded to them on the National Coal Board—people who were invited refused because they were not prepared to accept responsibility.'[1]

Indeed, miners, like other manual wage earners in nationalized industries wanted from nationalization no more than a guarantee against unemployment and an opportunity to extend labour's traditional activities in pursuit of more money for the same work. Still seized by *laissez-faire* doctrine, trade unionists could admit to their thought no positive collectivist concept of nationalization; and therefore, unwilling to seek either power or responsibility in the enterprises nationalized, they could get no farther than uneasy acquiescence in the unitary corporatism —the 'managerialism', as they began to call it—implicit in the new form of those enterprises: together with a determined struggle to preserve what they could of the practice and principles of uninhibited collective bargaining. The ideal of workers' control had, in short, failed to secure the manual wage earners' support.

---

[1] Ibid., 1947, p. 326; 1949, pp. 218, 415; National Union of Mineworkers *Journal*, 1948; Labour Party *Conference Report*, 1953, p. 132.

5

The Triumph of Sectionalism

We find, in fact, that a complete intellectual acceptance of the Doctrine of Supply and Demand has much the same results upon the attitudes of Trade Unionism as it has upon commercial life, and that it throws up, as leaders, much the same type of character in the one case as in the other. Those who know the Trade Union world will have no difficulty in recognizing, in certain of its sections, both in corporate policy and in the characters of individual leaders, the same strong, self-reliant and pugnacious spirit; the same impatience of sentiment, philanthropy and idealism; the same self-complacency at their own success in the fight, and the same contempt for those who have failed; above all the same conception of the social order, based on the axiom that 'to him that hath shall be given, and from him that hath not shall be taken away even that which he hath'. To the idealist who sees in Trade Unionism a great class upheaval of the oppressed against the oppressors, it comes as a shock to recognize, in the Trade Union official of this type, pushing the interests of his own clients at the expense of everybody else, merely another embodiment of the 'spirit of the bagman'.

SIDNEY AND BEATRICE WEBB, *Industrial Democracy*

THE REJECTION OF WAGE RESTRAINT

The Attlee government was both a consequence and a continuation of the crisis caused by the collapse of what a left-wing sociologist has called '*the largest empire in history, an empire qualitatively distinct in its immensity from all its rivals*'. This collapse entered its acute and final stage with the ignominious expulsion of the British from continental Europe at Dunkirk in 1940, and the destruction of British power in south-east Asia with the surrender of Singapore in 1942. Well before 1940, the domestic

problems inseparable from the manner and the substance of
the downfall of the British empire had begun to manifest
themselves in the context of British culture and British politics.
During the nineteenth and early twentieth centuries, democratic attitudes had been strengthened by the cult of utilitarian
laissez-faire, but weakened by the persistence of 'a strong
deference to the independent authority of government': a habit
which two American observers still thought to be the basis of
British political culture as late as 1963. But once Dunkirk and
Singapore had compounded the discredit ineluctably accruing
to government from Ypres and Passchendaele (not to speak of
Jarrow), such deference very largely ceased to characterize the
citizens of the United Kingdom.[1]

The traditional British ruling class continued to exist, yet
not so much as a group but as a collection of individuals, many
of whom were, in any event, altogether excluded from power
by the Labour victory of 1945. Something of a new ruling class
began to appear in the persons of the professional and wage-
earning parliamentarians led by Attlee. But these men lacked
even the shreds of traditional influence still possessed by the
Conservative opposition and its allies; and when the Conservatives were returned to governmental power by their
unearned election victory of 1951, the Labour leadership was
already suffering its own miniature crisis of confidence and
authority.

The Attlee government directed domestic affairs according to
principles generally established by the wartime coalition. A few
important industries were nationalized, but for the most part
Attlee and his ministers relied on a dwindling number of
physical controls over trade and production, and on the
methods of 'demand management' pioneered by the Treasury
under Churchill. The government hoped that such methods
would enable it to honour its 'full employment' pledge to the
unions while preserving the Gladstonian ideal of minimum
interference in the economy. 'Targets' (or 'estimates') were to
be approached by operating global fiscal and monetary rules,
backed by borrowing and redistributive taxation; and in

---

[1] Perry Anderson, 'Origins of the Present Crisis', in Perry Anderson and Robin
Blackburn (eds.), *Towards Socialism*, London, 1966, p. 21; Gabriel A. Almond and
Sidney Verba, *The Civic Culture*, Princeton, New Jersey, 1963, pp. 455, 493–4.

almost no instance was the government required to take any interventionist decision on precisely what was made or done, when or where, in the British economy. The results seemed, to Labour supporters, to be far from discreditable. Unemployment stood at 1·2 per cent of insured employees in 1945, and at 1·2 per cent of the estimated total number of employees in 1951; and even the temporary rise to 3·1 per cent unemployment in 1947 represented a lower level of peacetime unemployment than any recorded since 1920. Meanwhile, earnings rose 48 per cent, and the cost of living only 35 per cent; while, between 1946 and 1951, the gross national product rose 46 per cent.[1]

Such economic circumstances gave the unions great power, which the Attlee government sought to control in two ways. First, they continued until August 1951 the Conditions of Employment and National Arbitration Order (No. 1305) of July 1941, which created a national wages-arbitration system and put financial penalties on strikes. The number of employees engaged in stoppages fell from 447,000 in 1945 to 269,000 in 1950, at least partly due to this order. But neither the number, the length nor the size of industrial disputes accurately measures trade union strength, because trade unions may be able to secure their objectives merely by the threat of a stoppage. The Labour government, which was fully aware of this fact, therefore turned to a further instrument of industrial policy, namely, wage control. Fortified by the trade unions' many loyalties to the government, and by the unions' fears (after the fuel and sterling crises of 1947) of a repetition of the great postwar slump of the 1920s, Attlee's administration produced, in February 1948, a white paper on *Personal Incomes, Costs and Prices*, which rejected 'any general increase of individual money incomes'. The unions were not consulted on this document, but they did try to accept it. For the next two years, wage earnings rose no faster than, and may even have lagged behind, prices: so that, by the 1951 Labour Party Conference, a delegate could complain that 'the standard of life of the worker is gradu-

---

[1] Robert Bacon, George Sayers Bain, and John Pimlott, 'The Economic Environment', and 'The Labour Force', in A. H. Halsey (ed.), *Trends in British Society since 1900, A Guide to the Changing Social Structure of Britain*, London, 1972, pp. 82, 119, 121–2.

ally going lower' than 'ever we expected it to do under a Labour Government'.[1]

The Conservatives, remaining in popular estimation (even in the mid-1950s) the party that had mishandled the depression, and had perhaps not been entirely successful in its conduct of the war, chose to pursue many objectives popular with Labour supporters. Throughout the Conservatives' thirteen-year period in office, unemployment never reached the levels of 1946–7, but fluctuated between 1·2 and 2·6 per cent of the estimated total number of employees. During the Conservatives' first six years in office (1951–7), the gross national product increased by 49 per cent; earnings rose 51 per cent; and the cost of living rose 30 per cent. There is some evidence to suggest that, in this period, the share of the national income which went to wages and salaries rose; while the 'social wage' of public welfare services remained more or less constant. Moreover, after-tax money wages grew distinctly more equal. Between 1949 and 1959, the proportion of the population receiving after-tax money incomes of over £2,000 did rise from under half a per cent to over 1 per cent; but the proportion receiving after-tax incomes of £500–£2,000 rose from 11 to 47 per cent; and the proportion receiving after-tax incomes of under £500 fell from 87 to 51 per cent. However these figures may be interpreted, by the late 1950s 'affluence' and the 'affluent society' had become clichés of public discourse; and enough citizens found enough truth in these clichés to give the Conservatives over 49 per cent of the votes cast in the general elections of 1955 and 1959, a measure of support greater than any political party has since enjoyed.[2]

These developments must be attributed largely to favourable world economic conditions, partly to government policy. The Conservatives hoped and aimed to encourage the formation of a broad and prosperous group of skilled manual wage earners and lower-salaried clerical workers, an increasing proportion of whom would be house-owners. They sought this end by an economic policy markedly less interventionist than that pur-

---

[1] V. L. Allen, *Trade Unions and the Government*, London, 1960, pp. 269–70; H. A. Clegg and Rex Adams, *The Employers' Challenge*, Oxford, 1957, pp. 19–21; Gerald A. Dorfman, *Wage Politics in Britain, 1945–1967*, London, 1974, pp. 55–8, 68, 149; Labour Party *Conference Report*, 1951, p. 92.

[2] Halsey, pp. 83 ff., 119 ff., 237 ff.

sued by either the Attlee government or the wartime coalition; and they hoped to receive the voluntary co-operation of both employers and organized labour. Under Churchill especially, the Conservatives (in words attributed to the whilom General Secretary of the Trades Union Congress, George Woodcock) 'carefully avoided major strikes' by 'influencing wage settlements in trade unionism's favour'. In serious disputes the government appointed courts of inquiry, whose composition was designed to avoid the suggestion of government interference in collective bargaining, and whose establishment was intended to legitimate money wage increases, which—in the domestic and world economic conditions then prevalent— were very largely to be recouped in price increases. Meanwhile the government continued, and perhaps extended, the formal and informal links with the trade unions inherited from the Labour government. The Trades Union Congress fraternal delegate to the 1960 Labour Party conference boasted to the politicians so recently vanquished at the polls that:

> No Minister refuses to hear our views or to take them into account. Indeed, on a wide range of questions of industrial, economic or social significance we now operate machinery for regular consultation between governments and the representatives of industry. There our influence is powerful and continuous; not infrequently it is decisive. It is exercised on matters of principle as well as on detail. We look upon it as part of the process of collective bargaining and we have had a good education in that.

In short, the Trades Union Congress was now, unlike the Labour Party, a permanent part of government; and, quite characteristically, unions would, to that extent, industrialize government into a form of collective bargaining.[1]

The Conservatives got exceedingly little in return for what Anthony Crosland described as their 'almost deferential' attitude to organized labour. What they would most have wished to receive would very probably have been 'voluntary wage restraint'. During the 1950s academic observers of the industrial world tended to argue that wages and prices 'moved fairly close together', a view which suggested that trade unions caused no more than a part (and perhaps at that only a small part) of inflation. In the 1960s and 1970s academics admitted

---

[1] Dorfman, p. 83; Labour Party *Conference Report*, 1960, p. 169.

that wage increases had become 'abnormal', and that 'the trade union movement' helped 'to keep up inflationary pressure'. But whether post-war trade unionism were held to be a preponderant, a partial or even no cause of inflation, Conservative government and Labour opposition generally agreed, nevertheless, that unions could exert a major constraint on inflation.[1]

Thus, for example, Roy Jenkins argued in 1953 that 'the principle of a planned distribution of the national product must be carried into the field of wages'. This should be done, he proposed, not by means of a 'stultifying' wage-freeze such as that attempted by the Attlee administration, but by public determination of a 'global figure' for increases in incomes, which would then be distributed according to 'certain constant tests agreed upon' by 'the Government, the trade unions and . . . the employers'. A year earlier Aneurin Bevan had claimed that, 'most people are now convinced that a national wages policy is an inevitable corollary of full employment, if we are not to be engulfed by inflation.' Such a policy would consist, at least in its initial stages, of what Bevan called 'automatism': that is, the relation of increases in incomes to 'a cost of living index'.[2]

The Conservatives twice attempted a 'wages policy' during the years before the Suez crisis. Early in 1952 the government sought to relate wage increases to increases in output; and R. A. Butler, then Chancellor of the Exchequer, proposed in May 1952 that the unions draw up with the government rules whereby 'the national wage bill will advance in step with national production, but not outstrip it'. The General Council of the Trades Union Congress rejected the proposal; and the government continued to confine itself to monetary and fiscal methods of economic management. During the winter of 1955–6, however, the government decided to seek a 'standstill' or a 'plateau' in wages and prices, regardless of fluctuation in the volume of

---

[1] C. A. R. Crosland, *The Future of Socialism*, London, 1956, p. 33; Clegg and Adams, p. 74; Andrew Glyn and Bob Sutcliffe, *British Capitalism, Workers and the Profits Squeeze*, Harmondsworth, 1972, pp. 39, 43, 60, 65; Robin Blackburn and Alexander Cockburn, *The Incompatibles, Trade Union Militancy and Consensus*, Harmondsworth, 1967, p. 217.

[2] Roy Jenkins, *Pursuit of Progress, A Critical Analysis of the Achievement and Prospects of the Labour Party*, London, 1953, pp. 113, 179; Aneurin Bevan, *In Place of Fear*, London, 1952, p. 112.

production, or indeed in the productive efficiency of industry. The government then secured certain deferments of price increases in both publicly and privately owned sectors; but in March 1956 the General Council again expressed hostility to the government's policy. For some months, the government tried to change the General Council's mind, and to stiffen the engineering employers' resistance to the Confederation of Shipbuilding and Engineering Unions' forthcoming wage claim. By August, however, the conversion of the General Council was abandoned; and in March 1957 the engineering industry was advised to seek arbitration, in other words to settle on a compromise wage increase, but an increase nevertheless.[1]

Organized labour's arguments against 'wage restraint' or a 'wages policy' formed a pattern that has not greatly changed throughout the post-war era. One argument was that wage restraint was merely irrelevant. Since the trade unions had already 'displayed commendable restraint', the 'situation of constantly rising prices' was 'directly attributable to the policies of the present Government', the Transport and General Workers' Union leader Frank Cousins told the 1957 Trades Union Congress; and a Garment Workers' delegate explained to the Labour Party conference of the same year that increases in council-house rents, and taxation to pay for defence expenditure and concessions to surtax payers, made inflation inevitable. Defence expenditure in particular was much criticized. 'It would make our mouths water if we could merely say: "We won't spend money on armaments." Why, we could almost have free food for everybody!' exclaimed a Labour Party National Executive spokesman in 1954. A resolution declaring that 'the present level of defence expenditure' was 'largely responsible for the present inflationary situation' only failed to pass through the 1957 Trades Union Congress when a delegate pointed out that 'the major portion' of defence spending 'went in wages'.[2]

Trade unionists also argued that, for two reasons, wage restraint was undesirable. First, they claimed that wage increases would force employers to raise productivity by

---

[1] Clegg and Adams, pp. 27–8, 48–61; Dorfman, pp. 82, 89, 93, 98–9.
[2] Trade Union Congress *Report*, 1957, pp. 398–403, 434–5; Labour Party *Conference Report*, 1954, p. 179; 1957, pp. 199–200.

replacing labour-intensive with capital-intensive processes, a development held to be in the national interest (though a development about whose effect on employment trade union leaders remain silent). This claim was succinctly expressed by an Engineers' delegate who complained to the 1974 Trades Union Congress that 'unions have failed in their patriotic duty to force up wages so that investment has to take place. Low wages mean low investment and low productivity': and it was to reasoning such as this that Frank Haxell, the Electricians' leader, referred when he assured the 1955 Congress that the government 'will not prevent us defending national interests by improving the living standards of our people'. Secondly, trade unionists noted that wage restraint involved government intervention in 'voluntary' or 'free' collective bargaining, and a restriction of trade unions' freedoms; and they held such intervention and restriction to be harmful to industrial peace, if not dangerous to democratic principles. Frank Cousins declared in 1955 that 'we have stood firmly' against 'political instruction of unions', whether 'it is a Labour Government or not.' 'We are not prepared', he added, 'to tie our policy up to legislation . . . from a political party of whatever shade, telling us what we must do in relation to our industrial matters.'[1]

Finally, trade unionists claimed that wage restraint was impossible or unfair, or both, either because prices could not or would not be restrained, or because trade unionists would never obtain a share of the national income sufficient to warrant them seeking no further increase in that share. 'Wages have never caught up with prices since the first shot was fired in the industrial revolution', declared an Electrician in 1954. Cousins urged the 1957 Trades Union Congress to reject 'the principle of wage restraint while prices and profits were allowed to go uncontrolled'; and he summarized his views on wage restraint in the phrase (coined a year earlier) that, 'in a period of "freedom for all" we are a part of the all'. In 1956 the Railwaymen's leader Jim Campbell claimed that 'a *laissez-faire* philosophy', such as inspired the Conservative government, 'is completely incompatible with wage restraint'; but, he added, 'a planned economy' may 'create a climate where trade unions will not be

---

[1] Trades Union Congress *Report*, 1955, p. 402; 1974, p. 430; Labour Party *Conference Report*, 1955, p. 140.

compelled' to see wage increases to offset increased prices. By 1963, however, this hope had perhaps been extinguished: for a General Council document on 'Economic Development and Planning', published in that year, stated that 'trade unionists insist that in a free-for-all they are part of the all. They are still part of the all in the more dynamic conditions that . . . planning can create.'[1]

Organized labour resisted Conservative suggestions about wages largely because, by the 1950s, the unions no longer feared the mass unemployment which had appeared to threaten them in 1948. The unions also resisted a wages policy because they distrusted government (whether Labour or not, to use Cousins' words); and because any wages policy to which government was a party smacked of a repugnant collectivism. As Cousins' view of the 'free-for-all' indicated, the Conservative slogan of these years, 'Set the people free', met with a sympathetic response among trade unionists eager to abandon the collectivist false gods of 'workers' control' for an individualist 'affluence' more appropriate to their traditional convictions. By the 1950s trade unions were both stronger than ever and growing stronger; yet many trade unionists seemed to shrink not merely from the new responsibilities that such new power must bring, but even from the old responsibilities into which they had entered during the previous hundred years.

THE FRAGMENTATION OF LABOUR

One symptom of such recessiveness was the unions' tendency not merely to dissociate themselves from the Labour Party but to make a virtue of that dissociation. In 1953 Ben Gardner, General Secretary of the Amalgamated Engineering Union, wrote that 'unions must have their own independent view of political questions—and maintain their freedom to differ from any and every political party.' He agreed that the Labour Party was 'a trade union party in the sense that the unions formed it half a century ago'; but now, he complained, 'it has become a Party committed to larger responsibilities outside the industrial field'. Ten years later, Vic Feather, subsequently

[1] Trades Union Congress *Report*, 1954, p. 480; 1956, pp. 400, 402; 1957, p. 432; 1963, p. 495.

General Secretary of the Trades Union Congress, admitted that 'the Labour Party was originally formed by some trade unions'; but he attributed that fact to a 'particular set of circumstances at the time'. Trade unions, he argued, must never let their own work become 'secondary to the interests' of a 'political party'. In this period, a tradition grew up that both Party and unions 'had a job to do', and that neither should tell the other 'how to do their job'. Indeed, Lawther told the 1952 Labour Party conference that it had 'no right whatever to lay down a mandate as to how' the unions 'will act'. 'Not only have you no mandate', he declared, 'but even if you had', the unions 'would not accept it'.[1]

Yet the decay of post-war labour organization went further than the belief that trade unions and Labour Party were merely yoked by coincidence together. Writing in 1965, two International Socialists observed that though, in the past 'the workers' acted 'as a *class-as-a-whole*', 'struggles today are essentially local and fragmented'. Another commentator, somewhat to the right of these authors, attributed the unions' failure to co-ordinate their policies during the 1950s to a 'fundamental antipathy to planning', a 'mixture of innate conservatism, rugged individualism, and "I'm All Right Jack" . . . characteristic of modern British unionism'. Certainly most trade unionists opposed any increase in the strength of the Trades Union Congress. They did not mind the General Council of the Congress talking to the government, but they (and the Council) rejected any proposal that these talks should develop into negotiations binding on affiliated unions; and, in a similar fashion, they resisted any suggestion that the Congress might lead, or speak for, affiliated unions in collective bargaining with employers. As the Shop Workers' leader (and General Council member) Alan Birch put it, Congress intervention in collective bargaining would be a 'totalitarian' attack upon the 'democratic values' of trade unionism. 'The whole idea of a super body at the top . . . imposing limits upon the rights of trade unions to represent their members is foreign to every-

[1] Amalgamated Engineering Union *Journal*, February 1953, pp. 33–4; Victor Feather, *The Essence of Trade Unionism*, London, 1963, pp. 37–8; Peter Jenkins, *The Battle of Downing Street*, London, 1970, p. x; Labour Party *Conference Report*, 1952, p. 79.

thing we stand for in this country', George Woodcock declared in 1963. In any event, Congress could not guide member unions, especially on the delicate question of money: it would require 'the wisdom of Solomon', one General Council spokesman suggested, and it would meet with complete hostility from the unions. 'My job is to defend members', said the Boilermakers' leader Ted Hill in 1959, 'and I am going to defend them in the face of the Trades Union Congress and the Labour Party.'[1]

The unions affiliated to the Congress were, moreover, thoroughly divided among themselves. Sir Vincent Tewson, then General Secretary of the Trades Union Congress, remarked in 1957 that, 'we talk of "the Trade Union Movement" ' yet 'we have craft, industrial, and general workers' unions whose very theory and basis of organization leads to competition and overlapping.' After 1950 the number of unions affiliated to Congress substantially decreased through mergers and amalgamations; but relatively few larger and directly competing unions united with each other. The continued rivalry of the two biggest unions in Britain, the Transport and General Workers' Union and the Engineers, is further complicated by the claims of the National Union of General and Municipal Workers, on the one hand, and the craft unions on the other. The Boilermakers continue to dispute with all other shipbuilding unions; the National Union of Railwaymen continues to contest the claims of the Association of Locomotive Engineers and Firemen; and various white-collar unions vie for the loyalties of clerical and administrative workers in both the private and the public sector. Especially in metal manufacturing, and above all in the motor-car and ancillary industries, the uninhibited hostilities of different groups of manual workers, motivated by an enthusiastic *laissez-faire* love of self-government, have done little to promote labour solidarity. 'At regional and local level it is much more common for unions to pursue their separate interests', wrote Tom Lupton in 1976.[2]

[1] T. Cliff and C. Barker, *Incomes Policy, Legislation and Shop Stewards*, London, n.d., pp. 128, 132; Michael Shanks, *The Stagnant Society, A Warning*, Harmondsworth, 1961, pp. 118–19; Trades Union Congress *Report*, 1954, p. 472; 1955, p. 403; 1959, p. 336; 1963, p. 391; Labour Party *Conference Report*, 1959, p. 150.

[2] Trades Union Congress *Report*, 1957, p. 337; *The Guardian*, 5 January 1976.

These deficiencies have been compounded by manual workers' dislike of white-collar workers. By 1948 the trade unions once more organized 45 per cent of the total labour force, a level last reached in 1920; but by 1967 less than 42 per cent of the labour force were members of trade unions; and, even despite the exceptionally favourable social and economic circumstances of the period after 1969, it was not until 1974 that unions organized more than 50 per cent of the labour force. The stagnation of trade unionism is largely attributable to the rapid increase in the number of white-collar workers with whom, at least until very recently, manual workers have been apparently incapable of making common cause. Manual workers' unions' general distaste for the educated has long been notorious. 'In that dark period of 1931 it was the intellectuals who funked the issue', declared Lawther in 1952. It was the 'so-called intelligentsia in our party' who, through the machinations of an unwanted incomes policy, were endeavouring to destroy the labour movement, Hugh Scanlon suggested in 1968. Gaitskell remarked to the 1959 Labour Party conference that sometimes the party gave the idea that white-collar workers 'are not welcome in our ranks'. John Boyd, later the Engineers' General Secretary, was rather more explicit at the 1966 Trades Union Congress, when he told one white-collar union that 'in the main, you know (and somebody has got to say this) you represent people who produce nothing', and accused another white-collar union of being 'forty thousand Conservatives' who had 'run away from the struggle of the workshop floor'.[1]

These external shortcomings merely paralleled the serious internal weaknesses of labour industrial organization. Joseph Goldstein's classic study of the structure of the Transport and General Workers' Union, published in 1952, defined that institution as 'an oligarchy parading in democracy's trappings'. Stephen Fay, writing in 1969, more colourfully described the Engineers' union as 'a combination of Tammany and the Chinese Warlord system'. Many unions are now run by a very small fraction of the membership, which is enabled, by the

[1] Labour Party *Conference Report*, 1952, p. 89; 1959, p. 109; 1968, p. 142; Trades Union Congress *Report*, 1966, pp. 475–6; R. Price and G. S. Bain, 'Union Growth Revisited', *British Journal of Industrial Relations*, November 1976.

apathy of the majority and the intricacies of the rule book, to decide elections, monopolize official positions, and determine the union's policy on both industrial and political questions. In these circumstances, union members who strongly dissent from the officialdom of their own union have no recourse other than insubordination. Hence Clegg and Adams argued in the late 1950s that 'unofficial action' was 'one of the main guarantees of union democracy', since the officials could usually get decisions 'formally approved according to the constitution of the Union'. Almost all strikes are unofficial (although most *long* strikes are not); many unofficial strikes arise from conflicts between union members and union officials; and this can only intensify the irrationality and incoherence of the pressures to which unionized undertakings are subjected.[1]

The dissolution of a trade union into its constituent parts, indeed into the individuals who compose it, is a *laissez-faire* orthodoxy venerated by union leaders, and of course enshrined in the 1906 Trade Disputes Act. Feather assured the Royal Commission on Trade Unions and Employers' Associations in 1966 that a trade union was not a corporate body at all, but 'a voluntary society', 'a combination of workmen'. 'Any union is its members', he triumphantly concluded. Now, since 1940 this fiction has been progressively realized by the increase of shop stewards; the growth of their strength; and the decline of the powers of full-time union officials, many of whom have become no more than negotiators of minimal national conditions, which are subsequently improved by the shop stewards working side by side with union members in closed shops. The result has been at times a virtual severance of the relationships between the 'unofficial' work place organization of the union and its officially constituted leadership at branch, district and national level. In 1968 a member of the Engineers' union was quoted as saying, 'you've always got interest in the things that happen in the shop. You're not at all interested in the affairs of the "union"—except where it concerns yourself'. Two years earlier, Bill Carron, then the Engineers' President, commented

[1] Joseph Goldstein, *The Government of British Trade Unions, A Study of Apathy and the Democratic Process in the Transport and General Workers' Union*, London, 1952; Stephen Fay, *Measure for Measure: Reforming the Trade Unions*, London, 1970, p. 62; Clegg and Adams, pp. 15–16.

of his ten years in office, 'Looking backward, I feel very much like the victim who is about to put his last . . . sixpences into the ever-open maw of a one-arm bandit. I have repeatedly pulled the lever but, except for an occasional bit of fuss at the top, nothing ever happens at the bottom.'[1]

The character of post-war trade unionism, in short, reinforces the extreme sectionalism that labour organization has inherited from its utilitarian liberal-individualist tradition. Unions were 'being a bit too narrow-minded and too parochial in thinking only about their own problems', a left-wing delegate from the Association of Supervisory Staffs, Executives and Technicians discreetly suggested at the 1959 Labour Party conference. In 1957 Arthur Horner, the Communist leader of the National Union of Mineworkers, was franker. 'The only purpose of our existence', he said, 'is to take advantage of every possible opportunity to safeguard our members.' 'Safeguards', of course, meant more money. 'Unions have grown', said Alan Birch in 1958, 'by using their organization . . . for one purpose': to establish 'the best possible wages and conditions' through 'collective negotiation'. Appeals for union co-operation in wage restraint were, therefore, somewhat fanciful. A civil servant, speaking in the same debate, complemented Birch's remarks by declaring that, 'The trade unions will take one piece of advice on wages, and that is the view of their members. Everybody under the sun . . . can tell us what we should do'; but, he added, 'it will not make a scrap of difference.' That attitude did not change throughout the Conservatives' thirteen years of government. 'The job of a trade union leader is to look after the interests of his members', Feather stated in 1963. Hence, 'every political situation should be judged on its merits, and only from the standpoint of the members' interests.' Meanwhile, however, union members seem no more eager to strengthen their leaders' hands than they were in the mid-nineteenth century. By the 1970s, though weekly subscriptions to European unions represented about one hour's pay, sub-

[1] Royal Commission on Trade Unions and Employers' Associations, *Minutes of Evidence, 61, Tuesday 29 November 1966 and, 65, Tuesday 31 February 1967. Witness, Trades Union Congress*, London, 1967, pp. 2684, 2686; J. H. Goldthorpe, D. Lockwood, F. Bechhofer, and J. Platt, *The Affluent Worker: Industrial Attitudes and Behaviour*, Cambridge, 1968, pp. 103–4; Amalgamated Engineering Union *Journal*, June 1966, p. 235.

scriptions to British unions amounted to little more than ten minutes' pay.[1]

The reaffirmation of union sectionalism was probably assisted by the crisis in Labour Party thinking during the 1950s. Before the 1951 general election, Labour leaders were promising themselves that 'unemployment, reductions in social services' and 'catastrophic price increases' would 'surely follow a Tory victory'. By 1955, however, the economy had so far improved that Richard Crossman felt obliged to admit that 'unemployment is something which can be dealt with relatively easily by any Government which understands the economic system and has the right instruments for controlling and manipulating it'. The Conservatives seemed to constitute such a government; and under their administration, Crosland conceded, 'the rich are distinctly less rich, and the poor are much less poor'. By 1959, according to Gaitskell, the United Kingdom was characterized by 'full employment, new housing', indeed a 'new way of life based on the telly, the frig, the car': and all this had been achieved under Tory rule.[2]

Yet a society's level of prosperity—whether the destitution alleged to have marred the early nineteenth century, or the 'affluence' of the 1950s—is of little importance to most social and political theories. 'Affluence' is very probably a mere hedonistic irrelevance to normative collectivism, which is concerned with the creation of a complete, a perfected man, not a wealthy man. It is almost certainly a mere *tactical* irrelevance to whole hearted supporters of the utilitarian redistributive individualism which informs both the political and industrial organization of British labour; for whoever accepts such a creed sees the world as no more than the locus of various goods, on which the warring egoistic individuals, whose sum is society, have like designs and equal claims. Given a thoroughgoing normative collectivism, labour would have dismissed or

---

[1] Labour Party *Conference Report*, 1959, p. 114; Trades Union Congress *Report*, 1957, p. 437; 1958, pp. 418, 430; Feather, p. 39; *The Times*, 5 January 1976.

[2] Labour Party *Conference Report*, 1951, p. 75; 1959, p. 108; R. H. S. Crossmann, *Planning for Freedom*, London, 1965, p. 60; Crosland, p. 53.

despised post-war affluence; given an honest and self-confident individualism, it would simply have noted that the prizes of perfect competition had increased.

Trade unionists, on the whole, took the latter course. They were in the money business, and they simply raised their demands as the 1950s went on. Labour Party leaders, Labour intellectuals, and many Labour Party members found life more complicated. In the first place, they had long been used to conceal the stark self-interest of organized labour's redistributive demands by emphasizing, if not exaggerating, the poverty of those whose interests they promoted. The new prosperity made that exercise rather difficult. In his book *The Future of Socialism*, Crosland quoted Cole's statement that ' "the will to Socialism is based on a lively sense of wrongs crying for redress" '. 'When the wrongs were so manifest, we all knew what to do. . . . But now the certainty and simplicity are gone', commented Crosland, who added that Labour no longer had 'the same crusading spirit'. In the second place, the Labour Party had accustomed itself to equate 'capitalism' with evil and 'socialism' with good; to identify 'evil' and 'good', in a jejune though equivocal fashion, sometimes with different standards of living, sometimes with different relativities of income and wealth; and to promise itself a secure role in British politics over all those doubtless many generations which would elapse before the material abundance, or the material equality, of 'socialism' should replace the material scarcities, or material inequality, of 'capitalism'. All of a sudden, however, 'capitalism' seemed to have introduced material abundance, and to have nullified material inequality. Thus the 'framework' of 'most pre-war socialist discussion' had 'been rendered obsolete', Crosland reported. For 'traditional socialism was largely concerned with the evils of traditional capitalism', but 'traditional capitalism has been reformed . . . almost out of existence'. These considerations—reinforced by Labour's electoral defeats—drove not merely Crosland and those on the Labour right who thought with him, but even Crosland's opponents on the Labour left, to what they thought was a 'revision' of Labour's principles and policies.[1]

Aneurin Bevan, Labour's most famous 'anti-revisionist',

[1] Ibid., pp. 41, 96–7, 99.

argued that 'society' was 'an arena of conflicting social forces', namely, 'private property, poverty and democracy'. 'Poverty', Bevan freely admitted, meant little more than a perceived ability (available to at least ninety-nine per cent of the population) to make a material gain from a redistribution in wealth. Poverty was 'the general consciousness of unnecessary deprivation', 'resentment against inequality', or 'a knowledge of the possible, as contrasted with the actual'. 'Private property' meant a perceived liability (also available to at least ninety-nine per cent of the population) to make a material loss from a redistribution in wealth. 'Democracy' was the means whereby this redistribution would be sought. 'In a capitalist democracy', Bevan wrote at the beginning of the 1950s, 'either poverty will use democracy to win the struggle against property, or property, in fear of poverty will destroy democracy', by 'fascism and all forms of authoritarian government.' By the end of the 1950s, however, Bevan agreed that 'a very considerable number of young men and women', in the course of the previous ten years 'have had their material conditions improved and their status raised in consequence and their discontents have been reduced, so that temporarily their personalities are satisfied with the framework in which they live'. The political consequences of such conclusions, however qualified, were alarming for Labour: as many beside Bevan observed. If it was indeed possible for 'working people' to 'expect, without a change in society, an improved and guaranteed material standard of living', a constituency delegate told the 1955 Party conference, 'the necessity for a change in society is no longer there', and 'we have thrown overboard the whole basis for socialism'.[1]

'Socialism' based wholly on 'an improved and guaranteed material standard of living' may be an egalitarian, but is not a collectivist, doctrine. As an egalitarian doctrine, it would obtain the approval of the 'revisionists', for whom (as of course for their opponents), 'socialism' was 'basically about equality', in Crosland's words. And as egalitarians, the revisionists, and their opponents, sought to find new policies for Labour especially by denying whatever were the Conservatives' claims to have achieved 'affluence'. 'If we look honestly at Britain

---

[1] Bevan, pp. 2–3, 5; Labour Party *Conference Report*, 1955, pp. 115–16; 1956, p. 152.

today,' declared *Towards Equality, Labour's Policy for Social Justice*, published by the Party in 1956, 'we must admit that opportunities are far from equal; privilege in many forms remains strongly entrenched; the division of the nation's wealth is arbitrary and unjust; and in its essentials ours is—and is felt to be—a class society.' Yet such statements were little more than whistling in the dark, not merely because (as they confessed) Labour leaders did not think people in fact 'felt' Britain 'to be' so, but because it was quite unclear to the Party how to 'advance further towards a socialist society' of the egalitarian type.[1]

In practice further advance meant two kinds of changes. On the one hand, the Labour Party proposed to reorganize and expand government and municipal services in order to supply higher state-insurance benefits, better medical provisions, and a system of 'comprehensive secondary education' which would extend teaching of the quality provided by the grammar schools to every child in the country. These were the 'great social advances', the *'practical idealism'*, promised by the Party's 1959 election manifesto. On the other hand, the Party expected to facilitate still higher wage increases. 'When the nine hundred thousand members in our union think of equality', declared an Engineer in 1956, 'they think of the proper distribution of the wealth' which 'they have helped to create'; and Labour government would no doubt hasten a shift of that wealth in what Engineers thought was the right direction. Both kinds of change seemed very difficult to achieve. Expanded public services required higher taxation which now fell increasingly upon manual workers. 'When we try to attack' inequalities 'through the social services', Barbara Castle complained to the 1959 Party conference, 'we find that the wage earners they are designed to help have become their enemy because they have to carry the main burden of financing them through Pay As You Earn.' And, given the existing disposition of the gross national product, further wage increases would do little more than produce inflation. 'I feel . . . there is a limit to which we can go on arguing about the distribution of wealth at the

[1] Anthony Crosland, *Socialism Now, and Other Essays*, London, 1974, p. 15; Labour Party, *Towards Equality, Labour's Policy for Social Justice*, London, 1956, pp. 3, 5.

present level', confessed Fred Hayday, the Trades Union Congress Fraternal Delegate to the 1963 Party conference. Instead, he suggested, 'we have to co-operate to increase the wealth that is available for distribution.'[1]

These assumptions gave Labour politicians, whether of left or right, not much choice but to 'go for growth', as the saying was about 1960. Roy Jenkins's essay *The Labour Case*, published for the general election of 1959, put the point bluntly. 'The principal fault of the British economy today', he wrote, 'is that it does not grow.' But there must be 'more output' and a rise in 'productivity', if Britain was to achieve 'the extra goods and services' which were 'urgently' required for 'social justice' and 'a less stratified society'. That position reduced Labour to mere 'Butskellism', if not simple 'me-too-ism', since, if Jenkins were right, Labour could claim to do in the future no more and nothing else than the Conservatives then seemed to do, with great success, in the present. Yet perhaps Labour could claim to possess a special secret which would produce still faster or better growth. Thus Reg Prentice (who was himself later to become a Conservative, however) told the 1955 Labour Party conference that, 'if Mr. Butler can talk of doubling the standard of living in twenty-five years we can do better' by 'Socialist methods': not least because, through those methods, the 'new wealth' would 'benefit the whole community', not just a lucky few.[2]

An appeal to 'Socialist methods' did not help much, however. The Labour Party did continue to demand (in clause 4 of its Constitution) 'the common ownership of the means of production, distribution and exchange', and to look towards 'a socialist community based on fellowship, co-operation and service'. Yet the collectivism that might vitalize these phrases was lacking. As Hugh Clegg put it in 1951, in words which gained wide acceptance in the Party, 'democracy of the common purpose or general will—democracy based on an organic political theory—is only acceptable within a relatively small organization; if the organization is large enough it

---

[1] Labour Party, *The Future Labour Offers You*, London, n.d.; Labour Party *Conference Report*, 1956, p. 128; 1959, p. 85; 1963, p. 133.

[2] Roy Jenkins, *The Labour Case*, Harmondsworth, 1959, pp. 51–5; Labour Party *Conference Report*, 1955, p. 114.

becomes a sham and a cover for authoritarianism', with its 'toadies, tale-bearers', and 'multitude of functionaries'. The British economy, and British society, were certainly thought to be 'large enough' to bring forth these dire effects of 'organic political theory'. And in any event both Labour politicians and trade unionists remained more or less loyal to J. S. Mill. 'Society' and 'the community', argued the Trades Union Congress in its evidence to the Royal Commission on Trade Unions and Employers' Associations, were mere 'abstract conceptions', in reality composed of 'plural institutions, groups and individuals', whose behaviour 'can be most readily explained by reference to their interests'. 'The argument from national interest', the Congress declared, was simply 'but one of a rich repertoire employed by those whose interests are different to those of trade unionists.' The state should therefore have no more than a 'residuary role': 'its attitude' to industrial relations, for example, 'being one of abstention, of formal indifference'—so long as trade unions were 'competent' to bargain freely with employers. Of course, government could aid un- or ill-organized workers by establishing wages councils, by requiring employers to recognize unions, and so on: but this could be only 'the second best alternative' to 'free collective bargaining'.[1]

The 'Socialist method' of economic growth, in so far as it was purveyed by Labour and its backers, was therefore much the same as the 'capitalist' method; and this similarity was nowhere better seen in Labour's unease over nationalization. In the 1950s, as indeed for more than half-a-century earlier, nationalization meant, above all, a subsidy to producers in the form of higher wages and low unemployment. 'The people in the nationalized industries', Deakin complained in 1953, 'have regarded the change-over merely from the point of view of how much better-off they could become in the shortest possible time in the way of better wages and conditions'. 'I have been told very clearly by my own members employed in nationalized industries: "If you cannot get more out of this . . . we are going

[1] Ibid., 1960, pp. 12–13; H. A. Clegg, *Industrial Democracy and Nationalisation*, Oxford, 1951, pp. 16, 121; Royal Commission on Trades Unions and Employers' Associations, *Selected Written Evidence Submitted to the Royal Commission (Confederation of British Industry, the Trades Union Congress and Others)*, London, 1968, pp. 117, 135, 137, 140.

to vote Tory",' added Deakin. But getting more out of nationalization for producers meant getting less for consumers: 'Socialism can fly out of the door when another twenty shillings goes in the coal sack', as the Miners' leader Sam Watson warned, in 1955. Nationalization, in other words, seemed likely to win votes only from those who both were to be nationalized, and expected to get better pay and a safer job thereby; while the votes thus won might well be offset by votes lost from those who merely consumed the products of nationalized industries and had nothing to expect from nationalization but higher prices, along with higher taxes. Bevan recognized the dilemma in 1952, when he denied that 'we have discovered some royal road, some ingenious way of trying to achieve our socialist purposes which would not lead us through the old hard agony of public ownership.'[1]

In a sense, however, this was a commonplace difficulty. For the agony Bevan invited his fellow politicians to endure was little different from that daily suffered by trade union leaders who, having organized competing groups of wage earners, then have to reconcile their mutually incompatible claims. A difficulty of much greater theoretical significance arose from the very character of nationalization. That Labour remained true to its *laissez-faire* liberal individualism may be judged from the unequivocal clause of the Party's 1960 'Statement of Aims', which declared that Labour stood for the 'freedom of the individual against the glorification of the state'. Now, according to Labour, in the 1950s, the most feared threat to such freedom was 'managerialism'. Crossmann wrote in 1955,

> One of the main post-war features of the Western world has been the steady concentration of power in the hands of the managerial class. . . . The first task of Socialism . . . must be to expose this growth of irresponsible power; to challenge this new managerial oligarchy; to show that its . . . privileges are a threat to democracy and to demand that it should become not the master but the servant of the nation.

Naturally, the new 'managerial class' was sought above all in large industrial undertakings, among which British Railways and the National Coal Board began to seem, if not conspicuous,

[1] Labour Party *Conference Report*, 1952, p. 83; 1953, p. 132; 1955, p. 169.

nevertheless disturbing, examples. 'The boards of our nationalized industries', wrote Bevan in 1951, were 'a new and potenti-
ally dangerous problem'. 'We still have to ensure', he declared,
'that they are taking us towards democratic Socialism, not
towards the Managerial Society.' The 'statutory immunity' of
nationalized industries 'from direct parliamentary control' (a
device that sprang directly from Labour's *laissez-faire* doctrines)
was a threat to freedom, Bevan now claimed. Sheltered by this
immunity, he believed, 'the "management" is still associated
with the conception of alien ownership, and the "workers" are
still "hands".'[1]

One way of avoiding 'managerialism', while retaining
'public ownership' might seem to be to revive pre-war ideas of
workers' control. For if, as a constituency delegate to the 1958
Party conference put it, the 'workers' were to 'participate' in
management, let alone control industry, they must have a
'collective right to hire and fire the management'; and such a
right might appear to eliminate 'managerialism' once and for
all. Yet Labour politicians were not so certain. As Eirene White
observed to the 1960 Conference:

> industrial democracy . . . is a lovely phrase. But it is not so easy
> to carry out in practice . . . where we have free trade unions . . .
> very jealous, and rightly so, of their independence . . . who do not
> necessarily want to be absorbed into . . . management . . . because
> they believe that would interfere with their position as a bargain-
> ing authority. . . . If you tried to have a corporate organization of
> your industry, what happens to your free trade unions?

The question did not admit of any answer encouraging to the
admirers of 'free trade unions', to whom the proposal to curb
management by turning trade unionists into managers had
always seemed more than faintly ridiculous.[2]

Opposition to 'workers' control' received powerful reinforce-
ment from two books by Clegg: *Industrial Democracy and
Nationalization*, which appeared in 1951; and *A New Approach
to Industrial Democracy*, published in 1960. Clegg argued, from
the liberal-individualist presuppositions common to Labour
revisionists and anti-revisionists alike, that society necessarily

---

[1] Ibid., 1960, pp. 12–13; Crossmann, p. 63; Bevan, pp. 102–3.
[2] Labour Party *Conference Report*, 1958, p. 155; 1960, p. 230.

consists of conflicting and competing individuals whose struggles could only be superseded were one individual or group of individuals to overwhelm and exploit all other individuals. He therefore reasoned that 'organized opposition is a prerequisite of democracy', since by such opposition alone could individuals' democratic rights be protected. In 1951 he pointed to parliamentary Opposition as the paradigm of democratic institutions; while in 1960 he looked rather to 'pressure groups' as the basis of democracy. But at both dates his theme was the same, namely, that 'concentration of power is to be feared so much that opposition must be positively encouraged'; and that the trade unions—'industry's opposition', 'probably the most powerful, amongst the various pressure groups'—were the right instruments to achieve that end. 'The most important function of a trade union is to . . . defend the interests of its members', wrote Clegg. 'Trade unions owe their existence to the need felt by the workers for an organization to oppose managers and employers on their behalf.' Hence, he concluded, 'the trade union cannot become the organ of industrial management', because 'there would then be no one to oppose the management, and no hope of democracy.' The trade unions are therefore to be industry's permanent opposition, 'an opposition which can never become a government', and 'collective bargaining is the means to industrial democracy'. 'It is often said that trade unions are strong', wrote Clegg in 1960. 'For the purposes of industrial democracy it is difficult to see that the trade unions could be too strong.'[1]

If nationalization did little more than subsidize producers, at the risk of a managerialism which workers' control could not alleviate but only exacerbate, then further structural changes in industry seemed rather undesirable, at least to revisionists. Revisionism 'maintained contrary to traditional Marxist doctrine, that the ownership of the means of production was no longer the key factor which imparted to a society its essential character', Crosland wrote in 1974. In fact, however, this was not quite what revisionists argued. Revisionists did think that 'ownership of the means of production' influenced the character of society; for they held that state socialism or workers' control,

[1] Clegg, pp. 22, 114–15, 131, 141; *A New Approach to Industrial Democracy*, Oxford, 1960, pp. 20–1, 27.

for example, would jeopardize liberty, democracy and equality, while the 'mixed economy' of post-Attlee Britain protected liberty, democracy and equality. What revisionists meant to say was simply that the 'good' with which socialism had long been loosely equated should now be equated instead with the 'mixed economy': in other words, as Crosland put it, it was possible to achieve 'greater equality and other desirable ends within the framework of a mixed economy'. Revisionism, which started out from the assumption that the post-war world was a challenge to traditional socialism, ended up with the proposition that traditional socialism meant the post-war world.[1]

This dénouement did not seem a sufficient reward for a decade's debate, especially since there was no obvious way in which the revisionist equation could be translated into major acts of policy. Meanwhile, Labour had been defeated at two elections, in which, Gaitskell believed, 'nationalization—on balance—lost us votes'. This was partly because nationalization was blamed for high prices, partly because it was seen as an issue that committed the Party to what a much-publicized analysis of Labour's electoral fortunes described as 'the poor and labouring working-class'. Labour 'must explain to people that we are a working-class party but that the working-class was not just cloth-caps, mufflers and misery', Richard Marsh told the 1961 Party conference; and that explanation had to deal with Bevan's 'old hard agony of public ownership'. Little by little, therefore, Labour leaders tried to reduce their commitment to nationalization. From 1951 onwards, the Party indicated that only those undertakings which were 'failing the nation' would be nationalized. About the same time, Labour politicians began expressing the view that 'failing' industries might be dealt with by a government majority or minority shareholding, rather than by complete take-over, a view which was formally adopted in a policy statement published in 1957 under the title *Industry and Society*. And from about 1955, Gaitskell began to argue that nationalization was anyway simply a 'means' to an 'end', namely, the 'good' of 'socialism' (which revisionists now equated with the 'mixed economy'). 'If you look at the party constitution . . .' he declared, pointing in particular to Clause 4,

[1] Crosland, *Socialism Now*, p. 17; *Future of Socialism*, p. 74.

you will find among the seven objects this one: 'To secure for the workers by hand or by brain the full fruits of their industry and the most equitable distribution thereof that may be possible upon the basis of the common ownership of the means of production', and so on. The first part of that sentence is the object itself and . . . common ownership . . . is the means.

Perhaps, it seemed to Gaitskell and others by 1959, the need for a demonstration that nationalization was a mere 'means'—by the rewriting or even the elimination of Clause 4—might be the chief practical lesson of revisionism.[1]

Clause 4, Gaitskell told the 1959 Party conference, 'lays us open to continual misrepresentation' and 'should be brought up to date'. This proposal shocked many Party members especially as they feared that updating Clause 4 meant, in fact, deleting it. The clause had been inserted in the Constitution in 1918, not because Party members had suddenly been converted to socialism, but chiefly to differentiate Labour from the Liberals; now, forty years later, it was one of the few things that distinguished Labour from the Conservatives; and in 1959, as in 1918, to do without the clause seemed tantamount to doing without an identity. The notion was 'sacrilegious', declared one constituency delegate; but Paul Foot commented, rather less reverently, that 'the Party faithful could paste Clause 4 over their beds at night, but, provided no one re-wrote the Constitution in the morning they would happily work for the opposite.' Though they entertained opinions no more collectivist than those held by constituency delegates, trade unionists were particularly hostile to Gaitskell's plans. They saw the attack on Clause 4 as an attack on their influence over the Party, an influence they had been willing to let dwindle, but would not let lapse. Their anxiety was heightened by the fact that most leading revisionists (not all of whom openly opposed Clause 4, however) were precisely the type of 'middle-class intellectuals'—some being Oxbridge graduates, if occasionally of lower-class parentage, some even being Etonians or Wykehamists—whom trade unionists traditionally

---

[1] Labour Party *Conference Report*, 1951, p. 209; 1955, p. 175; 1959, p. 110; 1961, p. 98; Mark Abrams, Richard Rose, and Rita Hinden, *Must Labour Lose?*, Harmondsworth, 1960, *passim*.

feared and disliked as potential traitors to the 'Labour Movement'.[1]

Many bitter words were spoken on the subject of Clause 4. In March 1960 the National Executive Committee compromised on the issue by agreeing to leave the clause untouched, while adopting a new 'Statement of Aims'. The Statement affirmed Labour's support 'for democracy in industry and for the right of the workers' to 'full consultation in all vital decisions of management, especially those affecting conditions of work'. This, and Labour's other 'social and economic objectives', the Statement declared, in a clause said to have been proposed by Harold Wilson, 'can be achieved only through an expansion of common ownership sufficient to give the community power over the commanding heights of the economy'. The Statement of Aims was carried by almost a two thirds majority at the 1960 Party Conference; but then and thereafter the compromise formula remained undefined. The expansionist drive to the 'commanding heights' continued to be qualified by a certain loyalty to the much less aggressive concept of nationalizing only those undertakings that 'failed the nation'; and the mere eleven lines devoted to 'public ownership' in the Labour Party Manifesto of 1964 went no further than the re-nationalization of the steel industry and nationalization of water supplies.[2]

LABOUR NATIONALISM

By 1964, however, British politics had been profoundly modified, above all by certain events that occurred during 1956. In February of that year, Khrushchev made his secret speech to the Twentieth Congress of the Communist Party of the Soviet Union, criticizing Stalin's regime and 'cult of personality'. In July the Egyptian government, led by Nasser, nationalized the Suez Canal, in which the United Kingdom had held a controlling interest for the previous eighty-one years. At the end of October, certain groups in Hungary, emboldened by Khrushchev's secret speech, tried to secure

[1] Labour Party *Conference Report*, 1959, p. 112; Paul Foot, *The Politics of Harold Wilson*, Harmondsworth, 1968, p. 127.

[2] Ibid., p. 130; Labour Party *Conference Report*, 1960, pp. 12–13; Labour Party, *Let's Go with Labour for the New Britain*, London, n.d., p. 9.

independence from the Soviet Union; but were defeated by major Russian military operations in Budapest, ending, on 4 November, in the appointment of Kadar's pro-Soviet government. Almost at the same time the Israeli government invaded Sinai, and a joint Anglo-French expedition was sent to seize the Suez Canal. This conflict was strongly condemned by the United States; and Anglo-French military operations were abandoned on 6 November, the canal remaining in Egyptian hands. These developments had three important consequences. First, the state of war in central Europe and the Middle East, during October-November 1956, greatly intensified the already quite widespread fear of a 'Third World War', to be fought with nuclear weapons. Secondly, the secret speech and the suppression of the Hungarian uprising deeply discredited the Communist Parties of western Europe. Thirdly, the Suez fiasco demonstrated, even to those who had ignored the lessons of Dunkirk and Singapore, that the British empire was collapsing. Indeed the Anglo-French withdrawal greatly expedited the end of the United Kingdom's rule in Africa, where, during the decade after Suez, eleven succession states were formed from erstwhile British colonies.

The sudden and dramatic acceleration of imperial decline unsettled the Labour Party no less than the Conservatives. At the 1954 Labour Party conference, the chairman had expressed his 'thankfulness and pride in the influence which this country radiates all round the earth'. 'Britain still stands for something highly valued in this shifting, changing world,' he added. 'It seems that from Britain there still flows a creative energy, a civilizing force that is not just the residue of former imperial greatness.' That there was, in 1954, a rather substantial 'residue of former imperial greatness', especially in Africa, the chairman did not trouble to deny. Two years later, however, that 'residue' was strikingly diminished; whatever Britain stood for did seem to be rather less 'highly valued'; and the British 'creative energy' and 'civilizing force' appeared somewhat uncertain. Of course, Labour deplored the resort to force; but it may have deplored the unsuccessful outcome of the resort to force no less fervently. Norman Mackenzie, in his influential left-wing symposium *Conviction*, which appeared in 1958, lamented the 'humiliating . . . final futile fling of imperialism at Suez', which he identified as an episode in 'the long retreat of Britain from the first rank of world powers.' 'John Bull died at Dunkirk', declared Mackenzie, who found 'substance' in the view that 'we are dominated by the Americans, outwitted by the Russians, defied by the Egyptians', and 'out-sold by the Germans.'[1]

Indeed, from 1956 onwards, the Labour Party seemed to conceal the uncertainties left by the inconclusive revisionist debate beneath a rather thick layer of patriotism and nationalism. In every crisis the Labour Party spoke of 'Britain', and the 'British' position. At the 1969 Party conference, Harold Wilson condemned the government's 'humiliating' borrowings from the International Monetary Fund. He warned delegates that Britain was 'in danger of earning' the 'title of "The Sick Man of Europe" '. 'Labour does not wave flags', declared Wilson, 'but we do believe in Britain with a love of country and a dedication' to its 'role in the world which owes nothing to any cash nexus'. In 1962 Wilson condemned Britain's increasing involvement, on apparently disadvantageous terms, with the richer continental European countries. 'Now we look nervously over our shoulder to see what an eighty-six-year-old Chancellor says about us on German television', Wilson complained; and he added 'this country is getting a little tired of being pushed around.' At the 1962 Party conference Gaitskell condemned the government's proposal to seek membership of the European Economic Community, which, he said, meant 'the end of Britain as an independent . . . state'. 'It means the end of a thousand years of history', Gaitskell concluded. Labour, on the contrary, the Party leaders claimed, were about to open a new chapter in the thousand years of history, by creating what the 1963 policy document *Labour and the Scientific Revolution* called 'our national revival'. By 1964, when Wilson finally formed a Labour government, circumstances did not seem to favour such a revival. Yet a traditional British spirit would, it was hoped, overcome all outward difficulties. 'They misjudged our temper after Dunkirk', the new Labour prime minister told an enthusiastic Party conference, 'but we so mobilized' our 'strength that apparent defeat was turned into

[1] Labour Party *Conference Report*, 1954, p. 66; Norman Mackenzie (ed.), *Conviction*, London, 1958, pp. 12, 15.

a great victory. I believe that that spirit of Dunkirk will once again carry us through to success.'[1]

The 'authentic patriotic faith in our future' which the 1964 Labour election Manifesto promised to 'rekindle' was, however, a somewhat ambiguous creed. On the one hand, Labour made its commonplace appeals to manual wage earners' sectionalism. It was the *Conservatives'* fault that Britain was sunk in 'economic stagnation', and a 'dangerous national nostalgia'; the *upper classes* had enforced on an unwilling people the 'thirteen wasted years' that succeeded the 1951 general election; *capital* had failed to invest and to raise productivity, and had favoured the 'stop-go cycle' of inflation and deflation; and the pressures of 'the most snobbishly class-conscious society in the world' had inhibited advances in every sphere of national life. On the other hand, the Party proffered the somewhat novel suggestions that society was a collectivity; that blame for its faults fell, if in different measure, on all; and that correction of these faults could not be achieved solely by Labour government, increased social security, smaller defence forces, and higher wage awards. 'Our approach must not be what we can take out of the national pool, but what we can put into it', Wilson warned the 1964 Party conference. 'For only by a massive sense of dedication by every individual can we get the national sense of purpose that we need.' The idea that there could be a 'national purpose' this side of 'socialism' was a distinctly collectivist idea: and as such it consorted ill with Labour's cherished individualism.[2]

This ambiguity was well reflected in Michael Shanks's *The Stagnant Society*, which appeared in 1961, and which perhaps influenced Labour thinking in the 1960s no less than the doctrines presented in Crosland's *Future of Socialism* influenced Labour's thinking in the 1950s. As Shanks's title indicates, he, like many in the Labour Party, identified Britain as a 'stagnant society', failing to achieve the social and economic advances, not so much of Germany and France—whose successes Labour nationalism found too exasperating to be worth emulation—but of Sweden, which had long enjoyed the benefits of Social

[1] Labour Party *Conference Report*, 1961, p. 102; 1962, pp. 91, 159; 1963, p. 274; 1964, p. 112.
[2] Ibid., 1958, p. 78; 1964, p. 112; Jenkins, *Labour's Case*, pp. 9, 11; *Let's Go with Labour*, p. 23.

Democratic government. There were, Shanks claimed, 'economic techniques' which could bring Britain closer into line with Sweden; but 'at present' 'social, psychological and political frictions' were 'stopping the economic techniques from working effectively'. Shanks, like others, mistaking sectionalism based on utilitarian individualism for a class-consciousness attributable to some island version of Marxism, argued that British society was 'stagnant' because it was 'class-ridden'. Trade unionists and others might thus conclude that Shanks proposed to abolish Conservative government, the upper classes, capital, and niggardly employers, on the way to the Swedish style of 'socialism'. However, Shanks devoted much of his book to a vigorous attack on the trade unions, which were, he claimed, 'in many people's opinion, the greatest institutional barrier to Britain's becoming a genuinely dynamic society'. '*The unions*', he warned, '*are too often proving themselves the natural allies of the forces of stagnation and conservatism.*' In order to resolve this difficulty, Shanks proposed that managers should 'try to create a community spirit among their workers'; and that governments should attack the persistent 'antithesis of "We" and "They" ', which was 'one of the main deterrents to an efficient, dynamic industrial system'. Yet a managerially-promoted 'community spirit', not to speak of a government-led attack on the 'antithesis' between individuals and groups (which was held by liberal individualists to be the inevitable characteristic of a free society), would, no matter what abundance they promised, at once threaten the social principles dearest to both the industrial and the political organization of labour.[1]

Shanks' equivocation was necessarily imitated by Labour leaders. 'Through our domestic policies,' said Wilson in 1964, 'there run three golden threads: dynamism, compassion and concern for the liberty of the individual.' 'Liberty of the individual' meant a suitable preservation of the *laissez-faire* tradition, especially in the 'voluntary system of industrial relations', or 'free collective bargaining'; 'compassion' meant economic redistribution: and neither seriously offended against Labour's current version of the liberal individualist tradition. 'Dynamism', on the other hand, might or might not so offend. Under this heading, Labour proposed to create, in the words of

[1] Shanks, pp. 67–8, 93, 155, 158–9.

the 1958 policy document *Plan for Progress*, 'a dynamic economy'. Labour would 'energize and modernize our industries'—as the 1964 election manifesto had it—and thereby achieve a rapid growth of productivity and expansion of production.[1]

Now Labour leaders sometimes suggested that rapid economic growth could be achieved by a mixture of government investment and innovation that would prove quite painless, at least to Labour supporters. Wilson promised 'a Socialist-inspired scientific and technological revolution releasing energy on an enormous scale'. The 'scientific revolution' was to be completed without any inconvenience to trade unionists. 'What is science?' Frank Cousins asked himself. It was, he concluded, 'a vision with its working clothes on': and the 'vision' was the material abundance and/or equality of 'socialism', while the 'working clothes' were those of the white-coated expert who would secure those benefits by his own almost unaided efforts. But, at other times, Labour leaders hinted that rapid growth could not be achieved without a collective effort costly to all the people. 'The Britain that is going to be forged in the white heat of this revolution', said Wilson in 1963, 'will be no place for restrictive practices', or 'outdated methods on either side of industry'. Roy Jenkins stressed another aspect of the problem. 'Our bias must be for investment and against consumption', he told the 1958 Party conference. 'There is bound to be', he added, 'a degree of moderation in wage . . . demands.' Such talk as this (which was highly unacceptable to the trade unions) tended to be summarized in pledges to protect the existing relationship between sterling and other currencies, a relationship which possessed no clear-cut advantages for the British economy, yet could symbolize the British 'revival' for which Labour professed to be planning. 'The strength of the pound will be the first priority of our external policy', Wilson promised in 1958; and six years later, on taking office, he declared that the Labour government would 'take every measure' necessary 'ruthlessly to protect the pound'.[2]

[1] Labour Party *Conference Report*, 1964, p. 110; *Plan for Progress, Labour's Policy for Britain's Economic Expansion*, London, 1958, p. 5; *Let's Go with Labour*, p. 8.
[2] Labour Party *Conference Report*, 1958, pp. 143, 157; 1960, p. 151; 1963, pp. 140, 145; 1964, p. 112.

THE NEW LEFT

While Labour revisionism was transforming itself into Labour nationalism—and thereby opening up various possibilities of conflict between those Labour politicians who were enamoured of the apparent new collectivism, and those trade unionists who remained loyal to the latent old individualism—a rather different type of politics was also emerging on the left. These politics were expressed in what Ralph Samuel called the 'distinctively new pattern of socialist ideas' championed by a 'New Left', renewing the 'socialist tradition', and 'reaffirming the humanist, utopian and revolutionary elements' of that tradition. The New Left was from the first composed almost entirely of young intellectuals, who acquired their political convictions under the direct influence of one or more of the events of 1956: the sudden threat of nuclear war, the discrediting of Soviet Communism, and the Suez fiasco. 'The real growing points of socialism', wrote a New Left leader in 1959, were to be found in groups which shared something of 'the same spirit which moved people from Aldermaston to London last Easter, something of the anger at Hungary', and 'something of the outrage of . . . Suez'. These groups included members of the Campaign for Nuclear Disarmament, which organized Easter protest marches to or from the Atomic Weapons Research Establishment at Aldermaston; those recent ex-Communists who voiced their disillusion with 'Stalinism' in the periodical *The New Reasoner*; and the students and others who ran the *Universities and Left Review*, a publication which, as one of its editors put it, particularly appealed to 'the "scholarship boy" generation, who felt that without the serious stimulus of socialism they would lose their way for good in the lower reaches of Mr. Macmillan's Opportunity State'. Little by little, the New Left was to ramify into the Maoist International Marxists, the Trotskyist International Socialists, the eclectic readership of the *New Left Review*, and so on. Yet even in the mid-1970s, the movement preserved much of the distinctive though complex identity it had already enjoyed twenty years earlier.[1]

The New Left, taken as a whole, comprised by far the most

[1] *Universities and Left Review*, Autumn 1958, p. 68; Autumn 1969, pp. 1–2.

highly educated, and perhaps the most intelligent, group yet to appear anywhere near British manual labour. It was characterized by a strong ethical strain which led it to speak much of an 'outrage' that could no longer be stifled by the prevalent 'apathy'; and to demand what Kenneth Alexander described as 'a moral revolution' based on 'moral revulsion' from 'existing values'. It emphasized 'the humanist strengths of socialism', and rejected 'politics, too narrowly conceived', for wider concerns that included the 'cultural' themes developed in Raymond Williams's *Culture and Society*, and later in E. P. Thompson's *The Making of the English Working Classes*. (Indeed the New Left's 'cultural' emphasis rapidly came to include a libertarianism—hitherto quite foreign to the British left's public stance—indicated, for example, by the study of works such as Nabokov's *Lolita* and Lawrence's *Lady Chatterley's Lover*.) The leaders of the New Left strongly disliked the Communist Party, which was 'tainted', as Peter Sedgwick put it, by its 'acquiescence in frame-up, murder, and all-round political thuggery'; yet, at the same time, they condemned the Labour revisionists. This hostility was expressed above all in two ways. On the one hand, New Left spokesmen accused the revisionists of a complacent indifference towards the 'state of profound inequality and deprivation' in which British society lingered. On the other hand, the New Left urged the case for an *ethical* change in man, an end to the alienation inseparable from capitalism, that could not be secured by any change in *material* circumstances. 'The original Marxist conception of exploitation', wrote Ken Coates in 1967, involved 'the alienation of the product of labour from . . . the labourer . . . *at whatever* level of "affluence"'. The 'whole essence' of alienation, Coates claimed, was 'the private control of public resources', which was inseparable from the present order of society and could only be abolished along with it.[1]

Especially in its early days, the New Left was rather distant from trade unionism; and it was perhaps congruent with this remoteness from organized labour that the movement should

[1] E. P. Thompson (ed.), *Out of Apathy*, London, 1960, pp. 4, 266; *Universities and Left Review*, Autumn 1959, p. 7; *New Left Review*, January–February 1960, pp. 5, 62–3; November–December 1960, pp. 32 ff.; Blackburn and Cockburn, pp. 8, 15, 65, 71, 244.

display evidences of a collectivist idealism unusual in British politics. For the New Left did not simply affirm the policies of nationalization and workers' control—policies which, after all, could readily assume a somewhat individualist cast—but very often expounded and defended these and other measures in arguments that owed very little to the indigenous tradition of British political thought. Coates, for example, could dismiss the 'naive assumption that democracy is about counting up the opinions of the people. It is not:' he declared, 'it is about liberating their energies and opening their horizons to the widest human limits. Majorities for us can never be merely counted up; they must, as Trotsky once said, be *won over.*' E. P. Thompson condemned the North Atlantic Treaty Organization as an agency designed not to 'build the good society', but to 'preserve a philosophical tradition which teaches that no society can ever be good'. In so far as 'the Labour Movement' failed to recognize this, Thompson observed, it merely proved itself to be 'hedged in by a narrow empiricism'. The New Left's goal was not Labour redistributionism, '*Not* an equality of opportunity within an acquisitive society', as Thompson put it, but, in Coates's words, the creation of 'a new style of man', free, rational and fearless, in the manner of Marxist utopianism. That goal was, moreover, to be reached through the distinctly un-British device of 'revolution'. On the practical level, the New Left became leading exponents of agitation, beginning with the 'direct action' tactics of the Committee of One Hundred, which grew out of the Campaign for Nuclear Disarmament, and culminating in the anti-American riot in Grosvenor Square in 1968. On the theoretical level, various New Left writers advocated a revolutionary conflict. Thompson, who wrote a good deal about revolution, hoped in 1960 for 'a revolutionary breakthrough' when the next Labour government withdrew from N.A.T.O.; and two Oxford economists close to the concerns of the New Left looked forward hopefully in 1972 to 'a successful revolutionary struggle' aimed at 'eliminating the capitalist system'.[1]

Yet not merely are such statements somewhat rare in New

---

[1] Ibid., p. 82; 'The Insiders', in *Universities and Left Review*, Winter 1958, *passim*; Thompson, pp. 3, 179–80, 307; Ken Coates, *Essays on Industrial Democracy*, Nottingham, 1971, p. 26; Glyn and Sutcliffe, p. 212.

Left writings, but they are readily offset by other statements which indicate, on the part of New Left theorists, a firm commitment to a pluralism irreconcileable with full collectivism. The collectivist (and the socialist, who is but one type of collectivist) sees society as an actual or potential whole, a 'totality', or an 'organic unity'; while the individualist (including the advocate of *laissez-faire*, and the liberal democrat, who are but types of individualist) sees society as an aggregate, a plurality. Most New Left writers appear to be pluralists in one sense or another. Thus E. P. Thompson used the seemingly pluralistic term 'Society of Equals' to describe his ideal society. Perry Anderson insisted that 'socialism is not a monist praxis, but unity in multiplicity'; and Ken Coates, focusing more closely on one institution of a socialist world, emphasized that '*Socialist* factories' can never be 'monolithic'. Such convictions could narrow the range of revolutionary theory and practice available to the New Left. Bob Rowthorn, for example, strongly condemned 'a situation where the State, party machinery, trade union bureaucracies' become 'subordinate to the dominant class' who 'have the power to discipline recalcitrant elements': a situation which Rowthorn equated with the state of affairs in Britain in the mid-1960s, but which also corresponds quite closely to that thoroughly collectivist state of affairs, the dictatorship of the proletariat.[1]

The nub of the matter is of course the position of trade unions in socialism. Perry Anderson hinted that he might support Lenin's highly unindividualistic view that under socialism unions must be 'educational organizations', 'schools of communism'; but Anderson also insisted that trade unions must 'preserve their autonomy under socialism'. Stuart Hall, Ralph Samuel, Peter Sedgwick and Charles Taylor wrote in *The Insiders*, an early New Left pamphlet, that though there must be 'democratic control' of 'hiring and firing' and the 'wage contract' in what they called socialist industry, 'any scheme for industrial democracy must allow for an area of conflict between workers and . . . management.' The International Socialist Tony Cliff later went so far as to argue, not merely that 'a revolutionary socialist programme' must 'assert

---

[1] Thompson, pp. 289–90; Blackburn and Cockburn, pp. 225, 280; Coates, *Essays on Industrial Democracy*, p. 24.

the primacy of rank and file control', at 'the workplace, in the union and towards the State', but that 'the "bloody-minded-ness" of the workers' is 'the embryo' of socialism. That would be a position entirely unacceptable to Lenin who, in October 1917, wrote a decree which made the 'elected delegates of the workers' in the factories 'answerable to the State for the maintenance of the strictest order and discipline' and for the protection of any property that might pass through their hands; and rendered them liable to up to five years' imprison-ment for 'neglect of duty'.[1]

It would be a position acceptable to trade unions, however, or at least so New Left writers seem to have hoped. The New Left was rather critical of unions. Rowthorn, for example, called them 'largely apolitical'; Tom Nairn spoke of their 'sclerotic conservatism'. E. P. Thompson included 'key indus-trial workers . . . striking blindly in their own interest' among the *'ultras'* who 'hold the community to ransom'; and Kenneth Alexander exclaimed, 'If only the unions would understand' that 'nationalization has broader, more social functions' (than furthering wage earners' immediate self-interest, that is). Yet the New Left, almost from the start, saw the unions as the high road to socialism. Blackburn and Cockburn declared that the unions must seek 'a *new political destiny*'; Nairn believed that 'the key area' in which 'new socialist ideas and a new socialist movement could grow up' must be 'trade unionism'; and Alexander stated that 'the growth-cone around which social development can take place is the trade union movement'. Calling the New Left back to what he termed 'the realities of class power in our time', Thompson, writing in 1959, claimed that 'the community to which we look forward is potential only within our working-class movement. The "power to compel" must always remain with the organized workers, but the intellectuals may bring them hope, a sense of their own strength and potential life'.[2]

[1] Blackburn and Cockburn, p. 280; *The Insiders*, p. 63, in *University and Left Review*, Winter 1958; Tony Cliff, *The Employers' Offensive, Productivity Deals and How to Fight Them*, London, 1970, pp. 203, 222; V. I. Lenin, *Selected Works*, London, 1936, vol. 6, pp. 410–11.
[2] Blackburn and Cockburn, pp. 11, 223; Anderson and Blackburn, pp. 208–9, 216; Thompson, pp. 13, 284; *Universities and Left Review*, Spring 1959, p. 55.

UNILATERALISM

Though by 1959 trade unions had been free for some years to utilize their own sectional ' "power to compel" ', materially unaffected by any ideas extraneous to their traditional *laissez-faire* liberalism, this tranquillity was then already being disturbed. In the first place, both the inconclusive revisionist debate and the wave of nationalism in the Labour Party had concentrated the unions' chief political allies' attention on the possibilities of economic expansion. While 'nationalization' was to be rejected as a symbol and a policy too divisive, too class-conscious for Labour, and withal quite obsolete in the modern world, 'growth' was a symbol and a policy that seemed capable of uniting all groups and all classes behind a Labour Party newly able to claim a monopoly of relevance to the needs and aspirations of the day. The unions feared and resisted the transition from 'nationalization', of which they had grown fond, and which seemed to cause them no complications, to a 'growth', the achievement of which, they suspected, depended more or less completely on a sacrifice of their own historic policy of more money for the same work. Hence, very largely, the conflict over Clause 4.

Moreover, the substance and circumstances of the break-up of the extreme left, in the aftermath of the Secret Speech and the Hungarian uprising, caused the unions a mass of new uncertainties. The growth of the New Left (and especially of the Campaign for Nuclear Disarmament, of course) intensified anxieties about nuclear warfare inside as well as outside trade unions; and, though the New Left's initial dearth of authentic wage earners excluded it from trade union leadership during its first decade of existence, its novel and in some ways more challenging brand of leftism did impress certain trade unionists who had long taken their left-wing doctrines solely from the now reassuringly familiar teachings of the British Communist Party. That Party, meanwhile, desired to regain the ground it had lost as a result of the schism of 1956 and, thereby, to strengthen its hold on organized labour and its ability to promote those anti-American, pro-Soviet propaganda campaigns which had become virtually its only political rationale. No more promising or appropriate strategy offered itself to the

Communists than to intensify their long-standing demands for western nuclear disarmament, a policy still highly acceptable to the Soviet Union, and now modishly attractive to British public opinion, thanks to the efforts of the Communists' arch-rivals in the New Left.

Virtually the same strategy commended itself to the New Left, desirous of extending its influence over trade unions; to the old-fashioned Labour left opposed both to revisionism and to nationalism; and to those trade unionists who wished to punish the Labour Party's leaders for their attack on Clause 4. Had the unions retained their interest, such as it was, in socialistic notions like workers' control, all these groups could have followed up the defence of Clause 4, by organizing the unions to oblige the Labour Party not merely to abide by the truce on the issue achieved in the spring of 1960, but positively to realize the principles of Clause 4 in new and far-reaching socialist measures. But in fact the unions had ceased to interest themselves in workers' control; appeared to care for little else than wage increases; and remained steeped in an apolitical industrial sectionalism, the 'apathy' so exasperating to their left-wing critics. However, some trade unionists (often in important positions) had long been used to anti-American sentiments, fostered by the Communist Party, and fed by the reputation among them of American companies, both in Britain and in the United States. The same trade unionists, and others, had also long subscribed to an 'anti-militarism' compounded of a belief that 'defence spending' lowered their pay and reduced social-security and health benefits; an un-changing hostility to conscription, a measure which they regarded as the practical repudiation of liberal individualism, and the harbinger of direction of labour; and a preference for 'collective security', 'world peace', 'disarmament', and similar legitimations of a desire to ignore threats from other nations. Thus, though a continued campaign for nationalization seemed unlikely to gain the trade unions' official support, organized labour might be committed to a policy of unilateral British nuclear disarmament, and the expulsion of American military personnel and American nuclear weapons from the United Kingdom. Such a policy might perhaps achieve the 'revolutionary breakthrough' anticipated by E. P. Thompson;

and would certainly strengthen the Communists' position in the unions; assist the Soviet Union; and embarrass Labour leaders who remained on the whole loyal to an independent British nuclear deterrent and a peacetime military alliance with the United States, policies which had been pioneered by the Attlee government.

By no means all trade unionists were anti-American, pacifist, or unilateralists. But this could scarcely affect official trade union policy. The full-time national officers of the Amalgamated Engineering Union, which seemed briefly to go unilateralist in 1960, were elected by about 10 per cent of the union's total membership (a rather large constituency by labour standards). This 10 per cent of members, meeting in branches, also elected delegates to district committees, which then elected from among their members delegates to divisional committees, which then elected from among their members delegates to the national policy-making body. In short, while the unions' national leaders were directly appointed—but by a fraction of the membership only—it was that fraction's delegates' delegates' delegates who selected the policies that the national leaders were to execute. This procedure might still produce a policy which reflected the views of a majority of the members if the policy was one about which members cared, and in defence of which they were likely to act: as would be the case, for example, were the policy to indicate whether the union's national leaders should demand eight shillings and five pence or eight shillings and six pence from the Engineering Employers' Federation. The procedure was, however, rather unlikely to produce a policy at all representative of members' views if that policy was one towards which members were indifferent: as was the case, for example, when the national policy-making body voted 38 to 14 for unilateral nuclear disarmament early in 1960. Nevertheless, just as the national leaders could claim the whole membership's support when demanding eight shillings and sixpence from the Engineering Employers, so they were empowered to cast hundreds of thousands of votes in favour of unilateral nuclear disarmament when they attended the Trades Union Congress.

In September 1960, as a result of deliberations such as these, the Trades Union Congress carried by 52 per cent a resolution for the 'complete rejection of any defence policy based on the threat of the use' of nuclear weapons. The following month, thus encouraged, the trade unions carried this resolution through the Labour Party Conference by just over 50 per cent; and the Conference also voted 54 per cent in favour of a resolution brought in by the Engineers for 'the unilateral renunciation of the testing, manufacture, stock-piling and basing of all nuclear weapons in Great Britain'. This pleased the Soviet Union, the Communists, the New Left, and a large part of the Labour left. It did not please the Labour right, nor a certain part of the Labour left, who agreed that the Party's new commitment to unilateralism arose, not from a widespread and significant conviction among Party and trade union members that Britain should unilaterally renounce nuclear weapons, but from certain trade unionists' ability to foist unilateralism first on the unions (by manipulation of their rather deficient internal machinery of representation), and then on the Trades Union Congress and the Labour Party Conference (by use of the card vote system, which simply translated money power into policy-making power). The upshot of this process seemed to be the most spectacular reassertion of union power over the Labour Party and its parliamentarians since 1931. 'The vast majority of Labour Members of Parliament are utterly opposed to unilateralism', Gaitskell told the Conference. 'So what do you expect them to do?' he asked. 'Change their minds overnight? To go back on the pledges they gave to the people who elected them . . .? I do not believe that the Labour Members of Parliament are prepared to act as time-servers.'[1]

Gaitskell pledged himself to resist the Conference decision; and this he and his friends did, working through the Party and the trade unions by various means, including the organization of the Campaign for Democratic Socialism, the facilities of Industrial Research and Information Service Limited, and the activity of Catholic trade unionists. The results were quite striking. In January 1961, a joint conference of the Parliamentary Labour Party, the Labour Party National Executive Committee and the General Council of the Trades Union Congress produced a document called *Policy for Peace*, which

[1] Trades Union Congress *Report*, 1960, p. 408; Labour Party *Conference Report*, 1960, pp. 176–7, 201–2.

stated that 'we cannot renounce nuclear weapons so long as the Communist bloc possesses them'. Various unions then changed their policies; and in September 1961 the Trades Union Congress voted 74 per cent against 'unilateral disarmament by Britain' and in favour of *Policy for Peace*. The following month, as a matter of course, the Labour Party Conference voted 72 per cent in favour of *Policy for Peace* and 69 per cent against the 'complete rejection of any defence policy based on the threat of the use of . . . nuclear weapons'.[1]

In this way the centre and right-wing of the Parliamentary Labour Party foisted nuclear deterrence back on the trade unions: which then speedily foisted it back on the Labour Party conference. *Policy for Peace* could claim to be less unreal and less unrepresentative than the unilateralism of the previous year solely on the ground that, though the one constituted an outcome no less contrived than the other, *Policy for Peace* did coincide more closely with the views of most Labour parliamentarians, voters, and even party members, than did unilateralism. To this extent *Policy for Peace*, however secured, was a victory for common sense, if not for democracy. Moreover, the Trades Union Congress and Labour Party conference decisions of 1961 did leave the parliamentarians at least in control of themselves, though very probably not (in any important sense) of the trade unions: and to this extent *Policy for Peace* was a victory for the parliamentarians' Labour nationalism, which might otherwise have become even weaker than it eventually proved to be. Yet, whatever the substantive merits of unilateralism, the unilateralist episode did show the Labour Party to be prey to policies determined not by the thoughts and beliefs of its members and supporters, but by the almost arbitrary outcome of semi-secret power struggles within the associations that paid most of its bills. On the one hand, the consistency, the authority even, of the Labour Party seemed to disappear, because its politics seemed to be little more than a fortuitous importation from without; and on the other hand, the trade unions, without which the Labour Party would not exist, displayed, in their apparent choice and changes of policy

[1] Irving Richter, *Political Purpose in Trade Unions*, London, 1973, p. 145; Trades Union Congress *Report*, 1961, p. 435; Labour Party *Conference Report*, 1961, pp. 7–8, 194.

an inconsequence, a levity even, which suggested either that (as their friends might say) they were not political organizations at all or that, if they were, they were political organizations (as their enemies might say) of a culpable eccentricity.

PLANNING, PRODUCTIVITY, AND INCOMES POLICY

This was a matter of grave consequence, given the very serious domestic as well as foreign issues that Labour was required to ponder in the post-Suez era, and to deal with as a governing party from 1964 onwards. By about 1960, changes in world economic conditions, the shock of Suez, and the rapid expansion into Britain's export markets, not merely of the Federal Republic of Germany, but of France also, caused a reconsideration of British economic policy. The 'demand management' approach, which seemed so rewarding earlier in the 1950s, was held, after Suez, to have produced or permitted Shanks' 'stagnant society'. Certainly the gross national product was growing not merely rather slowly but at an ever slower rate. Furthermore, as so many politicians and economists had so long pointed out, demand management, full employment, and no restraint on collective bargaining produced an inflation that bore particularly heavily on the price of British manufactured exports. Between 1941 and 1950, for example, adult male earnings in metals, engineering and shipbuilding rose 44 per cent; but between 1950 and 1959 they rose 79 per cent. Increases of this magnitude could not be matched by increases in the productivity of wage earners in those industries.

The vague and general response to these problems was to look abroad. The French were thought to have derived much of their economic success from procedures known as 'indicative planning'. The Conservatives, led by a prime minister whose economic radicalism had begun in the 1930s, were encouraged by this unimpeachably capitalist if gallic form of interventionism; and they encouraged both civil servants and academics to investigate the possibilities of a British 'plan'. What 'planning' proved to mean in Britain was not much more than 'cost management', so to speak, or 'supply management'—and in particular the management of the supply of labour. There were pressing though not perhaps good reasons for this development. British interest in planning initially arose from a decline in exports, which was attributed to high prices, rather than lack of production, poor quality or bad design. Whereas greater production, higher quality or better design might well be achieved only by a degree of intervention that the government and public opinion disliked, distrusted, and in the last resort despised, lower prices *might* be secured by a species of 'management' not at all more interventionist than the 'demand management', which government and public opinion had come to know and even perhaps to love, but which was designed chiefly to secure high prices. To lower prices, it was necessary to lower costs; and since the input of fuel, raw materials, and capital equipment formed so small a proportion of the value of British exports, to lower total production costs meant, more than anything else, to lower labour costs. This could be done in two ways. The amount of work done for each pound of wages could be relatively or absolutely increased, or the amount of wages paid for each unit of work could be relatively or absolutely decreased.

In the 1930s, Labour had used the concept of 'planning' mainly to legitimate the specific nationalization schemes then being drafted by the Trades Union Congress. In the 1960s, 'planning' came to signify, first of all, 'talks': conferences, councils and so forth, between employers, employers and government, employers and trade union leaders, or all three. These talks were called for the general purpose of exchanging views on the likely future cost and character of British production. They were also called for the particular purpose of airing proposals on reducing production costs. Cost reduction by increases in work done—through introduction of shift working, new machines and lay-outs, more flexible practices, and so forth—was thought to be too technical for a government which was, in any event, debarred by force of custom and principle from the sort of activities which would enable it to influence cost reduction of this type. Such matters were therefore left to 'productivity bargaining' between employers and unions. But cost reduction by absolute or relative decreases in wages paid was regarded as an aim that could be achieved by measures not at all unlike those of demand management. These matters were therefore lumped together as the content of an 'incomes policy' which government would determine with or without negotiations with interested parties. Just what 'productivity bargaining' and 'incomes policy' meant, and in what manner and proportion they made up 'planning', was naturally subject to dispute; and, as naturally, those nearest to the unions tended to emphasize productivity rather than incomes. 'In a full employment economy', Gaitskell warned the 1961 Labour Party conference, 'there is a problem if incomes outrun the rise in productivity.' 'There are two ways of dealing with it', he claimed. 'You can . . . try to curb the rise in incomes; but you can do something else—you can try to increase productivity.' The Government's policy, he complained, was 'concentrated on curbing incomes', instead of 'concentrating, as they should, on increasing productivity'.[1]

Yet, however one interpreted or arranged 'planning' (on which Labour, not surprisingly, thought it ought to have something of a rightful monopoly), the term did raise some difficult issues of principle both for Labour politicians and for trade union leaders. Many of those difficulties were problems that arose from the relationship between planning (almost any sort of planning) and labour egalitarianism. That egalitarianism was, of course, asymmetrical: in other words, it established, in the minds of those who subscribed to it, the doctrine that one should get what others have, but that one should not lose what one has. This doctrine meant, among other things, that, while everyone tried to get what wages he could, lower-paid workers always demanded—by reference to the cost of living, their underrated skills, and so on—more money relative to higher-paid workers; and higher-paid workers always demanded—by reference to their 'differentials'—more money relative to lower paid workers. As George Brown put it in 1965, 'we have been operating the law of the jungle ourselves while condemning it for every other purpose'. An 'incomes policy' was soon thought to be inimical to the 'law of the jungle', because while that 'law' allowed all workers to demand what they liked (and exact what they could), the 'policy'—were it successful—might prevent some workers from getting much if anything, whatever their demands. Thus, for example, were the policy so devised as to allow the whole labour force only a very small

[1] Ibid., 1961, p. 151.

aggregate increment, that total might need to be given almost entirely to lower-paid workers (thereby narrowing higher-paid workers' differentials), simply in order to enable lower-paid workers to subsist in conditions of continuing increases in the price of the necessities of life. 'Some of our people have got to hold back, whilst some others go forward, but that, after all,' Brown declared, 'is the basis of Socialist belief.' Perhaps, however, he over-estimated labour's adherence to 'Socialist belief'. Jack Cooper, leader of the mainly lower-paid General and Municipal Workers, observed in 1967 that there were some people who 'mouth Socialism but are not prepared to hold those who are doing damned well back for a little while, so those who are worse off have a chance.'[1]

The tendency of the 'law of the jungle' to favour certain workers irrespective of their merits and claims, and the tendency of an incomes policy to modify such favouritism, was a problem the discussion of which left trade unionists rather unhappy. They were much more eager to debate the affront that incomes policy gave to another doctrine of their egalitarianism, namely the doctrine that all employees should get whatever they could from their employers. The trade union attitude was given neat if not original expression by Len Murray, General Secretary of the Trades Union Congress, who stated in June 1974 that 'the only long-term incomes policy we are interested in is . . . "More".' In this light, 'planning' seemed hostile to wage earners, *in toto*. The International Socialists Cliff and Barker asserted that '*capitalist planning*' was 'planning directed against the workers and their interests'. Incomes policy, Cliff argued, was 'aimed at forcing workers to abandon the straight wage claim in favour of a Productivity Deal' designed to make 'workers pay, by working harder, under worse conditions, for their wage increases.' Acquiescence in deals such as those to which Cliff alluded seemed highly unacceptable to trade unionists after more than a decade of apparently successful sectionalism. 'The members pay those who they have elected to lead them', the Boilermakers' leader Danny McGarvey told the 1966 Trades Union Congress. 'They pay us . . . to see that they get decent wages', he said, 'They do not pay trade union leaders to . . . line up with those

[1] Ibid., 1965, p. 227; 1967, p. 185.

who are prepared either to freeze or cut back the standard of living.'[1]

'Planning', 'productivity', and 'incomes policy', therefore, all had an unpleasing sound to trade unionists in the late 1950s and the 1960s. Yet trade unionists were pressed on all sides—by Labour nationalists as well as by Conservatives—to befriend these terms; while various critics readily pointed out what they held to be the drawbacks (even for trade unionists) in the current 'free-for-all': the relatively low level of national wealth, the apparent unfairness of certain wage earners' remuneration, the difficulty of finding resources to extend the social services. Trade unions responded to such pressures by alleging their willingness to co-operate in the new economic policies, while demanding some obscurely impossible concession as the price of their co-operation. Thus, for example, Bob Willis, a printers' leader, agreed, at the 1963 Trades Union Congress, that there could be 'sacrifices on the wages side' in 'a planned economy'. But, he added, 'it has to be a planned economy. It has to be one with which we are satisfied'. At the same Congress, Frank Cousins declared that, 'when we have achieved a measure of planning and a Socialist Government, and if I have to say to my members, "we must now exercise restraint", I will say it and when I say it, I will mean it.' As, on another occasion, Cousins indicated that, for him, 'Socialism' meant 'getting the rights of the workers adequately presented to the employers', the precise role of 'restraint' under 'a Socialist Government' is not easy to see. But Cousins' conditional promise seems in any event to have signified little: for he stated, elsewhere in his speech to the 1963 Congress, that 'we will not have wage restraint, whoever brings it and wraps it up for us'.[2]

Beside these egalitarian doubts about 'planning', 'productivity', and 'incomes policy', the new ideas raised considerable difficulties for organized labour's continuing *laissez-faire* libertarianism. The Trades Union Congress General Council's 1963 statement *Economic Development and Planning* did note that 'planning will to some extent limit the rights of individuals and

---

[1] *The Guardian*, 13 June 1974; Cliff and Barker, p. 7; Cliff, pp. 3, 21; Trades Union Congress *Report*, 1966, p. 474.

[2] Ibid., 1963, pp. 399, 402; Labour Party *Conference Report*, 1968, p. 123.

groups to act selfishly and in accordance with what they regard as their own interests', for 'Democracy itself involves giving up lesser freedoms for more important freedoms'. Yet even this highly uncharacteristic document warned that 'the fact of democracy itself sets limits to the planning process.' That theme was very popular with both Labour Party and trade union leaders. The government should work out 'targets of production and of exports', Gaitskell told the 1961 Labour Party conference. But he added, 'We have certainly got to get this agreed; it is no use dictating that kind of thing from Whitehall. . . . If you have a dictatorship you can order people about. . . . But we are not that sort of society and we shall not succeed in . . . planning unless we have full co-operation from both sides of industry.' In similar vein, George Brown vindicated his 'National Plan', published in 1965, by stating that 'It isn't a Plan to tell us what to do and when and how. That wouldn't be acceptable to a nation like ours.' And when Joe Gormley, the Mineworkers' president was invited to defend his union's epochal strike against the Conservative government's attempt to enforce its incomes policy in 1974, he asked, 'Who are they as a government to say what should be the wages of men who work at the coal face five days a week? Who are they to lay down the law in this democratic society we have?"[1]

Organized labour demanded that all 'planning' should be voluntary, if not optional, for one extremely simple reason. Any other type of planning would destroy both the purpose and the identity of trade unionism, as trade union leaders saw it. An incomes policy 'can constitute a very dangerous exercise for the trade unions', warned a Constructional Engineer in 1964, 'in so far as it sets aside the basic and historic role of the unions in fighting to secure wage increases on behalf of their members'. In that credo, the 'fighting' is as important as the 'wage increases'. 'There is always more satisfaction with a settlement which the two parties themselves agree is fair than there would have been . . . if the same settlement was made for them by the Government', explained Feather in his book

---

[1] Trades Union Congress *Report*, 1963, p. 486; Labour Party *Conference Report*, 1961, pp. 153–4; Department of Economic Affairs and Central Office of Information, *Working for Prosperity, The National Plan in Brief*, London, 1965, p. 2; *The Times*, 23 January 1974.

The Essence of Trade Unionism. Labour leaders are united on this one point, if on no other, that 'free trade unions' engaged in 'free collective bargaining' are fundamental to what they hold dear in politics. 'Statutory enforcement of wage and salary levels' was 'unacceptable to free men, freely bargaining in a free society', Clive Jenkins told the 1965 Party conference. Speaking of 'free collective bargaining' to the same audience, McGarvey reminded his fellow Party members that when a government 'takes that basic principle from democracy . . . democracy no longer exists'. A year later Cousins warned the Party that 'you cannot have a social democracy and at the same time control by legislation the activity of a free trade union Movement which is an essential part of that social democracy', and must therefore always be 'outside the realms of the law'.[1]

In view of the convictions of men like Jenkins, McGarvey and Cousins, even politicians allegedly committed to the 'common ownership' and 'popular administration and control' of the economy, as Clause 4 has it, had to tread warily when they came to implement their notions of 'planning'. At first they hoped precisely to 'plan' on a 'voluntary' basis, and to preserve all *laissez-faire* dogmas intact. People 'should regard wage agreements as sacrosanct', Callaghan told an approving Party conference in 1961. Four years later, after twelve months' responsibility for planning, George Brown could insist that, 'we are not proposing, nor will I ever have a hand in, legislation' to 'prevent negotiations freely taking place'. Within another twelve months, however, Brown, conceding the logical impossibility of so-called planning on a voluntary basis (the essence of which was the free activity of that which was to be planned) resorted to legislation very like that which he eschewed in 1965. In this way, said Cousins, the government began drifting 'into the totalitarian type of control'. By 1968 McGarvey, now fully aware of the significance of planning as conceived by the nationalist leadership of the Labour Party, was complaining that the 'oft worn phrase that the Government must govern' was becoming 'so repetitious that one is beginning to think that we are in Portugal or Spain or Eastern

[1] Trades Union Congress *Report*, 1964, p. 450; Feather, p. 9; Labour Party *Conference Report*, 1965, pp. 474, 482; 1966, p. 463.

Europe'. The 'foreignness' of it all, at least to organized labour, had already been taken up by George Woodcock in a speech to trade union executives in March 1967. In 'a Communist system where everything was regulated', observed Woodcock, '. . . you might say "We will have a . . . tight control of labour." I would not like it, and'—empiricist trump card of the liberal-individualist argument—'I do not think it would work anyhow.'[1]

The British attempt at 'planning' could be, given these attitudes, nothing else than a disastrous anticlimax. That attempt began with the Conservatives' renewed efforts during 1957–8 to slow down the rate of wage increases. In 1957 the government was defeated by a strike for higher wages in engineering; but in 1958 it succeeded in defeating a strike by the London busmen, who, said Jack Jones, on behalf of the Transport and General Workers' Union, were fighting against 'Government interference in collective bargaining and for the right of all our lads to share equally in any wage increase'. In July 1957, the government, following a recommendation of the Court of Inquiry into the engineering dispute, set up a Council on Prices, Productivity, and Incomes, chaired by Lord Cohen. Though merely instructed to review and report on changes in prices, productivity, and incomes, the Council soon aroused labour's hostility. 'To accept such a court' would 'spell the end of free collective bargaining and would put trade unionism into cold storage', McGarvey warned. The government allowed the Council to lapse in 1958, and did nothing further to halt wage increases till the sterling crisis of mid-1961 led it to introduce a 'pay pause'. The government also established a National Economic Development Council, whose title and scope were hoped to be sufficiently ill-defined to inveigle the Trades Union Congress into membership of, if not co-operation with, it. Congress refused to join the Council until the pay pause was ended; and condemned the pause, which was abandoned in December 1961. Congress then provided members for the National Economic Development Council which first met in May 1962. Were the Council to realize the goals of 'planning', incomes must be controlled; and

[1] Ibid., 1961, p. 95; 1965, p. 228; 1966, p. 222; 1968, p. 125; George Woodcock, *Incomes Policy*, n.p., n.d., p. 10 (Bodleian Library).

the government, having at least got the unions into the National Economic Development Council, appointed in July 1962 a National Incomes Commission, charged with the task of inquiring into wage claims in the light of the public interest. The government had also tried to replace the 'pay pause' with a 'guiding light' of $2\frac{1}{2}$ per cent wage increases; but this light was put out by the 1962 docks wage award of 9 per cent. Meanwhile, the cause of planning gained extra credit from the 'productivity package deal' settled at the Esso refinery at Fawley in July 1960, and celebrated in Allan Flanders's *The Fawley Productivity Agreements*, first published in 1964. The deal, wrote Flanders, would provide 'large increases' in pay 'in return for the unions' consent to certain defined changes in working practices that were hampering a more efficient utilization of labour'.[1]

By 1964 the Labour Party had for some time felt the need to follow as best it could the lead given by Conservative Ministers and by firms such as Esso. However, the trade unions' response to the Cohen Council and the National Incomes Commission made the Party cautious. As Crossman had put it in 1955, 'The success or failure of the next Labour Government will very largely depend on the readiness of the trade union leaders to adapt' to 'the requirements of a democratically planned society'; and that 'readiness' would not be increased by annoying trade unions years before Labour had even won a general election. Labour leaders therefore never mentioned a 'policy', let alone 'restraint', but spoke merely of a 'climate' in which unions would, so to speak, voluntarily plan along with government. Gaitskell told the 1958 Party conference that 'we do not want . . . a wage-freeze, but we do not want a wages spree either'. 'We believe', he said, 'that through our policy we can create a climate in which the unions would in their own interests be prepared to work with the Labour Government so that wages and productivity go up together.' The 'climate' which would thus brace the unions to their task would, naturally, include a Labour government, but it would also include all the good such a government would do, especially by way of

---

[1] Trades Union Congress *Report*, 1957, p. 439; 1958, p. 435; Allan Flanders, *The Fawley Productivity Agreements, A Case Study of Management and Collective Bargaining*, London, 1966, p. 13.

'social justice'. It was of course true, in a rather banal tactical sense, that unions would find it more difficult to attack a government formed from 'their own' party rather than one formed from what some trade unionists liked to call the 'class enemy': although the difference is perhaps a fine one. Yet it was a mistake to imagine that trade union leaders would feel noticeably beholden to a Labour government for measures of 'social justice' which they thought to be theirs by rights anyway; and 'climate' in this sense (rather than, say, a determined effort to change men's minds) has proved to serve strikingly little purpose.[1]

In any event, Labour leaders became disenchanted with the virtues of 'climate' long before they got back into government. With a certain prescience as to the practical meaning of the 'climate' approach, Gaitskell warned in 1961 that it was 'no use preaching ... planning, and when you get it ... practising anarchy. That way lies disaster ... both for ourselves and for our country.' By 1962 Callaghan could tell the Party conference that one of the conditions for 'real growth' was an 'incomes policy', though not 'wage restraint'. In 1963 the General Council of the Trades Union Congress announced the Copernican discovery that, in conditions of full employment, 'it is possible for incomes to get so out of line with output as to raise costs and prices'. The General Council also proposed to inform the Congress that it was necessary 'to ensure that money incomes' rose 'less rapidly than in the past'; though, under pressure from affiliated unions, Council members amended this formula to a more 'climate'-, and less 'policy'-, oriented acknowledgement of 'the desirability of creating a situation in which money incomes' did not rise 'more rapidly than output'. Congress voted 92 per cent to accept this amended statement; and a few weeks later the Party conference adopted a long composite resolution including provision for 'an incomes policy to include salaries, wages, dividends and profits'.[2]

Yet Labour had not, strictly speaking, adopted an 'incomes policy' by 1963, not least because, while the basic purpose of an

[1] Crossmann, *Planning for Freedom*, p. 70; Labour Party *Conference Report*, 1958, p. 170; 1961, p. 106.

[2] Ibid., 1961, p. 154; 1962, p. 219; 1963, pp. 189–90, 201; Trades Union Congress *Report*, 1963, pp. 491–2, 495.

incomes policy was to reduce wage costs, Labour had by no means agreed in 1963 whether, under its incomes policy, wages were to go down, stay still, or go up, either absolutely or relatively. As early as 1958 Cousins had said the unions did not accept 'a policy of wage restraint'. 'And we do not change our views . . .' he added, 'by a transference of government from one Party to another'. In 1961 he reaffirmed that, 'we are not willing to accept in any form, shape or disguise wage restraint'; and the 1963 Congress voted 52 per cent for a resolution that 'This Congress declares its complete opposition to any form of wage restraint'. These sentiments were then conveyed to the 1963 Party conference by various trade unionists, including the Shopworkers' leader Alfred Allen who warned delegates, just before they voted for an 'incomes policy', that 'wages is the life blood of the Trade Union Movement; it will be the life blood of the Trade Union Movement under a Tory Government or under a Labour Government.' Thus, though 'incomes policy' had become rather more fashionable by 1963, 'wage restraint' remained as unfashionable as ever. And, perhaps because they grasped this fact, Labour politicians described their new incomes policy as a policy for 'keeping prices down and planning incomes up'; for a 'planned growth of wages'; or for 'orderly growth of incomes and a more equitable distribution of the National Wealth'. Such phrases certainly did not threaten wage restraint; but they did not exactly promise reduction of wage costs either.[1]

When Labour was returned to power in 1964, however, the Party embarked on five years of what Peter Jenkins called 'prices and incomes diplomacy'. In December 1964, amid considerable publicity, government, employers' and union representatives signed a Declaration of Intent on Productivity, Prices and Incomes. A Prices and Incomes Board was established under the chairmanship of a Conservative ex-Member of Parliament, Aubrey Jones: who, trade unionists never tired of claiming, got £290 a week for the job, or slightly more than fifteen times the average male adult earnings in shipbuilding and engineering. For about a year and a half the government tried to operate a 'norm' of 3–3½ per cent increases all round;

[1] Ibid., pp. 396, 410, 495; Labour Party *Conference Report*, 1958, pp. 165–6; 1961, p. 97; 1963, pp. 189–90, 200; 1964, p. 148; 1965, p. 277.

but incomes rose nearly 10 per cent. Yet the Board had some effect. In seeking to lower labour costs, it took management's view of the value of different kinds of labour, and made great efforts to emphasize differentials. That is, it did try to remunerate more productive labour more highly than less productive. Trade unionists naturally responded by claiming, however implausibly, to be making a 'productivity deal' which made their labour more valuable. As Jones has since admitted, rather than see his Board 'flouted' by dissident unions, 'it seemed prudent' to endorse a settlement 'by "justifying" it on grounds of productivity'—in the hope that the deal would raise output per man-hour. In 1966, however, the government adopted two significant innovations. First, it introduced a system of compulsory reference of pay claims to the Board, an arrangement defended by Ray Gunter on the grounds that, 'we tried the voluntary system, but some would not play the rules of the game'. Secondly, together with the thoroughly deflationary 'July measures', the government ordered six months of 'freeze' followed by six months of 'severe restraint' on wages, a policy defended by Callaghan on the grounds that this 'might have been avoided' had there been 'complete fulfilment of the Declaration of Intent'. 'The Trade Union Movement was shocked and stunned' by these developments, as Harry Urwin of the Transport and General Workers put it in 1969. There was indeed what Jones called a 'further spread of the cult of "productivity bargaining" ' as unions evaded the 'severe restraint' of 1967; and, through these and other means, weekly wage earnings rose over 11 per cent between 1966 and 1968.[1]

The 1967 Trades Union Congress nevertheless disapproved even a cautious resolution favouring merely 'some planning and control of prices and incomes'; though the subsequent Party conference voted 60 per cent against a resolution, moved by McGarvey, condemning 'the present Prices and Incomes Policy which has been detrimental to the best interest of trade unionists and lower income groups'. Devaluation followed; deflationary measures were intensified; and by the autumn of

---

[1] Peter Jenkins, pp. 3, 8; Labour Party *Conference Report*, 1966, pp. 210–11, 244; 1969, p. 187; Aubrey Jones, *The New Inflation, The Politics of Prices and Incomes*, Harmondsworth, 1973, p. 82; Colin Crouch, *Class Conflict and the Industrial Relations Crisis*, London, 1977, pp. 123 ff.

1968 labour had lost any sympathy with 'incomes policy' that it might ever have had. Eighty-eight per cent of votes at the 1968 Trades Union Congress were cast for a resolution, moved by Cousins and seconded by Scanlon, rejecting incomes policy outright; and 82 per cent of votes at the following Party conference were cast, against the National Executive's recommendation, for a resolution calling for repeal of 'legislation restricting wage and salary movements', which had 'hindered both legitimate trade union activity and economic expansion'. The Wilson government tried to persist with a statutory $3\frac{1}{2}$ per cent ceiling on wage increases; but in 1969 the policy was abandoned, only to be succeeded by a highly inflationary 'wages explosion'.[1]

The new Conservative administration formed in June 1970 shunned and condemned a statutory incomes policy for nearly two and a half years. During November 1972 to February 1974, however, the Heath government, faced with ever-accelerating inflation, reversed its position, abandoned what had in fact been a bipartisan repudiation of all forms of 'planning', and introduced a three-stage incomes policy: first, a freeze; secondly, a ceiling of one pound a week plus 4 per cent per annum; and thirdly, a ceiling of 7 per cent plus flat rate 'threshold payments' to be introduced with each increase in the retail price index. It was in defence of 'stage three', challenged by the striking Mineworkers, that Heath called, and was defeated in, the first general election of 1974. The apparent humiliation of a government at the hands of a trade union was thus the sorry outcome of the effort, extending over more than fifteen years, to establish new types of governmental control over the British economy.

INDUSTRIAL DEMOCRACY

Just as organized labour was manifesting, in its triumphal opposition to 'incomes policy', the strength of the sectionalism that had succeeded to the early twentieth-century movement for workers' control, the doctrines of 'workers' control', and of its modern near-synonym 'industrial democracy' began to

---

[1] Trades Union Congress *Report*, 1967, pp. 528, 543; 1968, p. 572; Labour Party *Conference Report*, 1967, pp. 165, 201; 1968, pp. 122, 153.

arouse new interest in the world of labour. That interest can be overstated. One poll of trade unionists conducted in 1967 found little enthusiasm for 'workers' participation in management'; and a poll of full-time workers in organizations with twenty or more employees, conducted in 1974, indicated a positive desire for a 'bigger say in day-to-day running of the company', and 'workers having seats on the board', among only 19 and 3 per cent respectively of the sample surveyed. Moreover, the discussion of workers' control and industrial democracy in recent trade union and Labour Party conferences has been somewhat perfunctory. The chairman of the 1968 conference, for example, had to appeal for silence in what he reminded delegates was 'a very important debate' on a resolution for 'greater worker participation'. Nevertheless, new interest in these topics has been aroused among labour activists who, as the unilateralist episode shows, can wield a certain if rather illusory power by manipulating the defective representative machinery common to most labour organizations.[1]

Much of the revived interest in workers' control is due to the influence of the New Left. Lacking the single-mindedly pro-Soviet orientation of the Communist Party, the New Left felt a freedom to experiment within the existing structure of British society, even if this entailed some compromise with the principle of change by revolution adumbrated in the classic texts of Soviet communism. Many members of the New Left were bourgeois intellectuals much more anxious to promote and express 'values' in politics than were the rather less bourgeois members of the Communist Party, which had long devoted itself almost entirely to the militant cult of the pay-packet. Moreover, the 'humanist' emphases of the New Left led it to manifest these values in a sort of neo-Hegelian or young-Marxian concern with the 'alienation' of the labourer, the struggle to transcend which New Left scholars and propagandists tended to equate with the bolder passages of British labour history, notably pre-1920 syndicalism. Resurrecting the language of that period, New Leftists often spoke of

[1] Brian Lapping and Giles Radice, *More Power to the People, Young Fabian Essays on Democracy in Britain*, London, 1968; *The Times*, 13 January 1975; Labour Party *Conference Report*, 1968, p. 157; cf. Trades Union Congress *Report*, 1971, pp. 507–8.

a transformation of society to be achieved through the 'encroaching control' of powerful labour organizations such as those seen during 1914–20, or indeed since 1940. This glamorous reinterpretation of trade unionists' wage claims and other activities has enjoyed among trade unionists a vogue similar to that enjoyed by the Communists' 'revolutionary' propaganda in the 1920s and 1930s.[1]

About 1964, Ken Coates and others formed an Institute for Workers' Control based in Nottingham. After 1964, as numbers of wage earners' children began to graduate from universities, and the Trades Union Congress and its affiliates began to expand their research departments (not least to cope with the demands of 'planning'), young intellectuals of lower socio-economic origins and New Left views gained a certain influence over union policy through the briefs and position papers they wrote for national union leaders. Meanwhile older members of the New Left, a number of whom had gained senior posts in the universities, began to shape Labour Party policy documents, such as the 1967 Party report on *Industrial Democracy* (which was quite largely written by such men); and the new generation of trade union general and assistant secretaries, typified perhaps by Jack Jones and Hugh Scanlon, began to support New Left arguments, notably about workers' control.[2]

These developments soon influenced the course of Labour policy. At the 1965 Party conference, the National Executive agreed to set up a working party to study 'industrial democracy'; and in February 1966, Jack Jones, who chaired the working party's meetings, published in *Tribune* an article in which he advocated elected trade union representatives on company boards. About the same time, the General Council, prompted by David Lea of the Trades Union Congress research staff (who was later Secretary of Congress's Economic Department), agreed to include a general proposal for such 'worker directors' in its written evidence to the Royal Commission on Trade Unions and Employers' Associations. This was, the Council

---

[1] Thompson, p. 281.

[2] Coates, p. 32; Ken Coates and Wyn Williams (eds.), *How and Why Industry Must Be Democratised, Papers Submitted to the Workers' Control Conference (Nottingham, 30–31 March 1968)*, Nottingham, 1969, pp. 4, 68 ff., 163 ff.; Blackburn and Cockburn, pp. 156–7; Labour Party, *Report of the Labour Party Working Party on Industrial Democracy*, London, 1967, p. 5.

later noted, 'a major change in principle' in 'Congress's approach'. In 1967 the Labour Party Working Party on industrial democracy published its report advocating 'experiments' in 'workers' participation' and 'industrial democracy'. The 1968 Trades Union Congress carried by show of hands a resolution, moved by Jones, calling for 'a much wider degree of industrial democracy' through 'worker participation in management'; and the 1968 Party conference received a National Executive statement on 'Industrial Democracy' which declared that 'we favour experiments in placing representatives of the workers in a nationalized industry on the board of that industry'. In May 1974 the Labour government published a Green Paper, entitled *The Community and the Company*, which proposed the creation of supervisory boards of companies, one half of which would be representatives elected by the 'joint shop stewards' committee . . . in concert with the official trade union machinery'. In the autumn of 1974, the General Council carried through Congress a further statement on *Industrial Democracy*, which reaffirmed the proposal for 50 per cent of supervisory boards to be devoted to '*trade union representation*', by worker directors, who would be chosen 'via trade union machinery', remain able to continue 'lay or full time trade union work', and serve for two-year terms 'subject to recall and re-election'.[1]

These remarkable proposals, and the apparent transformation of policy that has produced them, are particularly favoured by white-collar unions: among which the National Association of Local Government Officers, the National Union of Public Employees, the Confederation of Health Service Employees, the Union of Post Office Workers, and the Association of Scientific, Technical and Management Staffs, have been the chief public spokesmen for the cause of 'industrial democracy'. On the other hand, the Electricians, the Engineers, the General and Municipal Workers, among other manual workers' unions, have been less enthusiastic: these three, in fact, carrying a resolution rejecting 'mandatory imposition of

[1] Blackburn and Cockburn, op. cit., pp. 156–7; *Working Party*, pp. 5, 7, 10; *Industrial Democracy, A Statement by the National Executive to the Annual Conference of the Labour Party*, London, 1968, p. 4; Lapping and Radice, p. 67; Trades Union Congress *Report*, 1968, pp. 531, 536; 1974, pp. 299–300, 306, 323–3; *The Times*, 30 May 1974; *Financial Times*, 27 January 1977.

supervisory boards with worker directors' at the same Congress that adopted the 1974 *Industrial Democracy* document.[1]

The white-collar unions' interest in 'industrial democracy' may not be unconnected with their members' possession of those clerical, not to say managerial, skills that are likely to make them (rather than the members of manual-workers' unions) preferred candidates for the proposed worker-directorships. If so, the white-collar unions' attitudes might be explained largely in terms of their desire to facilitate the professional advancement of their members, rather than in terms of a recent conversion to those corporatist or collectivist doctrines so long abhorred by unions. It is possible, too, that some very large unions of low-skilled manual workers might hope to offset their relative lack of industrial strength through the probable preponderance of their numbers in the factory ballots to be expected in schemes of industrial democracy. But certain manual wage earners may have supported industrial democracy out of social or political convictions. This could be because they believe that democratic principles require industrial changes of the sort proposed; and were these democratic principles the organicist or collectivist democratic principles of, say, Rousseau, or the Bolsheviks, this would indeed be a surprising change in the attitudes of British labour.

But there is some evidence that this is not so. Although manual wage earners are slow to specify the detail of the political theory that underlies whatever new interest they may have in workers' control, less hesitancy has been shown by certain Labour left-wingers who appear somewhat popular with, and undoubtedly appeal for the support of, the big manual trade unions. Chief among these left-wingers is Anthony Wedgwood Benn, who is openly and strongly committed to 'industrial democracy', and who has spoken much in varying contexts of 'the people', and 'democracy' generally. Benn's politics are scarcely organicist or collectivist, in a Rousseauesque or Bolshevik sense, however. Defending 'Marxism' in the Labour Party, in a statement to the National Executive Committee, Benn displayed his acquaintance with the works of authors such as Professor Nathaniel Micklem, 'the distinguished

[1] Labour Party *Conference Report*, 1967, pp. 254–61; Trades Union Congress *Report*, 1970, pp. 572–3; 1971, pp. 507–8; 1974, pp. 524, 526, 528.

Congregational preacher', but offered not a single word from Marx, whose views he illustrated by citing Laski's opinion that, 'the preservation of individuality' is 'the central aim of any ethic that Marxism can endorse'. Thus Benn claims that socialism is 'a study of the power structure, and the creation of countervailing powers'; and he values above all 'the idea of democratic self-government' most fully realized in Britain and the United States, where the 'same strong democratic pulse' is 'at work'. The United States constitution, with its Lockeian and even utilitarian principles, is, in Benn's view, 'fully democratic'; and 'the broad Atlantic' is 'a bridge uniting' British and American politics 'as one', while 'the English Channel is an almost unbridgeable gulf dividing us from the concepts of government' in the ascendant in continental Europe, and 'embodied in the Treaty of Rome'. Now were trade unionists to persist in such assumptions as these, as they seem to do, their attitudes to workers' control would remain consonant with the principles of liberal individualism; and would nowhere approach even the rather tentative collectivism embodied in German *Mitbestimmung*—let alone the Japanese 'life-long contract'.[1]

In any event, British manual workers seem as ready as ever to stay true to liberal individualism in the sense of holding almost no political principle that cannot be reduced to egoistic pursuit of material self-interest. Speaking for the National Executive at the 1968 Labour Party conference, the Foundry Workers' leader Bill Simpson vigorously upheld the democratic principles to which industry, he claimed, must at long last conform. 'I believe passionately', he said, 'that it is wrong that as soon as a works gate closes behind a worker the portcullis also comes down on his right as a citizen.' The Party's proposals for industrial democracy were, Simpson argued, 'our only chance of success' in creating the new kind of citizenship that was required; and, were these proposals to be realized, 'when we sit down . . . to discuss how machines are manned, how overtime is to be worked . . . we should also be able to discuss the rewards for bringing about these changes.'[2]

Simpson's observations point to certain further tactical considerations that have attracted at least some trade unionists to

---

[1] *The Guardian*, 7 May 1975; 13 December 1976; *The Times*, 29 June 1977.
[2] Labour Party *Conference Report*, 1968, pp. 160–1.

industrial democracy. Most of these considerations arise from difficulties created for trade unions by the Labour Party's attempt at 'planning'. One such difficulty was the unemployment necessarily caused by efforts to raise productivity in circumstances (such as those of the mid-1960s) when the demand for manufactured goods was rising only slowly. Productivity bargaining had contributed to such unemployment; and so had the rationalization promoted by the government, notably in electrical engineering where the AEI–GEC merger—and the attendant redundancies—became notorious among trade unionists. 'Industrial democracy' seemed to offer labour new powers to resist or delay such redundancies. 'The white heat of the technological revolution was not the cosy glow of industrial progress', said Benn in 1971, 'but what nuclear power did to the coal industry, containerization did to the docks' and 'computers do to clerical workers'. Hence, he concluded, 'the people' must be 'unleashed to control' technical change. In the same spirit, the working party on industrial democracy emphasized that 'the Government and the trade unions should urgently consider what can be done to strengthen the consideration of the interests of workers affected by company take-overs, mergers, and their associated "rationalization".' And in this spirit, too, some manual wage earners employed by Upper Clyde Shipbuilders Ltd., which the Heath government appeared to be about to rationalize out of existence in mid-1971, began, as they claimed, to take over the yard on 30 July of that year. Benn acclaimed this 'work-in' as 'the birth pangs of industrial democracy'. 'The workers in Upper Clyde shipbuilders have done more in ten weeks to advance industrial democracy than all the blueprints we have worked on over the last ten years', he told the 1971 Labour Party conference. Yet Jimmy Airlie, one of the leaders of the shop stewards' committee that organized the fourteen-month work-in, stated that 'our only purpose is to save . . . jobs'. 'If', he added, 'as a by-product, a new form of protest or control comes about then that is welcome—but it is not our aim.'[1]

---

[1] Ibid., 1971, pp. 250–1; *Report of the Labour Party Working Party on Industrial Democracy*, p. 9; Jack McGill, *Crisis on the Clyde, The Story of Upper Clyde Shipbuilders*, London, 1973, pp. 101, 103, 139; Alasdair Buchan, *The Right to Work, The Story of the Upper Clyde Confrontation*, London, 1972, p. 144.

Another, and perhaps more pressing, difficulty which unions hoped to circumvent by a resort to 'industrial democracy' was directly caused by productivity bargaining itself. Trade unionism is about wages, that is to say, more precisely, about more money for the same work. The productivity bargaining to which the desire to escape the Wilson government's incomes policy drove the unions in the 1960s, at best promised them more money for more work, and at worst threatened them with more money for much more work. As the General Council complained in 1974, the emphasis 'on obtaining increases in productivity and more efficient methods of working' changed 'the relationship between the work done and the monetary reward received'. The solution to the problem of productivity bargaining was sought in industrial democracy: the Trades Union Congress's written evidence to the Royal Commission passes straight from the one topic to the other; and the Jones working party insisted that 'effective participation by workers in the relevant decision making' was essential for industry to 'handle a rapid change', especially in 'improvement of labour utilization'.[1]

What the working party wanted may be expressed in the slogan 'open the books': which, in Ken Coates's words, is 'central, even crucial' to workers' control. 'Opening the books' was not 'a socialist demand', as one of Coates's fellow advocates of workers' control rightly noted; but it may be a device for dealing with productivity bargains. For management's technical expertise and financial secrecy may (so some trade unionists suspect) enable it to fool trade union negotiators; but once 'the books' are 'open', it will be denied this advantage, and productivity bargaining may be embarked on by trade-union negotiators safe in the knowledge that 'the relationship' between 'work done' and 'monetary reward' can only change in one direction. Thus the enormous emphasis on 'information' in recent discussion of 'industrial democracy'. 'The provision of information', was 'an essential background against which extensions to industrial democracy can occur', declared the General Council in 1974. As 'a first priority' it would therefore 'be necessary for trade union negotiators to examine

[1] Trades Union Congress *Report*, 1974, p. 294; Royal Commission, *Selected Written Evidence*, pp. 157–9; *Report of the Labour Party Working Party*, pp. 13–16.

information needs in the light of their objectives as far as improvements' in 'wage and non-wage benefits' were concerned. But the same point had been put, in racier phrases, eleven years earlier by a Battersea delegate to the Labour Party conference. What he wanted, he said, was 'workers' representatives' on 'boards of management', with 'no obligations and no commitments', but simply 'the capacity to lean over the shoulder of the employers, breathe down their necks, and know what is going on in their plans'.[1]

Given the single-minded demand for 'information', and the insistence on 'no obligations and no commitments', organized labour's traditional objections to 'workers' control' were now rather irrelevant. Those objections assumed that rational, collective economic activity should continue; and that, since the manual wage earner strongly desired to concentrate upon the liberal-individualist pursuit of personal or sectional self-interest, 'workers' control' would tend to eliminate such activity, which would sooner or later require some collective act (such as reducing labour costs, for example) counter to the pursuit of self-interest. In such circumstances, so the objections ran, either the demands of the workers' representatives would override the requirements of rational, collective economic policy, in which case conflict would bring the undertaking to a halt; or those demands would be sacrificed to the requirements of rational, collective economic policy, in which case compromise would ruin the workers. But certain national union leaders apparently hope to protect workers' representatives from both 'class collaboration' and excess 'militancy' by forcing 'planning agreements' upon companies. For the continuous preparation of such agreements, by governments, firms, and union leaders, would, they believe, give them the opportunity to guide the representative's steps. They would, however, be loath to guide them in a collectivist path. Speaking to the 1974 Trades Union Congress, Murray promised that, though the General Council favoured 'industrial democracy', 'We are not going to allow the essential functions of trade unions to be compromised'; and a few months earlier, he confided to *The Director* magazine that 'there are some campaigns to get the so-called two sides of

---

[1] Coates and Williams, pp. 4, 142; Trades Union Congress *Report*, 1974, p. 316; Labour Party *Conference Report*, 1963, p. 192.

industry together which I think myself are strictly for the birds'. 'In fact, I am a believer in creative tension,' he added.[1]

Organized labour's concept of the structure of 'industrial democracy' expresses just this attitude. Trade unionists regard industrial democracy as no more and no less than a fresh access of bargaining power. 'Industrial democracy is a natural extension of trade unionism and starts with the right to negotiate', said Jones in 1968. Hence the working party's major conclusion that 'we must develop industrial democracy on the basis of A SINGLE CHANNEL OF REPRESENTATION.' The 'single channel' has a corporatist and a utilitarian function. First, it excludes non-trade unionists from the representative process, thus preventing companies from using the non-unionists against the unions while, conversely, encouraging non-unionists to join unions. Secondly, it removes 'any distinction between subjects appropriate for bargaining and those appropriate for consultation': that is, it seeks to introduce a wage claim ('bargaining') into every discussion ('consultation') on any issue that might be raised by employers. As the National Executive put it in 1968, 'development of industrial democracy should be pursued through the creation of a single channel of communication between workers' representatives and management', so that 'all elements of management' would be 'within the sphere of negotiations'. The so-called worker directors in this scheme of industrial democracy would, in fact, be glorified negotiators. Because 'the trade union representatives will have a tough and responsible job', Murray reminded the 1974 Trades Union Congress, they would need training 'to ask the right questions about different forms of accounts'. This view has gained wide acceptance. When the Transport and General Workers' Union Convener at the Felixstowe Dock and Railway Company was elected a director of the company in 1975, he said, 'worker participation, when you look at it, in my opinion as a working man, is pounds, shilling and pence.'[2]

It is because the 'workers' representatives' on the supervisory boards are to be negotiators that trade unionists insist that

---

[1] Trades Union Congress *Report*, 1974, p. 522; John Elliott, *Conflict or Co-operation?*, London, 1978, pp. 36, 38; *The Director*, June 1974, p. 356.

[2] Trades Union Congress *Report*, 1968, p. 532; 1974, p. 524; *Report of the Labour Party Working Party*, p. 7; Elliott, pp. 130, 208, 249; Labour Party *Conference Report*, 1968, p. 345; *The Guardian*, 11 September 1975.

'these representatives should be free to continue to play a normal part in trade union activity'; and that they should be 'subject to recall and re-election' by those who appoint them. In no sense are the workers' representatives or directors to share even the mere legal liability of the other directors of an enterprise: indeed they are to be free to repudiate any liability whatever—just like any other trade unionist. 'We are not in any doubt that the right of workers and their organizations to withdraw from participation, from decision-making respons- ibility, from agreements . . . must be maintained', the Jones working party announced. 'Industrial democracy' must confer no obligations on wage earners who participate therein. Least of all must there be any new loyalties or commitments to the firm in which the industrial democrats work: for any such ties would confuse trade unionists' *laissez-faire* convictions that they live in a market in which they must be free to sell their labour to the highest bidder. 'Company-based schemes of co-owner- ship and profit-sharing' have been unacceptable to the Trades Union Congress, because such schemes might serve to give the wage earner 'a stake in the firm', so to speak, and inhibit him from withdrawing his labour at his own or his union's con- venience. A Labour Party study group fully acknowledged these dangers. Profit-sharing, it reported in 1973, 'can all too easily encourage workers' to think that they are 'part of a company "team" '. The worker directors, on the contrary, are to be motivated by the purest sectionalism: 'It will be important to ensure that the representatives of trade unionists in a particular enterprise do not become too centred on the problems of that firm', said Murray in 1974. 'They will need to keep firmly in the picture their relationship to their fellow-members'.[1]

THE ATTEMPT TO RESHAPE INDUSTRIAL RELATIONS

By 1974 public opinion was possibly more alert to the section- alism of such pronouncements than was the case earlier in the post-war period. During the late 1960s, as unions reacted against the development of Labour planning, strikes grew lengthier and more frequent, and involved an ever-increasing

[1] Trades Union Congress *Report*, 1974, pp. 307, 321, 324, 523; *Report of the Labour Party Working Party*, p. 30; Elliott, p. 189.

number of workers. In fact official strikes, such as the Seamen's strike of 1966, were increasing; but public attention remained largely concentrated on unofficial strikes, such as the demarcation dispute at Girling's in 1968, where a month's strike by twenty-two workers led to 5,000 other workers being laid off elsewhere in the motor-car industry. Academics, publicists and commentators began to express disquiet. Thus, for example, Alan Fox and Allan Flanders argued, in the *British Journal of Industrial Relations* in 1969, that 'the present condition of industrial relations', was chiefly characterized by 'unrestrained competition' which threatened 'a progressive breakdown of social regulation'. Stephen Fay noted, in 1970, an 'impression that the unions had somehow established a divine right to their legal immunity'; and indeed that labour organization sometimes seemed 'a monster which could no longer be controlled'.[1]

Demands for changes both in industrial relations and in trade unions increased. As early as 1960, Michael Shanks argued that 'it is hard to think of a more certain Conservative vote winner' than an election campaign fought on behalf of proposals to 'weaken the power of the unions'. Richard Marsh urged the Labour Party conference of that year to 'reorganize' the trade unions, which he described as 'the classic example of unplanned private enterprise'. Perhaps enthusiasm for action against the unions was slighter than some thought, however. Jack Jones observed, a few years later, that 'workpeople are in favour of doing something about unofficial strikes providing you don't actually do it to them when they are on strike for something they believe in'; and Shanks himself presciently warned that an anti-union election in the long run 'would probably be disastrous' both for the country and the party that adopted such a policy. Obviously no reform of unions or industrial relations could be undertaken without strong and extensive public support, yet such support was not guaranteed, even by the vehemence with which the unions were criticized in this period: partly because the public was not prepared to accept the difficulties and dangers of a conflict between government

---

[1] Michael Silver, 'Recent British Strike Trends: A Factual Analysis', *British Journal of Industrial Relations*, 1973, p. 97; Alan Fox and Allan Flanders, 'The Reform of Collective Bargaining: from Donovan to Durkheim', *B.J.I.R.*, 1969, pp. 163–4; Fay, p. 10.

and organized labour; partly because, in its heart of *laissez-faire* hearts, the public accepted the unions' right to do as they liked.[1]

Nevertheless, both Conservatives and Labour nationalists favoured change. In 1965 the Labour government appointed a Royal Commission on Trade Unions and Employer Associations under Lord Donovan. At the 1966 Labour Party conference, Wilson urged that 'conservatism' be 'eradicated from Trade Union thinking and outdated working practices'; and Callaghan emphasized that people 'arguing about their incomes' must 'accept that the strength of the two parties is not the only factor that will decide these issues in the future'. Successive Labour ministers with responsibility for union and industrial affairs, came to the conclusion—while the Donovan Commission was still sitting—that, as Peter Jenkins put it, 'no prices and incomes policy was likely to get very far, no Social Democratic society was likely to be constructed, until something radical was done to reform the structures and attitudes of the . . . trade unions.'[2]

What was to be done remained obscure. Some favoured secret ballots and other devices designed to make union policies more representative; others wanted to give agreements reached through collective bargaining a legal force sufficient to prevent unions bidding up wages by breaking them; and still others advocated various restraints on industrial action, such as 'cooling off periods' during which unions were obliged to continue negotiating and to desist from striking. The unions themselves argued either that reform was unnecessary and undesirable; or that, if some minor changes did prove useful, they should be implemented by the unions themselves spontaneously, voluntarily, and at times and by methods of their own choosing. John Edmonds, a research officer for the General and Municipal Workers' Union agreed, in 1968, that the government 'may retain the right to restrict actions of citizens and organizations in the public interest. But it ought not to interfere in the detailed internal affairs of a voluntary organization. That way lies government control and perversion

---

[1] Shanks, pp. 77–8; Labour Party *Conference Report*, 1960, pp. 141–2; Peter Jenkins, p. 145.

[2] Labour Party *Conference Report*, 1966, pp. 123, 164; Peter Jenkins, p. 9.

of the union movement's democratic purpose'. 'The democrat', he concluded, 'has to acknowledge that the unions must be left to reform themselves.'[1]

About the same time as Edmonds published these remarks, the Donovan Commission brought out its findings. The Commission's report was chiefly notable for the conflict it revealed between the critical, partly collectivist viewpoint expressed in a 'Note of Reservation' by Andrew Shonfield (then Director of Studies at the Royal Institute of International Affairs), and the more optimistic, traditional, voluntarist, and indeed *laissez-faire* viewpoint which apparently informed the opinions of the overwhelming majority of the Commissioners. In this sense, at least, the report witnessed to the continuing struggle, within the political consciousness of Britain, between continental organicist doctrines of society and an Anglo-American utilitarian individualism which regards society as a mere aggregate of competing interests.

In his book *Modern Capitalism*, published in 1965, Shonfield noted the prevalence in Britain of an 'old instinctive suspicion of positive government', which caused men to challenge the notion that the state could determine or promote any general good such as the 'collective economic interest'; and to deride the possibility that the state might call the people to a fuller citizenship, a positive freedom, in common pursuit of this or any other end. Indeed, Shonfield observed, in Britain 'the state is not visualized as the carrier of an overriding national interest, but rather as one among several—admittedly *primus inter pares*—who compete with one another on behalf of their individual and differing interests'. Moreover, the British, he concluded, 'allow effective power to slide into the hands of . . . corporations without subjecting them to public control—for the national doctrine insists that they are no more than free associations of individuals whose activities are essential to the emergence of a consensus.' Shonfield himself, in his 'Note of Reservation', sympathized with many of the tenets of liberal individualism: he much valued the 'liberty of the ordinary citizen' from external interference, for example; and he conceded the necessity of the 'strike weapon' in free collective bargaining 'so far ahead as one can see'. Yet, he argued,

[1] Lapping and Radice, p. 52.

British loyalty to the extremes of liberal individualism prevented optimum application of techniques of central direction and planning necessary to economic success in an age whose rapid technological innovation required deployment of vast resources of capital and labour. As a result, British economic growth remained slow; archaic practices predominated in industrial relations; and organized labour suffered not least.[1]

Shonfield favoured appointment, within enterprises, of directors 'to act as guardians of the workers' interests'. But he wanted trade unions to accept 'certain responsibilities towards society as a whole' and to conform to 'certain minimum standards of behaviour'; and he proposed to secure this end through the legal and quasi-legal activity of the whole society, which would be brought to bear on labour both through expanded statute law and through an 'independent judicial authority' embodied in some form of court or commission. By putting industrial affairs into the courts, so to speak, Shonfield apparently hoped to modify if not abolish *laissez-faire* by a mixture of exhortation and compulsion that brought the bi-partite corporatism of the British economy a little nearer to a collectivist system that embodied the long-opposed principle of 'positive government'.[2]

The majority of the Commission was much less ambitious and, indeed, much more loyal to the unions' own traditions and attitudes. It repudiated worker directors, above all because of the 'almost intolerable strain' under which such functionaries would be placed by the clash between the organized employees' interests and 'the interests of the company as a whole'. Indeed the Commissioners proposed no major change from the traditional system of 'voluntary collective bargaining', from which, as they put it (virtually echoing the Trades Union Congress), 'the State remained aloof'. That system, they suggested, 'is the best method of conducting industrial relations'; and any 'indecision and anarchy' which critics might allege to be actual or potential within the system could only be due to some aberration from, or misunderstanding of, the central tendencies of voluntary

---

[1] Andrew Shonfield, *Modern Capitalism, The Changing Balance of Public and Private Power*, London, 1969, pp. 89, 94, 119, 163; Royal Commission on Trade Unions and Employers' Associations, *Report*, London, 1968, p. 289.

[2] Ibid., pp. 257–9, 289–94.

collective bargaining. One such aberration or misunderstanding apparent to the Commissioners was the 'pretence' of a 'formal', so-say 'national' system of industry-wide agreements, which concealed and complicated the 'reality' of the 'informal' system of shopfloor bargaining within the firm or factory. The confusion and 'widespread ignorance' about the character and relationship of these 'two systems' inhibited the construction of 'speedy, clear and effective disputes procedure'.[1]

What was needed, then, according to the majority of the Donovan Commission, was the fragmentation of the somewhat unified industrial-relations system of Britain into suitable pieces, and the replacement of industry-wide by 'factory-wide', even perhaps shop-wide, agreements. The Commission thus vindicated the *laissez-faire* tradition; accepted the sectionalism of modern trade unionism; and rejected schemes to reconstruct trade unions or to co-ordinate collective bargaining on a national level, however defined. Since this course of action meant no more than following on the heels of labour organization as it vanished into the sectional fastnesses of the factory, the Commission did not find it necessary to commend the government to take any novel or special measures. A permanent Commission on Industrial Relations was to be created: but this would have little more than an advisory or educational role. As for the rest, the Donovan Commissioners assumed that the government would persist, whether rightly or wrongly, with 'norms' for pay increases, to which it would persuade unions to cleave; and employers would continue to hold out to the unions productivity bargains the benefits of which would be 'too persuasive' to be ignored.[2]

Two weeks before the Commission published its report, the Conservatives rushed out their proposals for the reform of industrial relations and trade unionism, under the title *Fair Deal at Work*. While remaining as loyal as possible to the liberal-individualist tradition, the Conservatives proved a good deal less *laissez-faire* than the commissioners. The authors of *Fair Deal at Work* proposed to restrict existing union privileges to organizations that both registered as trade unions, and complied with certain requirements (including secret ballots) for

[1] Ibid., pp. 10, 33, 50–1, 128, 257–9.
[2] Ibid., pp. 38, 40, 43.

the conduct of registered unions; to oblige such unions to enter into legally binding collective agreements; to prohibit them from striking without strike ballots and within a sixty-day cooling-off period; and to prescribe legal penalties for the breach of different regulations. These changes—which would of course virtually revolutionize the practice and attitudes of unions—appeared to receive quite wide public support. In 1969 one opinion poll found that over 60 per cent of the adult population favoured secret ballots, a cooling-off period, and fines on unco-operative unions; another claimed that 55 per cent of all voters (and 51 per cent of Labour voters) wanted legal limitations on the right to strike; and still another reported approval for the cooling-off period among trade union sponsored Members of Parliament.[1]

The apparent response to *Fair Deal at Work*, the alleged ineffectuality of the Donovan Commission's majority proposals, and the grave difficulties of carrying through an incomes policy against the opposition of the unreconstructed unions, convinced the government that it should and could change various rules of British industrial practice. Barbara Castle, as Secretary of State for Employment and Productivity, prepared, and the Cabinet endorsed, a document entitled *In Place of Strife*, which was published early in 1969. This document opened with the characteristically liberal-individualist credo that, 'there are necessarily conflicts of interest in industry'. But it proceeded to develop this credo with various proposals for new ways in which the government might, as Mill might have put it, prevent these conflicts causing 'harm to others'. These included permissive powers to promote changes in union rule-books; a 'discretionary reserve power' to secure a twenty-eight-day 'conciliation pause', and a strike ballot, in the event of an industrial dispute; and authority to exact financial penalties from unions which failed to heed directives issued by the Commission of Industrial Relations in cases of inter-union disputes. Such measures were, said Wilson, 'essential to our economic recovery, essential to our balance of payments, essential to full employment'.[2]

They were also abhorrent to trade union leaders. If these

---

[1] Fay, p. 85; Peter Jenkins, pp. 45–6.
[2] Ibid., pp. 40–1, 169.

proposals were put into practice, the game would be (after a century and a half of industrialization, and just as manual wage earners found it getting interesting), in a manner of speaking, up. The General Council denied that 'collective agreements' could 'be made legally enforceable'. It warned that the policy outlined by *In Place of Strife* put 'unreasonable and unworkable constraints on the freedom of working people to pursue their legitimate objectives'. Financial penalties would, said the Council, 'militate' against a 'genuine solution' of industrial problems; conciliation pauses were 'neither practicable nor desirable'; and compulsory strike ballots were 'completely misguided and quite unacceptable'. That these proposals were the work of a Labour government was ir- relevant. As a trade union Member of Parliament put it to the 1969 Party conference, 'the trade union movement are not prepared to be subservient to any government'. In March 1969 nearly 100 Labour Members abstained or voted against the government in a parliamentary debate on *In Place of Strife*; and the National Executive of the Labour Party overwhelm- ingly rejected 'legislation based on all' the recommendations of that document. On 5 June a special Trades Union Congress responded to the government's incorporation of these recom- mendations in an Industrial Relations Bill by voting 96 per cent 'to affirm that the trade union Movement is unalterably opposed' to 'financial penalties on workpeople or on trade unions in connection either with industrial disputes or with compulsory registration by trade unions of their rules.'[1]

The General Council might be thought to have led affiliated unions to make a stand in defence of those principles that Locke, Bentham and Mill held dear; it might also be thought to have affirmed the attitudes of the Slump. Certainly there was an odour of August 1931 about the situation in June 1969. But, whereas in 1931, some of the chief ministers of a Labour administration under MacDonald, the most collectivist leader in the Party's history, preferred to resign from office and to enter a coalition, in which they formed a small minority and for which they were generally reviled, in order to resist what they regarded as sectional union opposition to measures which, rightly or wrongly, they held to be necessary for the

[1] Trades Union Congress *Report*, 1969, pp. 191, 206, 217, 229–30, 243.

good of all, in 1969, the chief ministers of another Labour administration, under Wilson, the leading advocate of Labour nationalism, abandoned the measures which they had asserted were necessary for the good of all. On 18 June 1969 the Cabinet withdrew the Industrial Relations Bill in return for a 'Solemn and Binding Undertaking' by the Trades Union Congress to 'place an obligation on trade unions to take energetic steps to obtain an immediate resumption of work in unofficial disputes'. 'June 18 1969 will go down in history as a day in which democratic socialism was saved from committing hari-kari', said McGarvey at the 1969 Party conference. On that day, he indicated, Labour leaders, disabused of misunderstandings which could persist only in the 'very sheltered life' led by 'politicians', were taught a lesson by trade unionists who gained their wisdom in the struggle with 'enemies who are trying to get blood from us for as little money as possible'. 'It is the trade unions', McGarvey concluded, 'which is the eternal watchdog in this situation of democratic freedom.'[1]

It is perhaps a tribute to the indomitable optimism (or possibly stupidity) of politicians, however 'sheltered', that there is a postscript to the trade unions' decisive victory on 18 June 1969. Exactly a year after that date, the Conservatives, led by Edward Heath, were returned to power. At once they took up where Labour had left off; and within a year they had carried through Parliament an Industrial Relations Act, the most fundamental difference between which and Labour's ill-fated Industrial Relations Bill was that, whereas Labour intended to reshape the unions chiefly through the actions of a minister appointed to deal with them, the Conservatives intended to achieve the same end chiefly through the Shonfieldian 'independent judicial authority' of a National Industrial Relations Court. Yet a further year on, the Conservative government introduced its incomes policy, the provisions of which of course intensified the unions' hostility to the Industrial Relations Act. Almost all unions refused to register under the Act, and thus remained liable to actions for damages of up to £100,000. Both the Engineers and the Transport and General Workers were taken to the National Industrial Relations Court. The former union refused to acknowledge or appear before the

[1] Peter Jenkins, pp. 152–3, 160; Labour Party *Conference Report*, 1969, pp. 188–9.

Court, for which contempt it was mulcted in all of about £250,000; the latter did appear, and won a number of cases, although five members of its Docks section, who did commit contempt, were briefly imprisoned. Meanwhile the Mine-workers led the resistance to the government's incomes policy, causing black-outs by their strike in 1972, and three-day working by their strike in 1974.

Long before the 1974 strike, the government's power was ebbing away. In July 1972, when the National Industrial Relations Court released the five dockers, their contempt apparently unpurged, on the intervention of the Official Solicitor, the President of the Court, Sir John Donaldson, said he wished 'to make it clear' that neither the government nor anyone else had tried, 'otherwise than in open court, to influence' the court's decisions. Sir John Donaldson was endeavouring to deny that the government had engineered the dockers' release, not their imprisonment. For, after only a few months of the Act's operation, the Heath administration was suspected of abusing the law not to control the unions but to surrender to them. About this time Roy Jenkins warned that,

> In some quarters an attitude has grown up, implying that any action taken by any group of workers is automatically right: that anyone who questions the wisdom of a particular strike or the justice of a particular wage claim is a coward or a traitor: that confrontation is to be welcomed: that laws should only have force for those who agree with them.

Yet in a sense that attitude has always been implicit in the *laissez-faire* ideology of British labour, and was merely rendered explicit by the events of the early 1970s. That attitude, the trade unions' strength, and the apathy of the public, would seem to presage a somewhat problematical phase in British politics. With a certain *hubris* perhaps, on 19 June 1969 Heath commented of the Wilson government that 'although they still wear the trappings of office, the power resides elsewhere': and that comment could serve as a judgement on his own adminis-tration.[1]

---

[1] *The Times*, 28 July 1972; Roy Jenkins, *What Matters Now?*, London, 1972, p. 119; Peter Jenkins, p. 159.

6

Labour and Democracy

Let it be supposed . . . that every member of Parliament is sent by
working men and is himself a working man . . . and that all
govermental power is vested in the productive population. One
of the first acts of a government thus constituted would be to
interfere between the employer and the employed. Laws would
be made to increase wages and decrease the hours of labour—
machinery would in many cases be put down—the power of
refusing employment to obnoxious persons would be taken from
the employer—and the commercial regulations of society would
be subject to perpetual variations to meet the emergencies of
particular classes of producers. All these . . . changes . . . would
affect the relative position of the classes now constituting society,
without remedying the evils dependent upon this division—and
production would be carried on by complicated and ever-
changing arrangements—alternately depressing one class and
exalting another, and making society a hot bed of tyranny and
hatred.

> J. F. BRAY, *Labour's Wrongs and Labour's Remedy;
> or, the Age of Might and the Age of Right*

LABOUR'S CULTURE

The argument outlined in the first chapter of this book, and
illustrated in the four chapters which follow, is based on the
premise that, in Collingwood's phrase, 'all history is the history
of thought'. Much thought consists of specific responses to the
objective situations that confront men, but over the development of which they may, as individuals, have little control:
situations such as those caused by the Taff Vale judgement,
or the wars with Germany, or the financial crisis of August 1931.
Yet some thought consists of the attitudes and assumptions that

many men share, and that shape their individual and specific responses to objective situations. Sometimes such attitudes and assumptions are exploited by groups or individuals who use them, consciously or unconsciously, for ulterior purposes: and then attitudes and assumptions take on the ideological character of, for example, the appeal to racial superiority in order to legitimate inequitable treatment of ethnic groups, or the appeal to justice in order to further a wage claim. Sometimes such attitudes and assumptions merely serve to restrict the range of individuals' behaviour, by colouring their perception of situations, and by narrowing their notion of acceptable and appropriate responses to situations: and then attitudes and assumptions may be said to take on the character of the doctrinaire: then, indeed, as Winch put it, 'social relations are expressions of ideas about reality'.[1]

Certain doctrinaire and ideological attitudes may dominate the 'culture' of one or more 'nations' or 'countries'. When this happens, the habitual persistence of such thoughts tends to shape not merely the opinions but the actions of very many people. Hence different countries display specific patterns of social life at least in part attributable to their citizens' habit of thinking that some things and not other things are correct, proper, or commonsense. In other words, citizens of different countries have different cultures, because they have received a particular type of education, have come to acknowledge a particular kind of authority or rule, and are used to a particular sort of discourse. But fidelity to cultural norms corresponds, in a very rough and ready way, inversely to the individual's degree of education, and directly to the degree to which his opinions and actions are public in nature. The less educated an individual is, and the more he thinks and acts as a member of a group (whether that group be his country, a social organization, or a crowd) the more likely he is to conform to the culture in which he has been instructed. Hence the intellectual conservatism, the tenacious loyalty to cultural orthodoxies, so characteristic of the life and work of organizations of manual wage earners.

[1] R. G. Collingwood, *An Autobiography*, Harmondsworth, Middlesex, 1944, pp. 75–6; Peter Winch, *The Idea of a Social Science and its Relation to Philosophy*, London, 1958, p. 23.

The cultural orthodoxies peculiar to Britain (and, to a lesser extent, to the Anglo-American countries as a whole) may be described as utilitarian liberal-democratic individualism. According to this set of doctrines, any group of people, including society itself, is a collection rather than a collectivity, an aggregate of individuals rather than a totality with an organic structure. The freedom of individuals, whether in or out of groups, is perceived as the 'negative' absence of external impediments to motion: that is, of impediments to the exercise of will in utterance and action. Each individual counts for one and no more than one; he is of equal value to all other individuals, whatever that value may be. Individuals' pains and pleasures differ merely in quantity, not in quality: and—like individuals' aims, goals and interests—may only be perceived empirically from utterance and behaviour. In other words, men have only apparent wills and apparent interests, not real wills and real interests: and, of course, since individuals can only be aggregated, they can have no general will. Moreover, with very few exceptions, each individual is the best judge of his own interest although, by extension, the next best judges of his interest are likely to be those nearest him: his family, perhaps; his workmates or his peers more probably. Each individual is motivated by self-interest; and the optimum social mode is the unhindered pursuit of self-interest, since attempts to pursue the interests of others must be defeated by the error inseparable from the effort to determine the nature of others' interests. All human activity proceeds from conflict and competition; and perfect competition will be the most efficient means by which human resources are utilized, above all, but not only, in production. Though the exigencies of social life require a form of government, able to perform certain common services, government should observe the *laissez-faire* principle which teaches it in no wise to interfere in social life except to perfect competition by preserving such an equality between individuals as will prevent any individual from *harming others*: that is, from reducing the capacity of others to compete. In any event, government may well err, even in attempting this task, because it will be endeavouring to judge and pursue the interests of others; and, though government should represent the character and wishes of the people, it is itself but one collection of individuals, one section, among all the many collections or sections (each no more than the individuals which compose it) that go to make up society.

These specially British doctrines have dominated organized labour, its spokesmen and its admirers. Certain points stand out from the evidence cited here. In the 1830s Bray believed that 'an aggregate of individuals' did 'compose a nation'; in the 1960s the Trades Union Congress advised the Royal Commission on Trades Unions and Employers' Associations that 'society' and 'the community' were 'abstract conceptions' in fact composed of 'plural institutions, groups and individuals'. Likewise, each institution or group is a collection of individuals. 'Any union is its members', said Feather in 1966. Those members were to enjoy a strictly negative freedom. Liberty, according to the National Union of Working Classes, consisted of 'that power which belongs to a man of doing everything that does not infringe upon the rights of another'. Such rights meant to trade unionists the equality of each member of the group: and, so far as they were able, trade unions affirmed their members' equality by levying equal membership-dues (as opposed to insurance contributions, which varied with the benefits to be received). Trade unions also treated their members' interests in a purely quantitative sense by offering them only material aid: thus, for instance, until quite recently they provided their members with neither educational nor political services, and they have never concerned themselves with religion. Hence, once trade unions sought parliamentary representation they emphasized their egalitarianism, and soon adopted the view that 'socialism', as Crosland put it, was 'basically about equality'. Trade unions have always claimed to obey their members' wills, success in the empirical identification and furtherance of which, is, trade union leaders believe, the irrefutable evidence that establishes their organizations' claims to constitute a 'democratic movement'. 'My job is to defend members', claimed the Boilermakers' leader Ted Hill in 1959; and it was a conviction of the union's achievements in this respect which led Hill's successor, Danny McGarvey, to describe the trade unions, ten years later, as 'the eternal watchdog in this situation of democratic freedom'. Moreover, because trade unionists believe individuals are the best judge of their own interest, 'brains', 'professors' and 'middle-class intellectuals', who claim to know the true needs of manual wage earners, are rarely popular with organized labour. Nor, for that matter, are the officials at union headquarters. The leaders 'become "gentlemen" ', complained the authors of *The Miners' Next Step* in 1912: 'All leaders become corrupt, in spite of their own good intentions'.[1]

Trade unionists have traditionally believed that society is founded upon perfect competition between self-interested individuals. A hundred years ago, George Howell defined prevailing social and economic doctrine as the inculcation of self-love; and urged no one to feel surprise that the workman's 'one aim' was promotion of his own material interest, or, as Howell put it, 'screwing out of the employer' the largest possible wages 'for the least possible quantity of work'. Such attitudes shape trade unionism, and hence British society, today. Thus the white paper *The Regeneration of British Industry*, published in November 1975, noted the 'policies of confrontation' prevalent in industry; and the Central Policy Review Staff paper, *The Future of the British Car Industry*, which appeared a month later, remarked on the 'present "trench warfare" attitudes of management and labour' in motor-car manufacture. In such a society, self-help must be the individual's maxim, no less than self-love; and the great symbol of self-help is, in trade unionists' eyes, the strike, under the duress or menace of which they conduct 'free collective bargaining'.[2]

Trade unionists regard free collective bargaining as the optimum mode of industrial relations because such bargaining gives greatest scope to both self-help and to competition—between employees and employees as well as between employees and employers. Hence Feather's claim that, 'there is always more satisfaction with a settlement which the two parties themselves agree is fair than there would have been' if the same

[1] J. F. Bray, *Labour's Wrongs and Labour's Remedy; or, the Age of Might and the Age of Right*, Leeds, 1839, p. 34; Royal Commission on Trade Unions and Employers' Associations, *Minutes of Evidence*, 61, London, 1967, p. 2686; *Selected Written Evidence*, London, 1968, pp. 135, 137; Patricia Hollis (ed.), *Class and Conflict in Nineteenth Century England, 1815–1850*, London, 1973, p. 129; Anthony Crosland, *Socialism Now, And Other Essays*, London, 1974, p. 16; Labour Party *Conference Report*, 1959, p. 150; 1969, p. 189; *The Miners' Next Step*, Tonypandy, 1912, p. 13.

[2] George Howell, *The Conflicts of Capital and Labour*, London, 1878, p. 207; *The Times*, 6 November 1975; 17 December 1975.

settlement 'was made for them by the Government'. The Trades Union Congress claims that the state has merely 'a residuary role', its attitude to industrial relations in particular 'being one of abstention, of formal indifference', so long as trade unions are 'competent' to bargain freely with employers: and this latter day Millism was neatly summarized by Gormley's question, 'who are they as a government . . . to lay down the law in this democratic society we have?' These *laissez-faire* attitudes necessarily circumscribe the labour view of nationalization and planning. An opinion poll of full-time employees, conducted by Opinion Research Centre in Great Britain in November 1974 showed that two-thirds of those polled in the private sector were opposed to nationalization of their own company; and that only one-fifth of these workers thought that nationalization would enable their company to do a better job for its employees, its customers or the country. This scepticism reflects a long tradition of hostility to direct state intervention, manifest not merely in the right-wing opinions of a man like Morrison, with his objections to the 'old idea of Departmental nationalization' of 'a great business undertaking', but also in the left-wing opinions of a man like Strachey, with his horror of a 'horde of officials', and 'over-enthusiastic "planners" '.[1]

Thus the relatively limited role of government direction in the British economy results not so much from the machinations of the Treasury or the City, as left-wingers like to suggest, as from the conservatism of organized labour both in its trade union and its political forms. Laski's doctrine of the state as 'only one of the associations' to which the individual 'happens to belong' (an association which by definition pursues the good of a 'certain section' not 'the community as a whole'), illustrates the 'old instinctive suspicion of positive government' which Shonfield observed in British public discourse. Labour circles readily identify any divergence from a liberal *laissez-faire* disparagement of the State as something foreign. By contrast with English labour, 'continental workmen believe in the State, at least theoretically', observed George Howell in 1891; the Guild

[1] Victor Feather, *The Essence of Trade Unionism*, London, 1963, p. 9; Royal Commission on Trade Unions and Employers' Associations, *Selected Written Evidence*, pp. 117, 140; *The Times*, 23 January 1974; 13 January 1975; *House of Commons Debates*, vol. 250, col. 55; John Strachey, *The Theory and Practice of Socialism*, London, 1936, p. 141; *Why You Should Be a Socialist*, London, 1938, p. 65.

Socialist S. G. Hobson had no doubt in 1920 that the demand
for 'every national activity' to serve one 'great end' was
germanism; and, as recently as 1963, George Woodcock warned
that, 'the whole idea of a super body at the top . . . imposing
limits upon the rights of trade unions to represent their members
is foreign to everything we stand for in this country'.[1]

Labour's culture is, then, still largely shaped by the national
ideology, an ideology that frequently assumes a doctrinaire
character. Efforts have been made to challenge this ideology. In
the late nineteenth century, many intellectuals favoured what
E. E. Williams called a 'revolution' in 'the English mind and
habit', a revolution which would embody T. H. Green's ideal
of 'freedom in the positive sense' of 'the liberation of the powers
of all men equally for contributions to a common good'. Some
Labour leaders sought to continue these efforts during the
early twentieth century. MacDonald, for example, extolled the
'superior will and intelligence' of the state, which he described
as 'the embodiment of the general will' and 'the political
personality of the whole'. Tawney envisaged a 'functional
society', which would be 'organized primarily for the performance of *duties*, not the maintenance of *rights*'; and would be
marked by the 'discipline' of the 'necessity' of pursuing a
'common end'. Yet MacDonald was eventually expelled from
the party, while Tawney's true views were lost in hagiography.[2]

The post-war decades, and especially the years since Suez,
have seen the growth of a new Labour nationalism, symbolized
by Wilson's appeals to 'the Dunkirk spirit'. This nationalist
tendency has revived the ideas of men like MacDonald and
Tawney: hence Wilson's declaration in 1964 that, 'our approach
must be not what we can take out of the national pool, but
what we can put into it. For only by a massive sense of dedication by every individual can we get the national sense of
purpose that we need.' These emphases persist today. *The*

[1] Harold J. Laski, *Studies in the Problem of Sovereignty*, New Haven and London,
1917, p. 19; Andrew Shonfield, *Modern Capitalism, The Changing Balance of Public
and Private Power*, London, 1969, pp. 89, 94, 119, 163; George Howell, *Trade
Unionism New and Old*, London, 1891, p. 190; S. G. Hobson, *National Guilds and the
State*, London, 1920, p. 114; Trades Union Congress *Report*, p. 391.

[2] Ernest Edwin Williams, '*Made in Germany*', London, 1896, p. 164; Melvin
Richter, *The Politics of Conscience*, *T. H. Green and his Age*, London, 1964; J. Ramsay
MacDonald, *Socialism and Government*, London, 1909, vol. I, pp. 17, 78; vol. II,
p. 117; R. H. Tawney, *The Acquisitive Society*, London, 1926, pp. 14, 32, 96, 206.

Regeneration of British Industry declared that, 'above all, we must get away from policies of confrontation and work together in the national interest towards agreed objectives.'[1]

The survival of the nationalist strain in Labour Party thought was partly responsible for a further attempt at 'planning' after 1974. The spectacular wage increases that followed the fall of the Heath government accelerated the very rapid inflation of 1974–5, which greatly reduced many companies' liquidity and adversely affected their ability to export their products, in a world market which was, in any event, contracting. Unemployment rose sharply; the pound was severely devalued. The government responded by introducing a new incomes policy, which it justified in the strongest terms. Without this 'plan to save our country', the government stated, 'the British people will be engulfed by a general catastrophe of incalculable proportions'. The Trades Union Congress, thus solemnly admonished, abandoned hopes of 15 per cent wage increases, and accepted a universal flat rate £6 a week increase, a settlement described by Wilson as 'an achievement unexampled in peace or war by the free democratic trade union movement in this country'. A year later Congress accepted another period of controls on wage increases. Meanwhile, the government seemingly transformed its attitude to intervention in economic activity when it proposed to 'monitor' those areas of manufacturing that it controlled. Lord Ryder's report on British Leyland expressed the 'monitoring' doctrine in the proposal that each 'stage' of 'the injection of new finance by the Government' should depend on 'evidence of a tangible contribution by British Leyland's workforce and management to the reduction of industrial disputes and the improvement of productivity'.[2]

These events might indicate a major shift in British attitudes, away from individualism and towards collectivism. Indeed, in November 1975, the Central Policy Review Staff urged the government to 'sponsor a programme designed to achieve . . . fundamental changes in attitude' in the car industry, in order to improve 'productivity, quality and continuity in production': a proposal which, if meant and taken seriously, would amount

[1] Labour Party *Conference Report*, 1964, p. 112; *The Times*, 6 November 1975.
[2] Ibid., 25 April 1975; 26 June 1975; 11 July 1975; *The Attack on Inflation*, Cmnd. 6151, para. 48.

to a highly collectivist project of state-directed opinion formation. But as yet the evidence for a major change in attitudes (let alone a serious attempt at government-aided reformation of attitudes) is rather uncertain.[1]

First, the Trades Union Congress's approach to incomes policy was perhaps less novel than it might seem. The £6 a week increase represented, for all workers earning less than average incomes, a rise in basic wages of more than 10 per cent; and it resulted in an increase of average earnings of about 15 per cent. Even the figure of 10 per cent itself would scarcely seem an 'achievement' were it not for the 25–30 per cent increases of 1974–5. The 1975–6 policy, and that of 1976–7, which raised average money earnings by 12 per cent, were quite largely influenced by Jack Jones, who used his position in Congress and Party to favour his own low-paid members, and to compress differentials, in return for large money settlements which satisfied other unions until the fall in real earnings became apparent during 1977. Moreover, the trade unions' adherence to the income policies of 1975–7 was rather similar to their temporary adherence, under threat of unemployment, to the wage restraint of 1948–50. Indeed, the Trades Union Congress's document *The Development of the Social Contract* accepted the £6 limit as 'a temporary policy put forward for the coming year' to 'prevent massive unemployment': and, just as removal of the threat of unemployment led the trade unions back to an unadulterated *laissez-faire* sectionalism in the 1950s, so removal of the fear of 'economic catastrophe' may well expedite a return to tradition in the 1980s.[2]

Secondly, the government appears to be almost as loyal as ever to those doctrinaire *laissez-faire* views which require all approaches to state intervention in (and direction of) the economy to be as modest as possible, given the exigencies of the situation. At the end of 1975, Lord Ryder, whom the government had just appointed chairman of the National Enterprise Board (newly established to control state holdings in manufacturing undertakings) declared that the Board was 'going to be like any company in the private sector', and not at all like a government department, whether in a liberal or a socialist

---

[1] *The Times*, 17 December 1975.
[2] Ibid., 12 July 1975.

state. The Board's actions tended to confirm this view. The policy of 'monitoring', in the form of a threat not to finance the continuation of British Leyland as a mass producer, was applied to that company during negotiations on restrictive practices in October 1976, and again during the three-week toolmakers' strike in March 1977, but in neither case with apparent conviction or conspicuous success.[1]

A certain cautiousness seemed to characterize *The Regeneration of British Industry*, too, even though that document was in part the work of some of the most prominent left-wingers in the Labour Party. In 1972 Peter Self observed that 'the word "plan" '—that symbol of socialist enthusiasm—'is increasingly being replaced by the more flexible notion of strategy': and it was as a study in 'industrial strategy', not as prolegomena to a national plan, that the white paper was described. Yet the authors of the document called it 'not a strategy but a programme for developing a strategy': and the transition from 'plan' to 'strategy' to 'programme' is reminiscent of that from 'targets' to 'estimates' in the economic policy of the Attlee administrations. Subsequent events underlined this development. In 1976-7 the government spoke much of its 'industrial strategy': yet the chief items in this were the necessarily fragmented discussions of 'Sector Working Parties', whose deliberations, the government claimed, constituted a 'learning process' which could 'lay the foundations for a comprehensive and fully articulated national industrial strategy', at some unspecified future date.[2]

In short, just as the decisive change in industrial *structure* during 1945–51 left economic and social *attitudes* virtually unchanged, so the striking structural changes of the mid-1970s may also leave attitudes largely unaltered. For, if *cultural* determinants—ideas, attitudes and assumptions—shape social life, ownership of the means of production is not merely (in Crosland's phrase) 'no longer' but *never* 'the key factor' which imparts to a society 'its essential character'. Yet to argue that

[1] On incomes policy: see *The Times*, 12 July 1975; 17 November 1975. On the National Enterprise Board: see *The Times*, 2 March 1976. On British Leyland: see *The Times*, 6 and 7 October 1976; 16 March 1977; and *The Guardian*, 11 October 1976.
[2] *The Times*, 6 November 1975; 26 January 1976; 8 July 1976; Peter Self, *Administrative Theories and Politics, An Inquiry into the Structure and Processes of Modern Government*, London, 1972, p. 32.

political economists, rather than political economy, determine
the character of a society is not to argue that technology,
economic relationships or property structure do not affect
attitudes at all. Concentration of economic power in the hands
of the management of large firms (along with the associations
to which those firms are affiliated), of the leadership of trade
unions, and of the government, for instance, has undoubtedly
facilitated the movement from nineteenth-century liberal
individualism, not to full collectivism, but to a corporatist
compromise that has partly reshaped labour culture as well as
national culture.

This compromise was indicated in H. C. S. Dyer's remark
in 1897, that, 'I hope to see the day when every workman shall
belong to some Trade Society, and when every employer shall
also belong to an Employers' Trade Society'. Dyer's hope was
realized in the era of 'collective bargaining' that followed the
Victorians' struggle to get and keep unilateral job regulation.
Trade unionists acquiesced in that era, especially if they were
national leaders who stood to gain most from it. These men
naturally adopted the slogan of the Boilermakers' leaders in
1908 that, 'no true advance or good can come without true
and complete executive control'; and, by 1908 national union
leaders had sufficiently accepted the doctrines of corporatism
to advocate what Blatchford called a 'working-class party'
acting in 'the interests of the working-class'. The higher
sectionalism of national trade union officials and the leadership
of the Labour Party was not unmixed with a certain yearning
for the older ways—which retained their appeal to the 'rank
and file', of which so much began to be heard from the first
years of the twentieth century onwards. But corporatism was
vigorously promoted by influential labour theorists, and above
all by the Webbs, with their cult of 'collective bargaining', and
their talk of the sectional 'democracies', of 'Consumers, of
Producers, of Citizens' whose mutual trading was to be the
substance of the 'socialist commonwealth'.[1]

---

[1] *Conference Between the Employers' Federation of Engineering Associations and the
Amalgamated Society of Engineers . . . April 1897*, pp. 52, 84; *United Society of Boiler-
makers' and Iron and Steel Shipbuilders' Monthly Report*, May 1908, p. 21; Robert
Blatchford, *Britain for the British*, London, 1902, p. 148; Sidney and Beatrice Webb,
A Constitution for the Socialist Commonwealth in Great Britain, London, 1920, pp. 102–3,
167, 315.

The Webbs' corporatism led them to favour, first, 'municipal-ization', rather than 'nationalization', and then the independ-ent public-corporation type of nationalization, under which, in a Labour Party formulation of 1926, the corporation's officers would undertake 'day-by-day conduct', while the government would confine itself to 'questions of general policy'. The doctrine of the independent public corporation 'able to operate free from undesirable political restrictions', as Citrine put it, became the orthodoxy of the Labour governments of the 1940s. The 'social democratic revolution' thus proved, as a Chemical Workers' delegate not unjustly observed to the 1950 Trades Union Congress, to have been 'the managerial revolu-tion'. Yet the emergence of great managerial structures, such as those of the National Coal Board or British Rail, no less than those of Unilever or Imperial Chemical Industries, were in principle compatible with the corporatist views slowly pervad-ing even the 'rank and file' of labour: to whom, moreover, corporatism offered certain compensations through the increas-ing 'tripartism' of public affairs.[1]

'Tripartism', the determination of state policy by negotiation between government, representatives of management and trade unionists, derives theoretical justification from the Laskian view of government as just one of the 'associations' that compose society. It derived its first practical impetus from the Mond-Turner conferences, with their concept of 'industry as a whole', and their efforts to promote the interests of industry as a whole through joint approaches to government. Since the Second World War the ideal of the Mond-Turner conferences has become a reality. Though the Heath government collapsed in 1974 amid accusations of 'confrontation' with trade unions, two years earlier its efforts to secure an incomes policy by agreement with the Confederation of British Industry and the Trades Union Congress were provoking accusations of 'corpor-atism': and, such accusations notwithstanding, the subsequent Labour administrations followed the same tripartist course. 'We have sought to work through consensus and agreement with the TUC and the CBI', said Wilson in defence of the £6-a-week policy. 'We were right to do that.' Heath agreed.

---

[1] W. M. Citrine, *Problems of Nationalized Industries*, Sidney Ball Lecture, 30 October 1951 (typescript), p. 1; Trades Union Congress *Report*, 1950, p. 513.

'He fully and unequivocally supported the agreement between the Government and trade unions' on wages, he told the House of Commons in July 1976. 'It was in the national interest', not least because 'those countries which had had greatest success in dealing with the industrial situation were those which had the closest form of consultation with both sides of industry.'[1]

Perhaps organized labour concurred. 'Governments treat the T.U.C. as a sort of Industrial Parliament' to obtain the views of 'the trade union Movement' and 'to secure the approval of the T.U.C. for . . . legislation which will have a day to day influence on the work of the trade unions', the Trades Union Congress told the Donovan Commission in 1968. From 1974 onwards, the unions, in pursuit of the 'Social Contract', seemed still closer to government. Jack Jones strongly defended both the Wilson and the Callaghan administrations, not least against Labour left-wingers; and the Engineers, under Scanlon's leadership, arrived in the spring of 1977 at the unusual position of supporting the state-appointed management of British Leyland against their own craftsmen members. Yet the unions' direct involvement in the formation of government economic policy had its limitations. Both in 1976 and in 1977 the government attempted to control incomes unilaterally by budgetary measures to which the unions were not privy; while throughout this period the sector working parties discussing the trilaterally agreed 'industrial strategy' had 'real difficulties in recruiting enough interested trade unionists'.[2]

Nevertheless, by accepting tripartism, in however qualified a form, the Trades Union Congress had largely succeeded to the role of national union leadership earlier in the history of collective bargaining. In the 1900s national union leaders bargained with the organized employers. In the 1960s and 1970s, national union leaders' representatives bargained with the organized employers and the government. Naturally, such a role has caused the Trades Union Congress much the same difficulties as national union leaders had earlier endured, and not least the difficulties of enforcing unattractive but inescapable agreements. The Trades Union Congress's extended sphere of

---

[1] *The Times*, 12 July 1975; 8 July 1976; Royal Commission on Trade Unions and Employers' Associations, *Selected Written Evidence*, p. 138.

[2] *The Guardian*, 14 August 1976.

activity seems so far to provoke among its affiliates less hostility than was aroused among union members by the efforts at collective bargaining of the national union officials of the early twentieth century. Yet there is little sign of a change in the outlook and *mores* of organized labour sufficient to establish the argument that the new system of industrial relations has brought the attitudes of trade unionists nearer to collectivism. On the contrary, labour culture, if now converted into corporatism, nevertheless preserves (to return to Collingwood's terminology) very substantial 'residues' of individualism 'incapsulated' within itself.[1]

The persistence of individualism, despite the continued growth of tripartist habits of thought and action among trade unionists was illustrated, at the beginning of 1977, during the campaign to elect a successor to Jones as General Secretary of the Transport and General Workers' Union. Jones's own candidate, Moss Evans, pledged himself 'to continue the policies that have been determined by the union over the many years that Jack Jones has been its general secretary'. He was challenged by Frank Cousin's son John, who, though not even a union official, managed to poll 16 per cent, and came second to Evans who received only 46 per cent, and was thus the first candidate to be elected to lead the union on a minority vote. Cousins urged the Union's members not to forget that 'the only safeguard against the corporate state' was Parliament. The 'special political relationship' of unions and government, associated with the 'Social Contract', ought to end. 'The name of the game today is looking after our own people', said Cousins in the course of a speech advocating a 'return to free collective bargaining', a policy shortly afterwards adopted, despite Jones's opposition, by the Union's conference. Labour's loyalty to sectionalism seemed little changed.[2]

THE INDUSTRIALIZATION OF POLITICS

Writing in London (and not least from English experience) in 1848, Marx and Engels argued that,

[1] Collingwood, p. 95.
[2] On Cousins: see *The Sun*, 19 January 1977; *The Guardian*, 19 January 1977; *The Times*, 15 February 1977. On Evans: see *The Times*, 22 April 1977.

The bourgeoisie, wherever it has got the upper hand, has put an end to all feudal, patriarchal, idyllic relations. It has pitilessly torn asunder the motley feudal ties that bound man to his 'natural superiors', and has left no other nexus between man and man than naked self-interest, than callous 'cash payment'. It has drowned the most heavenly ecstasies of religious fervour, of chivalrous enthusiasm, of philistine sentimentalism, in the icy water of egotistical calculation. It has resolved personal worth into exchange value, and in place of the numberless indefeasible chartered freedoms, has set up that single, unconscionable freedom—Free Trade.

In short, the 'bourgeoisie' (the 'empirical businessmen' so closely linked in the young Marx's mind with 'political economists') had adopted an ideology of *laissez-faire* liberal individualism: of 'naked self-interest', of 'egotistical calculation', and of 'Free Trade'. Moreover, the bourgeoisie had adopted this ideology in a pronouncedly utilitarian, materialist form that encouraged it to reconstruct society on the basis of 'callous "cash payment"', and to evaluate individuals by reference not to 'personal worth' but to 'exchange value'. And though these intellectual developments affected 'society as a whole', and tended towards a more or less homogeneous 'epoch of the bourgeoisie', the empirical businessmen had in fact enforced their doctrines only 'wherever' they 'got the upper hand': in those countries, and those sectors of human life, where conditions were most favourable to them.[1]

The argument of this book is that the 'bourgeoisie', precisely in the sense of *laissez-faire* liberal individualists (or 'political economists' for short), have 'got the upper hand', especially in certain cultural conditions: and Engels made a Marxist nod towards such an argument when he remarked in his notes to the *Communist Manifesto* that, 'generally speaking, for the economic development of the bourgeoisie, England is here taken as the typical country, for its political development, France'. Yet within countries that afford cultural conditions favourable to the growth of the bourgeois ideology, certain sectors may present conditions that accelerate, or indeed modify, the growth of that ideology. This argument, which is more akin to

---

[1] K. Marx and F. Engels, *Manifesto of the Communist Party*, London, 1938, pp. 5, 9–10, 12; Karl Marx, *Economic and Philosophical Manuscripts of 1844*, Moscow, 1961, p. 118.

Marxism than would be any *universalist* variant of the cultural argument, may be illustrated by reference to Hegel's triad of the family, civil society and the state. In Hegel's schema, the family, the domestic sphere, is 'specifically characterized by love', a sentiment that would allow relatively little scope for *laissez-faire* liberal individualism, even in a *laissez-faire* liberal-individualist country. So, too, even in such a country, the state, the political sphere which is 'the end and actuality of both the substantial universal order and the public life devoted thereto', would provide relatively fewer opportunities for the development of the bourgeois ideology than would the 'battlefield' of civil society, where 'each member is his own end, everything else is nothing to him' and 'where everyone's individual private interests meet everyone else'.[1]

This approach has a certain commonsense strength. One would, after all, expect to find loyalty to *laissez-faire* principles less pronounced in the family than on the stock exchange. In other words, though 'economic activity' does not have the '*capital* importance' in shaping men's 'way of thinking and feeling', attributed to it by Goldmann, it may well have considerable effect upon the intensity and consistency with which a general 'way of thinking and feeling' is in fact thought and felt by particular individuals and groups. Sectoral influences may also affect the emphases of different parts of an ideology. The utilitarian, materialist element in liberal individualism may be quite subordinate in certain contexts. Karl Popper, for instance, presents the distinctively liberal-individualist argument that 'Science and more especially scientific progress, are the results' of 'the *free competition of thought*'; but this philosopher's liberal individualism stresses utilitarian materialism much less than would the liberal individualism of the authors of *The Miners' Next Step* who favoured competition with the capitalists 'until we have extracted the whole of the employers' profits'.[2]

Many observers, trade unionists among them, distinguished both 'political' and 'industrial' sectors in the life of nineteenth-century Britain: that is, the sectors of polity; and of production, and, more especially, of factory production. Both areas were

[1] Marx and Engels, p. 11; T. M. Knox (ed. and transl.), *Hegel's Philosophy of Right*, Oxford, 1952, pp. 110, 189, 267.
[2] Karl R. Popper, *The Poverty of Historicism*, London, 1960, pp. 154-5.

much influenced by liberal individualism. But the political sphere, closely linked to the pre-industrial past by the traditions of the monarchy, the established church and the ancient universities, 'incapsulated' rather large 'residues' of earlier patterns of thought within its version of the increasingly prevalent liberal-individualist doctrines. Despite the ever greater weight of utilitarian criteria of convenience and efficiency, moreover, the political form of these doctrines remained, to a great extent, that of the large general normative principles characteristic of the world in which the polity is formed, re-formed, and debated: principles which express that world's concern for the qualitative, and its continuous formulation of universal, binding laws and rules. Hence in the political sphere, liberal individualism expressed itself, for example, in Gladstone's moralistic campaigns against inequity and inequality, and for freedom, self-determination, and self-government. Such campaigns were major features of the strictly political debate, about sovereignty, government, and law-making powers, that developed through the movements for parliamentary reform and home rule, the introduction of the secret ballot, and the formation of mass political parties divided on specifically political issues.

But the industrial sphere was much influenced by nonconformity and had little to do with the ancient universities. Though rarely if ever republican, the new industrial entrepreneurs were pioneers often deliberately distancing themselves from the past; and, as a self-conscious group, they (and still more organized labour) were so novel an entity that they had rather few objective links with the past. As has been noted, though both Marx's 'bourgeoisie' and his 'proletariat' were necessarily divided from each other by their mutual predilection for what a self-styled 'primitive' trade unionist at the 1944 Trades Union Congress called 'a good wrestling match', they were in fact united by their common hostility to the pre- or non-industrial order. They were united, too, by common cultural and social attitudes, fidelity to the Webbs' 'spirit of the bagman', and a preference for political principles readily reducible to egoistic pursuit of material self-interest. Their world was characterized, in short, by debates about money.[1]

[1] Trades Union Congress *Report*, 1944, p. 227.

The political sphere of life long antedates the industrial, at least so far as the industrial is characterized by machine tools and factory production. Yet as R. M. McIver put it, in 1926, 'the new economic power was no child of the state'. Indeed, most of those who disposed of this new power seemed at first to shun the state, or any large problem that might divert them from their material concerns. Thus, as the Webbs remark, 'political or religious wrangling . . . were penalized by fines' in the early trade unions. Organized labour's continuing unease about politics is well documented. 'It has been the boast of trade unionists that they belong to no political party;' said the President of the 1885 Trades Union Congress, who added, 'I hope they never will as it is now understood.' Nearly eighty years later, when the trade unions had 'their own' party, Feather, shortly to become General Secretary of the Trades Union Congress, advised fellow trade unionists that, 'every political situation should be judged on its merits, and only from the standpoint of the members' interests'. And in 1974, when Congress was most enthusiastically proclaiming the 'Social Contract', Feather's successor, Murray, stated that 'We can never be the agents of a political party—or of the State.'[1]

Meanwhile labour has shown a marked loyalty to the commercial. Early trade unions modelled themselves on, and indeed often became, friendly societies. Trade unionists and their allies formed the co-operative societies, with their dividends, share capital, interest, and now trading stamps. The trade unionists' Labour Party, a Miner told fellow delegates to the 1913 Trades Union Congress, was 'the best investment we ever made'; and four years later that Party's first manifesto promised the people that, when Labour's era of nationalization arrived, there would be an 'equitable sharing of the proceeds', virtually in the form of a dividend. Since the First World War, Labour's stress on 'socialism', and indeed 'compassion', has perhaps somewhat diluted the commercial element in the Party's character. But utilitarian materialism still seems quite popular. While 'building up the case for socialism' in 1913, Snowden warned that, 'if under a system of private landowning and

---

[1] Sidney and Beatrice Webb, *Industrial Democracy*, London, 1902, pp. 4–5; R. M. McIver, *The Modern State*, Oxford, 1926, p. 139; Trades Union Congress *Report*, 1885, p. 17; Feather, p. 39; *The Director*, June 1974, p. 364.

private capitalism, the condition of every individual in the community was all that could be desired, there would be no argument for a change of the system'. The same point was made by the constituency delegate to the 1955 Party Conference, who argued that, if it were possible for 'working people' to 'expect, without a change in society, an improved and guaranteed material standard of living', the 'necessity for change in society is no longer there', and 'we have thrown overboard the whole basis for socialism'.[1]

The Labour Party's strongly utilitarian variant of *laissez-faire* liberal individualism indicates the degree to which the party is itself one necessary element in the modern industrialization of British politics. The Labour Party was founded as a trade union in politics. As Blatchford observed in 1902, a trade union was 'a combination of workers to defend their own interests from the encroachments of the employers', and a Labour Party was the same thing 'in Parliament and on Municipal bodies'. Once the Labour Party began to challenge existing political parties, political institutions in general did tend to become trade unions or quasi-trade unions, and to adopt the industrial habits and procedures of organized labour. Doubtless, however, the tendency towards imitation of the Labour Party is nowhere fully completed; and at least one special circumstance seems to distinguish the relationship between the quasi-trade union which is the Labour Party, and the truly industrial associations that finance it, from the relationship between other such quasi-trade unions and industrial associations which support them. This is the one-directional nature of the relationship that trade unions apparently wish to maintain between the so-say 'political' and the industrial properly so-called.[2]

The asymmetry in this relationship differentiates Britain from any situation where the 'political' and the 'industrial' are merely conflated. McIver argued in quite general terms that, 'economic forces . . . may proclaim ever so loudly the principles of *laissez-faire*, but when they cry, "let us alone to pursue our aims", they do not address to themselves the reciprocal of that

---

[1] Trades Union Congress *Report*, 1913, p. 227; Philip Snowden, *Socialism and Syndicalism*, London, n.d., p. 17; Labour Party *Conference Report*, 1955, p. 116.

[2] Blatchford, p. 149.

command, they do not promise in turn to cease exerting influence on the government of the state.' Yet this is especially true of trade unions. For, while manufacturing firms have (largely in response to the trade union example) increasingly sought to influence 'politics', they have in their turn accepted an increasing regulation of their internal affairs, through statute law and administrative action. Such reciprocity is, however, anathema to trade unions, who resist all efforts to regulate their affairs, whether by Conservative or by Labour governments. Hence a National Union of General and Municipal Workers' research officer's belief that, 'the democrat has to acknowledge that the unions must be left to reform themselves'. In this sense, then, trade unionists and others who 'industrialize' politics, have no desire to 'politicize' industry in general, or unions in particular: on the contrary they wish to keep unions outside the polity, 'outside the realms of the law', as Cousins put it.[1]

The conversion of political parties into a sort of trade union is inextricably linked with the transformation of the Victorians' strictly political debates about the distribution of political power into debates about the distribution of money. Those trade unionists who have used political terminology have traditionally done so chiefly when discussing the realm of the 'ultimate'. In 1834 the Grand National Consolidated Trades Union carefully distinguished between its 'design', which was 'in the first instance' to raise wages and diminish 'hours of labour', and its 'great and ultimate object', which was 'to establish the paramount rights of Industry and Humanity'; while Clynes insisted, more than seventy years later, that the Labour Party was a party of 'immediate legislation', not 'ultimate objects'. Immediate legislation meant, in practice, more money for wage earners. As Cole and Mellor remarked in 1918, 'in Great Britain, where men have been . . . constitutionally averse from idealism . . . Socialism has been almost purely a doctrine of distribution of income'. The redistribution of money to wage earners has been achieved partly by welfare measures financed out of taxation, partly by maintenance of a low level of unemployment (and hence a high level of trade-union bargaining strength), and partly by specific assistance to

[1] McIver, p. 300; Trades Union Congress *Report*, 1966, p. 463.

individual sectors of the economy, which have been wholly or part-nationalized. Were 'governmental power' to be 'vested in the productive population', Bray observed, 'the commercial regulations of society would be subject to perpetual variations to meet the emergencies of particular classes of producers'. Now, as ever, organized labour seems to view such 'variations' as utilitarian expedients, rather than as steps towards socialism (or even as means towards long-term economic advance). Hence Arthur Deakin's complaint, in 1953, that 'the people in the nationalized industries have regarded the change-over merely from the point of view of how much better off they could become in the shortest possible time in the way of better wages and conditions.'[1]

When the substance of 'politics' becomes money, the conduct of 'politics' becomes a kind of collective bargaining. As the Shopworkers' leader Alan Birch noted in 1958, 'unions have grown by using their organization' for 'one purpose: to establish the best possible wages and conditions' through 'collective negotiation'. Another member of the Shopworkers' union said, at the 1974 Trades Union Congress,

> At last we have been able to get over the message that wages are only one part of the total package that the worker is entitled to enjoy. The whole range of economic and social policies pursued by governments . . . has a direct effect on our general living standards. . . . But there are items which, even under free collective bargaining, are not established across the negotiating table between the unions and the employers. I would love to be able to negotiate the defence expenditure across the negotiating table.

These remarks indicate the way in which some trade unionists have converted the 'political' into the 'industrial'. 'The whole range of economic and social policies', including 'defence expenditure', is to be subsumed within 'the total package the worker is entitled to enjoy', and therefore to bargain over. Such policies are to be determined, not within the overtly political structures of society, but 'across the negotiating table between

---

[1] *Rules and Regulations of the Grand National Consolidated Trades' Union of Great Britain and Ireland*, London, 1834, pp. 22–3; Labour Party *Conference Report*, 1908, p. 58; 1953, p. 132; G. D. H. Cole and W. Mellor, *The Meaning of Industrial Freedom*, London, 1918, p. 6; Bray, p. 213.

the unions and the employers'. Who 'the unions' and 'the employers' are, in the context of 'defence expenditure', for example, is unclear. What is clear is that the formulation of all national decisions by negotiation between 'unions' and 'employers' would represent the total assimilation of the 'political' to the 'industrial'.[1]

The concomitant to this process is the employment of 'industrial action' for 'political' ends. In 1919 some Labour Party members thought it 'unwise and undemocratic' to 'substitute industrial action' for traditional parliamentary methods of obtaining the political power necessary to implement the Party's proposals. The objection was occasioned by Smillie's apparent certainty that the Miners would be right 'to use the power of their organization in order to improve their conditions by means of nationalization'. The exercise, both of that power and of the power of several other unions, in order to secure a 'drastic reorganization' of the coal industry, seven years later, emphasized the nature of such a resort to industrial action. The General Strike of 1926 was an attempt to supersede the decision-making power of Parliament, to supplant the Labour Party as an instrument for the formation and articulation of public opinion, and to substitute the constraint necessarily exerted by a widespread concerted stoppage of work for the development of policy through discussion and debate. In certain senses, it has been suggested here, such an undertaking does appear to be 'unconstitutional'. Moreover, whether a strike is or is not the best way to fix wages, it can rarely if ever be the best way to determine the organization of society.[2]

These points continue to be acknowledged, if in a rather strange way, by Labour leaders. When Wilson condemned the Ulster Workers' Council for calling the strike that brought down the power-sharing executive in Northern Ireland in May 1974, he complained that the Ulster Workers were 'like a group of workers holding the country to ransom not on something they feel strongly about—on wages and so on—but saying that people must pull out of the Commonwealth, go into a republic. You cannot have a strike to get a major constitutional

[1] Trades Union Congress *Report*, 1958, p. 418; 1974, pp. 424–5.
[2] Labour Party *Conference Report*, 1919, pp. 113, 118.

change of government.' The Ulster Workers' action, he concluded, was 'totally unconstitutional'. As critics noted, Wilson
implied that workers 'holding the country to ransom' act
constitutionally when they act on 'something they feel strongly
about', provided that something is 'wages and so on', not 'a
major constitutional change of government'. Wilson did not
argue that 'holding the country to ransom' was an unacceptable
method of dealing with wages; nor did he assert that such a
proceeding was an unacceptable method of dealing with the
questions he summarized as 'so on', that is, questions between
'wages' and 'a major constitutional change of government' such
as abolishing the monarchy. The extent of Wilson's 'so on'—
which would include labour's objectives in 1926 and in 1971–4
—seemed to indicate the degree to which politics have been
industrialized; while his apparent approval of industrial action
in the pursuit of industrial politics confirmed many people in
the fear that society was in danger of becoming, as Bray put it,
'a hot bed of tyranny and hatred'. After 1974 such fears declined; yet the problem of the relationship of the 'industrial'
and the 'political' remains. That problem is simple. The
doctrinaire application of 'industrial' methods to politics
involves a confusion harmful to industry and polity alike. For,
popular orthodoxy notwithstanding, a nation is more than its
trade unions, and its affairs cannot be conducted as if they were
merely a series of wage claims.[1]

VARIETIES OF DEMOCRACY

Despite the pressures of the last hundred years or so, the
ideology that informs and sustains British national life remains
fundamentally inimical to collectivism. In parts that ideology is
corporatist; but even its corporatism is tinged with an apparently indelible nostalgia for Victorian *laissez-faire*. Nowhere
are the doctrines of *laissez-faire* more faithfully preserved than
among the trade unions, for all their socialist language; and
the *laissez-faire* liberal individualism of organized labour is
characterized by an unusually powerful strain of utilitarianism.
The growth of organized labour has been a major factor in the
development of the corporatist elements in the social and

[1] *The Times*, 30 May 1974; 3 June 1974.

political structure of modern Britain, and above all in the emergence of the tripartist system of determining national economic policy. Meanwhile, organized labour's influence has industrialized politics, by converting political institutions into quasi-trade unions, by transforming political argument into debates about money, and by settling such debates through methods akin to those of collective bargaining. Finally, organized labour's power confers upon it an anomalous autonomy and immunity which trade unionists, and others, justify by traditional liberal-individualist arguments that trade unions are 'only' their members, 'only people', and that people should be free to do what they like.

The United Kingdom is believed to be a democratic country; and it is precisely the prevalence of *laissez-faire* liberal individualism, in thought and action, that provides most people's evidence for this belief. In the popular view, democracy occurs when men are free and equal; are safe to say and do more or less what they like; are able to pursue their lives, and follow their interests, unhindered by government interference; and can expect that, if government does act, it will act in conformity with their wishes and in accordance with universal and equal laws. But the identification of the United Kingdom as a democratic country must be qualified in certain respects. First, however 'democracy' may be defined, it will occur in its purest form in men's minds. Secondly, the principle upon which much (but by no means all) of men's life is conducted, actually or ideally, is not strictly a democratic but a representative principle, which necessarily curtails freedom, and reduces equality by the explicit or implicit grant of powers by the represented to the representative. Thirdly, freedom and equality, and men's 'democratic rights' in general, are further abridged by the obligations, the responsibilities imposed upon men by the requirements of any form of society as complex as the representative system of politics. Fourthly, it is not always clear that laws are of equal and universal application. Thus just as many men cling to individualism in an increasingly corporatist society, so they cling to the utilitarian *laissez-faire* liberal-individualist variety of democracy in a largely (though not entirely) representative social and political system.

Divergences between the corporatist reality and individualist

convictions, or between the representative reality and democratic convictions, may well cause dissatisfaction. The representative system, as exemplified in the working of the British
Parliament, for instance, is operated by a rather small élite
commanding at least a certain degree of authority and quite
often acting in defiance of the apparent wishes of very many
citizens. These things do not seem particularly democratic.
In defence of the claim that they are democratic, the parliamentarians argue that, if they are an élite they are an élite
recently appointed and readily dismissed; that any élite
characteristics they may possess arise not from privilege but
from their appointment by those who themselves could become
representatives in their turn; that their authority is derived
from the mandate given them by the voters who chose them;
and that, were they to exceed, or default on, their mandate,
the voters would be free (in no more than three or four years
time) to vote against them. Finally, the parliamentarians
would add that they do make universal and equal laws: and
that their special position in society is necessary to that work.

This kind of argument has serious weaknesses. Any such
argument rests on two assumptions, the democratic validity of
elections and the democratic formation and application of laws.
But it is not at all clear that elections are always if ever
democratic, or indeed representative. Parliamentarians are
appointed, not by the people, but at most by a majority; and
often they are not even appointed by a majority. At highly
important junctures in public affairs—in 1929, 1951, and 1974
—the group of parliamentarians who have had the largest
number of seats in the House of Commons, and have therefore
formed a government, received fewer votes than the group of
parliamentarians with the second largest number of seats. In
1951 the Labour Party, which then had to leave office to make
way for what proved to be thirteen years of Conservative
government, polled more votes than any party has polled
before or since. In any event, a majority of the votes cast at an
election is simply the quantity of votes cast for particular
candidates (chosen, so far as the people are concerned, in a
more or less arbitrary fashion) whom a majority of electors
happen to prefer to other candidates (equally arbitrarily
chosen), rarely on grounds of the candidates' qualities or

intentions, but usually on the ground of their association with a party. Parties and their candidates publish manifestos at election time; but few voters read them, and fewer agree with everything that they read; manifestos are, moreover, written in rather general if not tendentious language; and governments usually do things not mentioned in manifestos, and fail to do things that are mentioned in manifestos. The parliamentarians' claim to derive a 'mandate' from elections is therefore suspect. It becomes still more suspect, when, as in the exercise of tripartism, governments take decisions in consultation with, and on the advice of, groups with no formal or public standing in the election process.

The parliamentarians' claim to be part of a democratic system is further weakened by the uneven application of laws. There are differences in the way criminal law is applied to different cases; and these differences sometimes seem to derive from the socio-economic status of the accused. There are also differences in the way statutes do or do not affect certain individuals and groups. Among various prominent examples, those most relevant to the issues under consideration here, are the unique immunity from actions for damages, conferred on trade unions from the 1906 Trade Disputes Act onwards; and the special freedom of trade unions from public supervision, confirmed by the withdrawal of the Labour Party's Industrial Relations Bill in 1969, and the repeal of the Conservative Party's Industrial Relations Act in 1974.

These deficiencies of the representative system, as it is operated in Britain today, are rendered more serious by the limited extent of representation in national life. True, the House of Commons is elected, if in a rather unsatisfactory manner; but neither the House of Lords nor the Crown, both of which play important parts in the political process, are elective in any sense whatever. There is no representative machinery in the armed forces, in most industrial and financial undertakings, or in schools. The representative machinery operative in colleges, churches and other voluntary associations, including political parties and trade unions, is usually more or less defective. Yet such institutions' leaders may exercise significant influence over the formation of public policy: which, by that very fact, is made less representative, and probably less democratic also.

Of course, some social organizations influence public policy less than do others. The present power of organized labour, together with the industrialization of politics, raises special problems for democracy and for representation. 'For the purposes of industrial democracy', wrote Clegg in 1960, 'it is difficult to see that the trade unions could be too strong.' This would perhaps be so, if trade unions were themselves 'democratic' (or at least representative), and if they exerted a democratic influence on the world about them. Yet, as Clegg and Adams observed in 1957, the expansion of trade unions, and the development of their constitutions has been such, that nowadays 'unofficial action' is 'one of the main guarantees of union democracy'. It was noted, in connection with the unilateralist episode, that about 1960 the national policy of the Amalgamated Engineering Union was formed by the delegates of the delegates of the delegates of 10 per cent of the membership. In 1960, and since, this system has given unrepresentative power to left-wingers; and, indeed, the introduction, against left-wing objections, of postal balloting in national union elections, was followed by important changes in the political complexion of the Engineers' national leadership in 1975. Similar faults occur in the franchise and electoral machinery of other unions. Much union policy is therefore both unrepresentative and undemocratic. In 1897, the Webbs noted that trade unions 'are perpetually meddling' with 'issues of . . . politics, upon which the bulk of their constituents have either no opinions', or shared the opinions of the Conservative and Liberal parties:

> Resolutions abolishing the House of Lords, secularizing education, rehabilitating silver, establishing a system of peasant proprietorship, enfranchising leaseholds, or 'nationalizing the means of production, distribution, and exchange',—questions in which the Trade Unionists, as such, are not more interested, not better informed, nor yet more united than other citizens,—find a place on Trade Union agendas, and either get formally passed through sheer indifference, or become the source of discord, recrimination, and disruption.

A similar point was made in 1975, by Bryan Magee, who agreed that 'it is virtually impossible' for 'a politically-minded union official' to 'get his men to act against their convictions in anything to do with the job'; but claimed that, 'he can get them to pass resolutions about Chile or Vietnam with comparative ease'.[1]

These problems are exacerbated by the character of the larger organizations of labour. Many union resolutions— whether on the House of Lords or on Vietnam—are remitted to the Trades Union Congress, the delegates to which are appointed by affiliated unions. Congress 'composites' most such resolutions into omnibus formulas, for or against which the affiliated unions' delegates cast—in concert, and often on the basis of agreements entered into before the public debate—not their own votes but the votes of those of their members for whom the Union has chosen to pay dues to the Trades Union Congress. The representative nature of the British political system vests authority in numbers; and, by alleging a mandate from millions of trade unionists, the few hundred men who vote either way in a Trades Union Congress ballot, claim for themselves a quite unreal authority. This authority is then reinforced by a repetition of the entire process at the Labour Party conference. Labour Party leaders naturally tend to discount the significance of certain resolutions, which, nevertheless, are said to have received millions of votes at Congress or Conference. Then the Webbs' 'discord, recrimination, and disruption' may well occur; and Labour's consistency, credibility, and authority are impaired.

So far, however, this 'card vote' concept of mandate, of the representative who is empowered by the represented, not to cast his own vote but to cast *their* proxy votes for them, has gone no farther than the Labour Party conference. Yet in 1975 a Labour Member of Parliament claimed that, because the 290 Members who voted with the Labour government on the Trade Union and Labour Relations (Amendment) Bill on 6 November of that year, had been voted for by 17,643,472 electors, while the 241 Members who voted against the government had been voted for by 10,493,015 electors, 'one finds that the Government's position was backed by 17,643,472 electors and opposed by 10,493,015, which gives the Government a

[1] H. A. Clegg, *A New Approach to Industrial Democracy*, Oxford, 1960, p. 115; H. A. Clegg and Rex Adams, *The Employers' Challenge*, Oxford, 1957, p. 15; Webbs, pp. 838-9; *The Times*, 10 November 1975.

democratic majority of 62·7 per cent'. Some millions of the electors who thus found themselves 'backing' the 'Government's position' were, in fact, Liberal voters; while several thousand of those who thus 'opposed' the 'Government's position' were Labour voters, whose elected Member chose on this occasion to vote with the Conservatives. Such anomalies are commonplace to the devotees of the card-vote, although their notion of 'democracy' may well seem somewhat arbitrary, even to those who are willing to equate the democratic with the representative.[1]

But the supporters of the card-vote kind of democracy may now be putting more pressure on Parliament. At the end of 1975, the General Secretary of the National Union of Railwaymen had to tender his 'humble apologies' to the Speaker of the House of Commons for stating that the ten Members sponsored by the union knew there was 'no area' of railway policy 'in which they can deviate from what we are expecting of them'. Six months earlier, the Yorkshire Area Council of the National Union of Mineworkers ruled that 'no miners' M.P. shall vote or speak against union policy on any issue which affects the coal-mining industry', or 'actively campaign or work against the union policy on any other major issue'. These utterances breathe the spirit of the period after 1969, when trade unionists began five years of almost unbroken conflict with the parliamentarians by destroying the Industrial Relations Bill, whose provisions were described by Wilson as 'essential to our economic recovery, essential to our balance of payments, essential to full employment'. That conflict may or may not have ended.[2]

In any event, such conflict raises, for the representative system, and for that system's power to conform to the democratic principles of the equality of both citizens and laws, not only the constitutional issue of parliamentary 'privilege', but the substantive issue of the content of government policy. The corporatist notion of a sectional claim to a special place in the policy-making process was always implicit in the project of labour representation, and has been reasserted by the post-war practice of tripartism. Now, realization of that claim offends

[1] Ibid., 17 November 1975.
[2] Ibid., 26 June 1975; 18 December 1975.

against 'democracy'—since it is fundamentally inegalitarian—and it offends against the principle of mutual obligations and responsibilities—since as practised by organized labour, at any rate, it is highly arbitrary. The extraordinary conduct of organized labour in 1960–1, when, in two successive years, the Trades Union Congress and the Labour Party first rejected and then affirmed a nuclear defence policy, has already been noted. Not the least problematical aspect of the events of those years was the ability of Congress and Party to put the weight of millions of votes behind a policy originating among a rather small and unrepresentative group of activists.

In recent years, that ability has seemed as great as ever. During 1972–3, Stuart Holland, an adviser to Labour ministers, and a research fellow of Sussex University, advocated in various party policy-committees a proposal to nationalize twenty-five of the largest manufacturing and financial companies. This proposal was adopted by the 1973 Labour Party conference, and actively promoted by Benn, as Secretary of State for Industry, in the spring and summer of 1974. M. H. Brewer observed, in a report on this episode in *The Guardian*, that 'Stuart Holland had virtually single handedly committed a great party to his particular view in . . . industrial policy'. Whatever its merits, the twenty-five companies proposal was almost certainly unrepresentative of the views of many Labour Party members, let alone Labour voters. It was publicly dismissed by Wilson, and omitted from Labour manifestos and from government white papers in 1974. Yet it remains *Conference* policy; and as such will very probably continue to influence Party deliberations. It is not easy to argue that such a situation enhances the democratic claims of the British political system, at least in so far as those claims are expressed in liberal-individualist terms.[1]

The methods whereby organizations of labour form their policies were further illustrated by the proposals that the Trades Union Congress and Labour Party put to the Royal Commission on the Press. In May 1975 the Trades Union Congress proposed reserving 'day-to-day discretion' over the 'content' of newspapers to their editors, subject to a supervisory board, half of whose members would be union representatives.

[1] *The Guardian*, 3 November 1975; *The Times*, 26 January 1976.

Papers would be printed on presses belonging to a National Press Finance Corporation, itself controlled by a supervisory board, half of whose members would be union representatives, and half government nominees. There would also be a Communications Council 'to keep the operation' of 'all the mass media under permanent review'. Such innovations, the Congress believed, would reform the 'anti-trade union bias in both news coverage and editorial treatment', and would prevent developments such as press support for the Industrial Relations Act, on which issue 'the owners of the press actually played the role of the representatives of capital'.[1]

This scheme for press control may have great merit from other than individualist standpoints. But it is highly unlikely to conform to the views of trade unionists and Labour Party members, even though it has been formally approved by the Trades Union Congress. The proposals are apparently the work of the Trades Union Congress Research Department, and seem to have travelled through the Congress's bureaucratic machinery 'through sheer indifference', as the Webbs would put it. Likewise the Labour Party's press proposals, which follow Congress's proposals quite closely (but stress the desirability of an Advertising Revenue Board, empowered to control all advertising, redistribute revenues between papers on the basis of circulation, and set up new newspapers), seem to be a production of the Labour Party Research Department. The Party proposals have been adopted by the Party Conference and put to the Royal Commission as evidence. Yet, the Labour Member of Parliament John Mackintosh observed, after these events, that, 'it is not clear who thought out the evidence. It was not submitted to the Parliamentary Labour Party, and many M.P.s are unaware of the contents of the document.'[2]

Such cases illustrate the way in which a system based on liberal individualism, no less than any other system, can give great, if momentary, strength to those who control the resources of institutions. As Shonfield observed, the British 'allow effective power to slide into the hands of . . . corporations without subjecting them to public control—for the national doctrine insists that they are no more than free associations of

---

[1] Ibid., 25 May 1975.
[2] Ibid., 7 November 1975.

individuals whose activities are essential to the emergence of a consensus'. The New Left has undoubtedly profited by this tendency. But whether their apparently collectivist views, thus buttressed by an irresponsible organizational power, will be accepted by the members of labour organizations, or whether indeed those views will prove to be in reality as collectivist as they may seem, is doubtful. Just as bi-metallism and secular education, to take two examples from the 1890s, have so far failed to appeal to British public opinion, some more recent proposals may lack popularity commensurate with the publicity they have received.[1]

Meanwhile many people, in trade unions and Labour Party alike, will argue that organized labour has no monopoly on the unrepresentative, let alone the undemocratic. These people's favourite counter-example is the firm, whose management is almost always entirely appointive and, moreover, in its higher echelons at least, is very largely recruited from upper socio-economic groups. The firm typically displays virtually no democratic ethos, and no representative machinery, it is argued: yet the firm may have complete power over its employees' livelihood. In theory, at least, the current demand for industrial democracy arises from the desire to reform this major obstacle to a democratic way of life. In practice, the industrial democracy movement may be interpreted either as a revival of the somewhat collectivist workers' control movement of the years up to 1950 or as a new lease of life for the section-alism that has grown up largely unchecked since 1950. If the movement were the former, it might transform the meaning of democracy and of representation, as these things are now understood in Britain; if the latter, it would very probably leave the British social and political system no more and no less democratic and representative than it has been heretofore. And only in the former case, of course, would it be necessary to conclude that the cultural constraints described in this book were ceasing to shape the consciousness of British people in general, and of British labour in particular.

The movement for workers' control in the first half of the present century was anti-élitist in character. Syndicalists argued that the representative system centred on Parliament

[1] Shonfield, pp. 89, 94, 119, 163.

could only generate successive undemocratic ruling classes; and that, rather than build up the Labour Party to become a new élite to oppress the people, the 'workers' should seize power themselves, through an expropriatory general strike, and organize what the *Miners' Next Step* called a 'real democracy in real life'. This 'democracy' would, in fact, be representative: since it would consist of government by a set of industry-wide unions, acting through elected representatives. Syndicalists hoped to curb these representatives by a system of frequent elections and recall sufficient to render the officers subservient to the people, or democratic rank and file. Yet, even under this system, the syndicalist society would look curiously like a unitary corporatism, run by a new breed of employer-employees, responsible only to the employee-employers of their own industry, and quite free of control from the wider community, if such still existed. It was the lack of any representation of (and responsibility to) the people outside each sectional industry that caused the Webbs to oppose the syndicalist scheme, which, they suggested, was similar to an arrangement whereby not a union's members but the charwoman at union headquarters elected the union's general secretary.[1]

But after the First World War, schemes of workers' control were advocated by several unions, and fought for by the Miners. The collapse of the General Strike perhaps depressed demands for workers' control; but in the early 1930s, Charles Dukes of the National Union of General and Municipal Workers urged the Trades Union Congress to seek statutory provision for a representative system of workers' control, in which the trade unions would be 'the recognized nucleus of representation', and in which trade unionists would occupy half the managerial positions in each undertaking. This proposal did not immediately appeal to the General Council of the Trades Union Congress, which favoured trade union nomination, rather than shopfloor election, of any worker directors, and virtual representation of the employees' interests rather than actual direct representation of the employees themselves. When the Attlee government nationalized the mines and the railways, it borrowed the General Council's ideas in preference to Dukes's. In general, the Attlee version of

[1] *The Miners' Next Step*, p. 30.

nationalization satisfied trade unionists' utilitarian demands for better wages and conditions, rather than any demand there may have been for new industrial and social structures.[1]

The failure of the attempt to secure workers' control was chiefly due to three factors. First, those who favoured workers' control did not convince their opponents that industrial employees had the managerial skills necessary to such a system. Workers' control seemed to Laski, for instance, as absurd as the patient controlling the doctor; and the Trades Union Congress insisted on 'competence' as a criterion for all appointments to nationalized undertakings. Secondly, the spectres of such creations as the employer-employee and the employee-employer provoked influential trade unionists and politicians to argue that workers' control posed an insoluble problem of conflict of interests. Hence Morrison's warning that, in a system of workers' control, either the representatives would think only 'of their interests with sectional minds . . . and your socialist undertaking will be in danger of failure', or, if they thought otherwise, within a year, they would be condemned as men who had 'gone over to the boss class' and could no longer be trusted. And this conflict of interests was demonstrated during the early 1940s in the joint production-committees promoted by the Communists to increase armaments production. Thirdly, though the movement for workers' control was from the first shaped by the *democratic* liberal-individualist ideology, as soon as it reached the details of possible systems, it was inescapably confronted with the problems of mutual obligations and responsibilities, inseparable from *representative* machinery, even if abhorrent to the democratic ethos. 'People who were invited' to take managerial posts in nationalized industries, 'refused because they were not prepared to accept responsibility', as Deakin put it.[2]

In the 1960s trade unionists and Labour Party members, led by Jack Jones, began to advocate a type of 'industrial democracy' little different from the workers' control scheme of Charles Dukes. Some industrial democrats, such as Benn and the Foundry Workers' leader Bill Simpson, argued that a man's

---

[1] Trades Union Congress *Report*, 1933, p. 371.

[2] Harold J. Laski, *A Grammar of Politics*, London, 1941, p. 442; Labour Party *Conference Report*, 1932, p. 214; 1953, p. 132.

democratic 'right as a citizen' should be extended to his life in the workplace. Yet the appeal of 'industrial democracy' lay chiefly in the opportunities it offered for prevention of redundancies and greater information on company profits. 'Open the books' was the slogan that summarized these utilitarian concerns, which Jones and fellow members of the Labour Party Working Party on Industrial Democracy hoped to further by means of 'A SINGLE CHANNEL OF REPRESENTATION'. Such unified machinery would submit all issues of employment, investment and manufacture to negotiation between the directors (half of whom would be trade union representatives) and the stewards representing the shop floor employees. 'Industrial democracy', said Ian Mikardo in the House of Commons in mid-1975, 'was a situation where every single decision was negotiable and the subject of collective bargaining': a situation which, in short, merely paralleled within the factory the industrialization of politics outside the factory.[1]

Present day trade unionists have a higher opinion of their own managerial skills than trade unionists of the interwar period had of theirs. The earlier technical objections against the Dukes-Jones proposals therefore now have less force, at least in public debate. Yet the problem of the conflict of interest causes as much concern as ever, especially to the skilled manual wage earners' unions who oppose the industrial democrats' plans. Their position was expressed as early as 1960 by Eirene White's warning that 'free trade unions' believed that 'their position as a bargaining authority' would be harmed if they were 'absorbed' into management. Though white-collar unions seemed to like the Trades Union Congress's version of industrial democracy (the Union of Post Office Workers securing a reorganization of the Post Office partly in line with Congress policy), and though the Transport and General Workers' Union, dominated by its general secretary, supported schemes for worker directors, many manual workers' unions—notably the Electricians, the Engineers and the General and Municipal Workers—rejected the proposals put forward by Jones and Murray. Opinion polls conducted during 1976–7 indicated that, while about 50–60 per cent of adult employees favoured 'worker directors', most believed that such functionaries should

[1] Ibid., 1968, pp. 160–1; *The Times*, 3 July 1975.

not be imposed by law. Moreover, trade unionists as well as non-trade unionists rejected both the appointment of worker directors by trade unionists only, and the occupation by worker directors of half or more of the seats on company boards. Thus public opinion seemed much closer to the Engineers than to the Transport and General Workers, and the Trades Union Congress. Meanwhile, worker-director or other 'participation' schemes introduced on government instructions—in the British Steel Corporation, British Leyland and Chrysler, for example— remained unpopular; and even shipbuilding employees demanding to be nationalized objected to becoming worker-directors as a perquisite of nationalization.[1]

Of course most trade union and left-wing opponents of the new Trades Union Congress orthodoxy on 'industrial demo-cracy' feared 'that involvement as company . . . directors will compromise the union's bargaining function'. Such fears could only be strengthened by the enthusiasm for participation and industrial democracy being expressed in managerial and property-owning circles. Sir Arnold Weinstock suggested that General Electric should develop a system of participation in which every member of the company could make 'the optimum contribution to its well-being and his own' in 'an intelligent and productive harmony'. Lord Ryder understood his scheme for participation in the state-controlled British Leyland as 'a framework removed from the normal arrangements for collec-tive bargaining, in which agreement can be reached on the action required' in 'an atmosphere of joint problem-solving'; and he counselled trade unionists to 'ensure that the right people' act as representatives 'to exercise these responsibilities', not least so as to raise the quantity and quality of production, and to reduce industrial disputes.[2]

The greater economic success of other members of the European Economic Community, at least some of whom

[1] On conflict of interest: see Labour Party *Conference Report*, 1960, p. 230; *The Times*, 25 April 1975; 5 December 1975; *The Financial Times*, 19 October 1975. On the Post Office: see *The Times*, 15 June 1976. On union hostility to worker-director schemes: see *The Guardian*, 26 January 1976; 2 and 10 March 1976; 3 January 1977; *The Times*, 29 January 1976. On opinion polls: see *The Financial Times*, 12 November 1976; 26 January 1977; *The Sunday Times*, 30 January 1977.

[2] John Elliott, *Conflict or Co-operation?*, London, 1978, pp. 114–15; *The Guardian*, 26 January 1976; *The Times*, 25 April 1975.

seemed more advanced than the United Kingdom in the implementation of worker-participation policies, coupled with the Community's promotion of such policies, may have increased the responsiveness of men like Lord Ryder to trade union demands for industrial democracy, such as they were. Speaking to the 1976 Labour Party conference, for the first time as prime minister, Callaghan noted that successive governments 'have failed to ignite the fires of industrial growth in the ways that Germany, France and Japan, with their different political and economic philosophies, have done'. He argued that 'unless there is agreement on the place of the human being in our industrial society we shall push and pull at the economic levers in vain'; and he observed that 'more and more active trade unionists' were 'becoming more vocal in their opposition to small bands of disrupters in industry, and were recognizing that there was a joint responsibility to make the factory work.' The notion that such a responsibility might be realized by the application in the United Kingdom of European (specifically *German*) principles that had brought strength and prosperity to those countries that adopted them, was but the latest in a long series of British attempts to adjust the individualist tradition to the challenge of continental collectivism, a series in which the unsuccessful effort to emulate *French* 'planning' during the 1950s and 1960s was a not inconsiderable item. Of course, as Lord Plowden remarked, there were indeed, even in the 1970s, 'fundamental differences between Germany and Britain—differences in trade union objectives, attitudes and organization, as well as in social and political traditions, experience and behaviour'. Yet it was quite widely reported in the late 1970s that the European example of employee participation was working powerfully on the government and its advisers. 'There is reason to think', wrote Michael Shanks, that the desire to be 'in the mainstream of European thinking' on industrial democracy 'carries much weight in Whitehall': where (and elsewhere), as *The Times'* correspondent Peter Hennessy observed, 'all protagonists in the argument cite in their support the West German experience where co-determination has been a feature.'[1]

Though European innovations may have inspired the Labour

[1] Ibid., 29 September 1976; 10 January 1977; 15 February 1977.

government to yield to union demands, those demands were in any event fairly pressing. The government tried to offset its lack of electoral support by securing demonstrations of trade union loyalty, which were said to indicate a degree and kind of *popular* support available to the Labour Party alone. In return for such demonstrations, trade union leaders required various concessions among which, according to Jones, was an industrial-democracy statute. When a back-benchers' bill on the subject got into committee through a whips' error, the government decided to act. But since industrial democracy seemed unlikely to be widely or enthusiastically welcomed, even among trade unionists, the government proposed not to seek immediate legal enactment of the relevant Trades Union Congress resolutions, but to prepare public opinion by appointing a preliminary committee of inquiry. But those trade union leaders who wanted industrial democracy apparently feared that a committee of inquiry would either merely express the general dislike of these newfangled schemes, or rewrite them so as to deny the unions the material benefits looked for in this connection, or both. The Trades Union Congress therefore 'imposed terms of reference on the Committee of Inquiry', according to one trade union leader. These were that 'accepting the need for a radical extension of industrial democracy . . . by means of representation on boards of directors, and accepting the essential role of trade union organizations in this process', the Committee was to 'consider how such an extension can best be achieved, taking into account in particular the proposals of the Trades Union Congress'. Possibly because of the number of questions begged by these terms, four months elapsed before, in December 1975, the government could announce the appointment of the committee, which was to be chaired by Lord Bullock.[1]

Of its eleven members, one resigned; one produced a note of dissent; three signed one report; and seven signed another. Although Eric Batstone, who wrote one of the committee's two research papers on European employee-participation projects found that 'worker directors have generally had little effect on anything', the majority report stated that 'board level repre-

---

[1] *The Guardian*, 26 January 1976; Elliott, pp. 216–18, 220; *Report of the Committee of Inquiry on Industrial Democracy*, Cmnd. 6706, 1977, p. v.

sentation' of organized labour 'will have beneficial effects on the performance of British companies'. The majority based this belief partly on 'experience in other European countries', not least Germany. 'It is now twenty-five years', observed the majority, since 'co-determination was introduced in the Federal Republic of Germany', a country whose economy had been 'among the most successful in the world—not least in avoiding the industrial conflict which has cost Britain so dear'. Yet any suggestion that the collectivist traditions of German society were now to be followed in Britain was speedily scouted. 'In our view', the majority declared, 'a study of the West German system shows how difficult it would be to introduce something similar into the United Kingdom', because 'the formalistic approach' of the West Germans 'cuts right across the flexible tradition' of British law and industrial practice. The committee observed that

> Many submissions emphasised the importance of a flexible approach to . . . industrial democracy. . . . From quite different sides there was considerable opposition to the idea that a law might try to define too closely the method of selection . . . constituencies and . . . structure of boards. Many submissions warned the Committee against copying continental systems, particularly the West German system where the law defines these matters very closely.

Thus, the Bullock majority, like Andrew Shonfield, in his 'Note of Reservation' to the Donovan Commission's report, and like the Federal Republic of Germany, favoured worker-directors; but, unlike both Shonfield and the Germans, they remained more or less faithful to the individualist doctrine of a residual or arbitral role for law and the state; and rejected any collectivist reliance on the legal and quasi-legal activity of the whole society. 'Neither companies nor unions would welcome being put in a statutory straightjacket', the majority believed.[1]

Yet if the majority had been entirely unshaken in their loyalty to individualism, they would presumably have been more sympathetic to the historic objections to schemes of workers' control and industrial democracy. On the contrary, in line with the attitudes of Jack Jones and David Lea, who were

---

[1] Industrial Democracy Committee, *Industrial Democracy, European Experience*, London, 1976, p. 35; *Report of the Committee of Inquiry*, pp. 25, 37, 50, 56, 72–3, 117.

among the seven signatories of the majority report, they discounted these objections. 'Board level representation does not raise any new issues of principle for trade unions which already engage in collective bargaining. It simply creates additional means by which they may influence the managerial process', stated the majority in a passage with distinct corporatist overtones. Indeed, though the Bullock report proposed that worker directors could only be appointed in a company at least one third of whose employees (whether union members or not) desired such an arrangement, it also proposed that the only representation to be offered to employees was, like the Trades Union Congress's own scheme, to be controlled solely by trade unions; and it might be thought that the majority favoured an exclusive corporatist collaboration between organized management and organized labour. The *minority* report stated that

> It is one of the great strengths of political democracy . . . that every citizen has equal political rights and that no one has to belong to a particular . . . organization to exercise those rights. . . . It would make a mockery of democracy . . . to limit the rights of employees in any system of industrial democracy to those who have opted for collective representation through a Trade Union.

The majority proposals of the Bullock Committee certainly infringed the principle of equal rights, as thus stated; and, especially in view of the peculiar character of representation within unions, might well be thought to reinforce the trend towards corporatism in contemporary Britain.[1]

That this was not the intention of the authors of those proposals can be seen at various points in their argument. The trade unions had displayed their greatest semblance of full-blown corporatism in their advocacy of 'parity': that is to say, of the reservation to trade unionists of half the seats on boards of management. For were parity to be realized, trade union board members would need to solve the problems of both conflict and compromise of interest if the enterprise managed was to survive; and it was the claim of Jones, Murray and others that these problems could be solved, in the context of continuing private ownership of property, which most sharply differentiated their opinions from those of the earlier champions

---

[1] Ibid., pp. 117–18, 125, 175.

of workers' control. The Bullock majority seem to have doubted these claims, however, and, despite disclaimers, to have concentrated most of their energies on what their report calls 'the problem of deadlock': namely, the breakdown of management consequent upon the importation, into the board, of labour representatives, armed with veto-power, and imbued with the assumptions, attitudes and habits of behaviour characteristic of British individualism.[1]

For despite the majority's interest in European methods, the Bullock report treated conflict as an axiom of social and economic life. To those who objected that employee participation of the kind envisaged must jeopardize the sectionalist independence of trade unions, the majority replied that

> trade unions must retain their independence. But we do not see why this independence need be compromised by representation on the board. If . . . employee representatives are equal in number to the shareholder representatives, and . . . are backed by the trade unions in the company, they will carry both weight and influence on the board. Indeed, they will be able where necessary to oppose a policy not only on the board but also in collective bargaining. . . .

The Bullock version of industrial democracy would, in short, guarantee in their fullest form the negative freedoms of trade unionism. In order to achieve this end, however, the majority had to redefine 'parity', which had been interpreted by the Transport and General Workers and others, at least as late as mid-1976, as a 50–50 division of board seats between employees and employers, in the form '$2x + y$'. According to the $2x + y$ rule, the board would consist of 'an equal number of employee and shareholder representatives' (i.e. $2x$), plus 'a third group' of directors 'co-opted with the agreement of a majority of each of the other two groups' (i.e. y). In other words, since the ineluctable algebra of $x + y > x$ would in the end permit employee representatives to be outvoted, trade-union appointed worker directors, though able to boast of 'parity' with 'the employers', could always escape the onus of an unpleasant or unpopular management decision, and let the company go on as though they had never existed.[2]

[1] Ibid., p. 98.
[2] Ibid., pp. 96, 124; *The Guardian*, 6 July 1976; *The Times*, 25 May 1976.

But the Bullock majority's solicitude for traditional trade union methods and attitudes went further still. An unthinking or over-zealous trade union leader might fail or scorn to see the efficacy of the y-component as a safeguard for his conscience and reputation; and might seek merely to parcel out the y-directorships on a fifty-fifty basis. To prevent the 'deadlock' that could thus ensue, it was to be a basic rule of Bullock boards *that y be an odd number*. Of course, though the last, or casting-vote director of the y-component would both salve the trade union directors' consciences and prevent 'deadlock' in the running of the company, his appointment might itself cause 'deadlock' in cases where the logic of the system was misunderstood. To escape from this difficulty, the Bullock majority proposed the creation of an independent 'Industrial Democracy Commission', 'to be called in to provide conciliation'; and 'in the last resort', to 'decide that specified persons should form the third group on the board'. Hence, where algebra failed, a public body could act to guarantee the fundamental principle, adumbrated by the Labour Party working party in 1967, that, whatever else industrial democracy entailed, 'the right of the workers and their organizations to withdraw from participation, from decision-making responsibility, from agreements . . . must be maintained'.[1]

In many ways, this scheme was a *tour de force*. But neither the majority's cautiously judicious approach to the possibility of greater collectivism in British society, nor the ingenuity of its proposal for the composition of company boards, could disguise the unreality of its recommendations. Those recommendations expressed the preferences of a few national trade union leaders; they were no more representative of the views of any significant proportion of that half of the employed population which belongs to unions than were, say, the 1973 Labour Party conference's decision to nationalize the twenty-five largest British companies, or the 1975 Trades Union Congress proposal to control the press. Indeed the Bullock majority recommendations were, in a sense, necessarily groundless.

First, as was noted by John Elliott, the Industrial Editor of *The Financial Times*, and perhaps the Bullock report's most influential sympathizer, the committee's 'terms of reference did

[1] *Report of the Committee of Inquiry*, pp. 96, 104, 154.

eventually dictate the contents of the report', which 'tended to move on some key issues from an assertion of a need for change, to a statement of the TUC solution, to a little-analysed report of opposing views, to an assertion that the TUC solution was right'. Second, that 'solution' was the work of the Trades Union Congress only in the arbitrary or 'card vote' sense: it did not represent trade unionists' attitudes towards industrial democracy, which the General Council had no means of discovering. Lastly, 'the TUC solution' to the problems of industrial organization illustrated, in this instance almost to the point of caricature, the confusion inevitably attendant on labour's traditional usage of a highly collectivist language—the socialist language of Clause 4—in a profoundly individualist sense. And precisely by 'accepting the need for a radical extension of industrial democracy', and by 'taking into account the proposals of the Trades Union Congress', the committee were obliged to translate these historic ambiguities into faithful but nonetheless remarkable institutional forms.[1]

This obligation exposed the Bullock report to public condemnation of unusual persistence and severity. Peter Jenkins claimed in *The Guardian* that the 'report of the majority of the Bullock Committee (short title the Jones Report)' was 'a travesty of democracy', an 'insult to the general public . . . the equivalent roughly of extending the franchise to the rotten boroughs'. Similar and lengthier, if sometimes less harsh, judgements appeared in the rest of the press, and in the statements of the Confederation of British Industry and other management organizations. Yet these criticisms were perhaps less indicative of the strength of the individualist *laissez-faire* loyalties that the Bullock report offended than were, for example, the comments of communists. The Communist Party's industrial organizer Bert Ramelson warned that 'workers should not be stampeded into accepting the Bullock Report merely because for their own reasons the CBI and other big business representatives are making a big hooha against it'. The *Morning Star* reaffirmed its support for the kind of industrial democracy that the trade union *avant-garde* of the 1960s had hoped for, by declaring that 'all important policy decisions—forward manpower planning, investment and location of new plant etc, etc, etc,—should be

[1] Elliott, pp. 221–2.

put on the bargaining table'. But it could not stomach the Bullock report, for all the majority's efforts to realize such hopes in practical form. The Bullock proposals, the paper declared, were 'designed to suck the workers and their leaders yet deeper into the embrace of the shareholders and big business magnates'; and in so doing would institutionalize 'class collaboration' at the company level.[1]

Trade union doubts about industrial democracy as understood by Bullock were perhaps most clearly expressed by John Lyons, general secretary of the Electrical Power Engineers' Association, in a careful restatement of Morrison's arguments:

> It is because employee representatives on boards à la Bullock will tie the unions into the management process, and . . . take away their ability to remain independent when they want to, that there is such a fundamental difference between collective bargaining and Bullock.
>
> In practical terms, if employee representatives on boards agree to rationalizations, redundancies, etc, as they will be bound to do from time to time, then to that extent the trade unions representing the staffs in the company . . . concerned will be compromised in their collective bargaining positions. That is utterly unavoidable.
>
> To argue that they will still retain all their independence is either a fiction or, if not, an expression of extraordinary naivety. If trade unions were consistently to repudiate the decisions of the representatives of their own workforces on boards of management then the whole exercise would be quite abortive for industry and trade unions alike.

These observations suggest that the unitary corporatism, hinted at in the Attlee nationalization measures, and openly expressed in the wartime joint production committees, aroused in the 1970s objections no less vigorous than those rehearsed so many times in earlier years.[2]

The Labour government took note of these objections. The prime minister gave the drafting of a white paper on industrial democracy to a Cabinet committee chaired by Shirley Williams, the Secretary of State for Education and Science, who had already publicly expressed the view that, however desirable

---

[1] *The Guardian*, 27 January 1977; *The Morning Star*, 27 January 1977.
[2] *The Times*, 2 March 1977.

industrial 'participation' might be, 'the sharing of responsibility' in industry was 'much more difficult'. The *Industrial Democracy* white paper, published in May 1978, politely rejected the Bullock report, which had certainly 'illuminated the major issues' but had also aroused 'sharp divisions of view'. The white paper was, however, as anxious as the report to treat collectivism with caution. Britain could of course 'learn' from European co-determination, but only so far as 'the unique development of the British system of industrial relations' would permit; shared responsibility and 'positive partnership' was the objective, but in industry some conflict is 'inevitable, even healthy'. Above all, the government desired, the white paper stated, to 'avoid inflexible legislation': and it was admitted in particular that 'the Government's consultations following publication of the Bullock report have not so far resulted in consensus on the principle of whether employees should be given a statutory right to representation at board level'.[1]

Despite the absence of such consensus, the white paper (manifesting in this respect some vestiges of the spirit of the 'Social Contract' period) did propose legislation on industrial democracy, which was, after all, indubitably one of the Trades Union Congress's demands upon the government. Yet it proposed legislation with a diffidence rather foreign to that period; and it envisaged an institutional framework quite different from that favoured either by Bullock or the Trades Union Congress. That framework embodied two major principles: first, the minimum trade union 'share of responsibility' compatible with the notion of worker directorships; and, second, the minimum trade union power compatible with a system of employee representation controlled by trade unionists.

The first principle was observed in the scheme to give employee representatives only 'up to one third' of the seats on a 'policy board', which would 'not become involved in—or responsible for—the day-to-day running of the company': management in this sense being reserved to 'professional' managers, eligible for membership not only of the 'management board' but of the policy board as well. These provisions excluded Bullock's and the Trades Union Congress's concepts of 'parity' between worker and other directors. The second

---

[1] Elliott, p. 249; *Industrial Democracy*, Cmnd. 7231, pp. 1–2, 6.

principle was recognized both in a declaration 'that there should be no question' of employee directors 'being mandated to vote in accordance with the instructions of those by whom they are appointed', and in a proposal for 'any substantial homogeneous group of employees', whether unionized or not, to secure, on appeal to the Industrial Democracy Commission, 'a requirement for elections based on nomination of candidates' by *any* 'groups of at least 100 employees whether or not they are members of trade unions'. These provisions excluded Bullock's and the Trades Union Congress's notions of a 'single channel' of representation.[1]

This relatively cautious approach reflects, as far as the medium of late-twentieth-century 'industrial democracy' allows, the more modest traditions of bipartite corporatism developed in nearly a hundred years of 'collective bargaining'. For the corporatist schema of competing 'substantial homogeneous groups' is axiomatic to the white paper: though bolder unitary projects, whether of employer or employee hegemony, are rejected by it. The document's essential conservatism—Germanic two-tier boards notwithstanding—may well have secured it quite widespread acceptance: at least, the public's apparent indifference to the white paper suggests as much. Whether realization of the government's proposals would remove the confusions hitherto ineradicable from the conduct of national affairs is another matter. For it seems more likely that solutions to the problems of the representative system in Britain, and remedies for the ills of industrial politics, must be found in combinations of *laissez-faire* and collectivism as yet unenvisaged, and in forms of labour and concepts of democracy as yet unknown.

[1] Ibid., pp. 7, 9.

Index